Criminal Law for AS and A-Level

plus the rule of law, an introduction to the non-substantive law

(the English legal system and the nature of law)

Sally Russell LLB (Hons), PGCE

Key features

- Tasks and self-test questions throughout (with answers at www.drsr.org)
- Key cases with key principles highlighted
- Examples to bring the law to life
- Links between the law and the English legal system
- Links between the law and the nature of law in relation to various concepts
- Summaries with diagrams for the main points of each area
- Examination and evaluation pointers
- Examination guidance and question practice
- Free interactive exercises at www.drsr.org
- Free guide for teachers also at www.drsr.org

My main objective has been to combine legal accuracy with a style that is accessible to all students, so I hope you will find this book both stimulating and helpful. Fully updated with recent cases and laws it is written in a lively, clear and accessible way and is designed to help students of all learning styles to understand the subject. AQA would only give approval to one publisher so this book does not carry an official badge of approval. However the AQA Portfolio Curriculum team kindly gave help and advice on content and assessment and I am grateful to them.

Although aimed at A-Level the book provides a good base for 1st Year LLB, CILEx and other courses, and can be used as a self-study guide.

Other books by Sally Russell

As new books may be available by the time you read this, I have not listed my other books by title. They currently include crime and tort at AS and A2 level for both the AQA and OCR examination boards. Also, *'the law explained'* series offers a more in-depth coverage of individual areas with additional tasks, examples and examination practice. These cover much of crime and tort as well as the various concepts of law. This means you can pick those topics for which you need more guidance (all the answers to tasks are included in the booklets).

For the most up to date list of what is available, please check my author's page on Amazon or visit my website at www.drsr.org. All my books are available in both Kindle and paperback.

Table of contents

Table of contents 2
Introduction: Things you need to know and links to other areas 5
Part 1: Criminal law for Year 1 A-level and AS (7161) 9
Chapter 1: The Nature of Law and the Rule of law 10
    The nature of law 10
    Linking the concepts with the law 13
    The rule of law 14
Chapter 2: Actus reus: Conduct, circumstances, consequences and causation 17
    Conduct 17
    Consequences and causation 20
Chapter 3 Mens rea 26
    Intention 26
    Recklessness 30
Chapter 4 Strict liability 34
    Statutory nature of strict liability 34
    Interpretation by the courts 35
    social utility (usefulness) and public policy 36
    Arguments for and against imposing strict liability 37
Chapter 5 Common assault: Assault and Battery 41
    Assault 41
    Battery 44
    Consent 44
Chapter 6 Assault occasioning actual bodily harm (ABH) under s 47 of the Offences against the Person Act 1861 48
    Actus reus 48
    Mens rea 50
Chapter 7 Grievous bodily harm (GBH) and wounding under s 20 and s 18 of the Offences against the Person Act 1861 53
    Actus reus for s 18 and s 20 53
    Mens rea for s 20 56
    Mens rea for s 18 56
Summary and examination practice: Non-fatal offences against the person 60
    Problems and proposals for reform of the non-fatal offences 61
The AS examination (7161) 63
    About the examination 63
    Examination guidance 65
    Examination paper for AS 69
The Bridge 72
    Evaluation of the non-fatal offences against the person and proposals for reform 72
    Background of proposed reforms 73
    The Law Commission Report (No 361) 2015 73

The nature of law (concepts)	75
Part 2: Criminal law for A-level 7162	81
Chapter 8 Murder	83
Actus reus	83
Mens rea	86
Chapter 9: Voluntary manslaughter under the Coroners and Justice Act 2009 – Loss of control	92
Did D's act result from a loss of self-control?	92
Did the loss of self-control have a qualifying trigger?	93
Would a person of D's sex and age have reacted in the same way in D's circumstances?	97
Chapter 10 Voluntary manslaughter under the Homicide Act 1957 – Diminished responsibility	103
An abnormality of mental functioning	104
Arising from a recognised medical condition	104
Substantially impaired D's ability	107
Provides an explanation for D's acts and omissions in doing or being a party to the killing	108
Chapter 11 Gross negligence manslaughter and constructive or unlawful act manslaughter	113
Gross negligence manslaughter	113
Unlawful act or constructive manslaughter	118
Summary and evaluation of the fatal offences	126
Chapter 12 Theft	133
Actus reus	134
Mens rea	140
Chapter 13 Robbery	148
Actus reus	148
Mens rea	151
Chapter 14 Attempts	153
Actus reus: more than merely preparatory	153
Attempts to do the impossible	154
Mens rea	155
Summary and evaluation of the property offences and attempt	158
Chapter 15 Insanity and Automatism	160
Insanity	160
Automatism	165
Chapter 16 Intoxication	169
Involuntary intoxication	169
Voluntary intoxication	170
Chapter 17 Self-defence and the prevention of crime	176
Prevention of crime	176
Self-defence	176
Chapter 18 Duress and duress of circumstances	182
Duress	183
Self-induced duress	185
Duress of circumstances	185

Summary and evaluation of the defences and their effect ... 190
Chapter 19: The A-level Examination (7162) ... 192
   About the exams ... 192
   Examination guidance ... 194
   Examination paper Task 50 ... 198
Appendix: Abbreviations and acknowledgements ... 202
Acknowledgements ... 202
Index of cases ... 204

Introduction: Things you need to know and links to other areas

This book covers all the criminal law for AQA for both Year 1 and Year 2 (AS and A-Level), as well as the rule of law and an introduction to the nature of law. AS criminal law is much the same as the first year of A-level criminal law, but it is not identical. You may well share your lessons so I have included a little more evaluation of the law than is strictly needed for AS (where evaluation is limited to the advantages and disadvantages of various procedures and institutions) because A-level students need to evaluate the Year 1 criminal law topics and relate them to concepts such as fault or justice. Also, evaluation is useful when looking at the rule of law, which is similar to justice as it involves fairness, and which AS students *do* need.

Part 1 covers the nature and general elements of criminal liability, followed by the five non-fatal offences against the person. This is the material you need for both AS and A-level criminal law Year 1.

Part 2 covers the fatal offences against the person, property offences, attempted crimes and defences for Year 2. This is the additional material you need for A-level criminal law Year 2.

More on how the key features can help:

- **Examples help you to see how the law relates to real life situations**
- **Tasks and self-test questions help you to check your understanding**
- **Examination pointers help with application**
- **Evaluation pointers help you to see problems with the law, which are relevant to the development and reform of the law as well as to the rule of law and justice (both of which require fairness and clarity)**
- **Key cases show you the important cases to know, and where a principle of law is established this is clearly stated**
- **Summaries and diagrams help to make the law clear and accessible**
- **Links between the criminal law and the English legal system show you how to deal with questions which mix these**
- **Links between the criminal law and the nature of law show you how to deal with questions which mix these**

Answers to tasks and self-test questions are on my website at www.drsr.org. Click on 'Answers to tasks' on the right. For some interactive exercises, click on 'Free Exercises' on the top menu then the book cover. Note that the Interactive exercises for Year 1 are attached to the AS book. Click on the cover for this book for Year 2.

At the end of Part 1, there is a summary of all the offences and examination practice. Although there is no need to take an external examination at the end of Year 1, you may wish to do so if you are not 100% sure about doing the full A-Level. The AS won't count towards the A-level but if you decide to go no further you will have a law qualification at AS level.

Part 1 is followed by 'The Bridge'. This section links Year 1 and Year 2. It includes an evaluation of the law so far, along with proposals for reform, which you will need for Year 2. The Bridge also explains the nature of law and the role of law in society, and provides examples to illustrate these from within the areas already covered. This will set you up for Year 2, where you will need to be able to discuss the nature and role of law in relation to all areas of law, including the new offences you will meet in Year 2. Examples are given in each Chapter for Part 2.

It is a bit early to talk about examinations (covered at the end of Parts 1 and 2) but there are a couple of things you need to know now, firstly so you can use the book effectively and secondly so you can understand the links to other areas as required throughout the course.

In some questions, you will be asked to apply the law to a set of facts, in others to evaluate it. There are 'pointers' throughout the book to help with this. Two questions are mixed, linking crime (the substantive law) to the English legal system (the non-substantive law). Throughout this book references to the English legal system refer both to this and to law-making.

There are links in each Chapter to help with this. Here's what these three aids to learning include.

Examination pointers

These relate to legal rules and application of the law. For application of the law you need to identify the specific legal rules that apply to the given facts. Then you need to apply those rules logically to the facts in order to reach a sustainable conclusion. The law for application is the current law and latest case developments.

Evaluation pointers

These cover criticisms of the law. They are for evaluation questions where you may be asked to provide a critique of the law on a particular topic or a particular legal rule. Any problems with the law will suggest that the rule of law is not being upheld (AS) or justice not achieved (A-level) as both these require fairness and clarity. The evaluation pointer may show the law has improved in some way, too, as any critique should include the good points and any developments can be relevant to several areas including sources of law, influences on Parliament and law reform. The law for evaluation may need to include developments or advantages and disadvantages, not just the latest cases and principles.

Links

In Part 1 the links are to the English legal system (note though that the rule of law is covered by the evaluation pointers so not included in the links). In Part 2 the links are to both the English legal system and the nature of law (concepts of law such as justice). The links are needed for the mixed questions on each paper. There is more on this under 'more on the two mixed questions'.

A few terms need explaining.

Substantive law means the particular topic, like crime and tort.

Non-substantive means the nature rather than the substance of law. This includes the English legal system and various legal theories. The first is needed for both AS and A-level, the latter only for A-level.

Extended writing questions can be on the application or evaluation of the law, or a mix of both of these. They require that you provide "an extended answer which shows a clear logical and sustained line of reasoning leading to a valid conclusion". There are two extended writing questions on each of the AS papers and three on each of the A-level papers.

Application: You will need to explain the relevant rules of law to decide on a particular offence and then apply those rules as discussed above. You will need to support what you say by using cases and principles to illustrate your points and then reach a conclusion based on your application.

Evaluation: This could require e.g., a discussion of how far the rules on a certain area of law or procedure are satisfactory (for both AS and A-level) and/or whether the rules achieve justice (for A-level). You may need to discuss whether there is need for reform of the law in a particular area, or whether proposals for reform have been suggested (especially any by the Law Commission as this body was set up to investigate the law and suggest reforms).

Whatever you need to discuss, try to produce a balanced argument. Where there is debate on an issue there are usually valid arguments on both sides, so don't strive to write what you think examiners want to see; they will be much more impressed by independent thought. Have an opinion, but look at the issue from the other point of view too to show that you have considered the arguments before reaching that opinion.

For more detail on what non-substantive areas are in each of the examination papers see the two 'examination practice' sections at the end of Parts 1 and 2 of this book. However, you need to be able to link the criminal law to the non-substantive areas as you work through the course, so here is a short guide to get you started.

More on the two mixed questions

You will have to link the substantive law to the English legal system for the AS examination. There are two mixed questions on each paper. One is based on a scenario and one is not. Here is a diagram to show how the links might work between the criminal law and the parts of the English legal system which are on Paper 1 AS. The links to the nature of law for Year 2 are introduced in the first Chapter. This means you can start thinking about these as you work through your course.

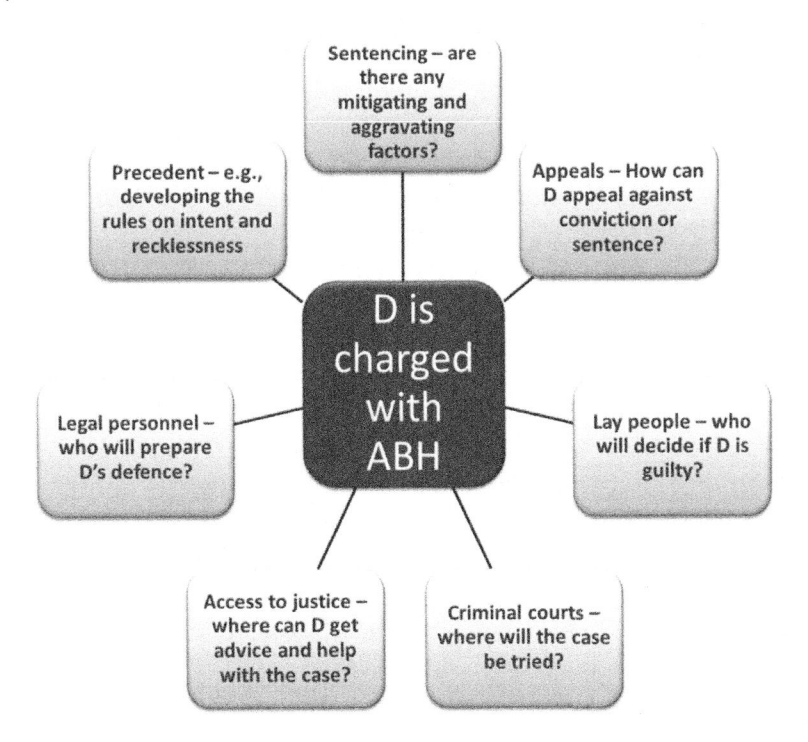

D is charged with ABH

- Sentencing – are there any mitigating and aggravating factors?
- Precedent – e.g., developing the rules on intent and recklessness
- Appeals – How can D appeal against conviction or sentence?
- Legal personnel – who will prepare D's defence?
- Lay people – who will decide if D is guilty?
- Access to justice – where can D get advice and help with the case?
- Criminal courts – where will the case be tried?

I have not included the areas that are not on both the AS and A-level papers (the rule of law, law reform and statutory interpretation). Bear this in mind depending on which examination you are taking. The rule of law (AS) is a very similar concept to justice (A-level) as both require fairness and clarity in the law. The evaluation pointers cover problems in the law, so all students can use these to discuss either of the concepts. Law reform is needed for AS criminal law and statutory interpretation is needed for A-level criminal law. At the end of each Chapter is a reminder to look back at this diagram to see what parts of the English legal system the particular topic you have just studied could link to (look for the linked rings symbol). Think of the topic as being in the central box and see how it can link to any of the outer boxes (adding law reform or statutory interpretation as appropriate). There may not always be a strong link in a particular examination question, but there will be one. However, as most of the substantive law can link to any part of the English legal system there is no way of knowing where the link will be made, so it is best to think about it for all areas. Also note that any cases establishing new principles are indicative of the development of the law and can be related to many areas of law-making.

Examples

People charged with a crime need to obtain legal advice and representation (access to justice) from a member of the legal profession such as a solicitor (legal personnel). Funding may be needed to help pay for preparing the case (access to justice) or in lodging an appeal against conviction or sentence (appeals). The type of offence will determine which court (criminal courts) and whether magistrates or a jury will decide on the facts if the defendant (D) is guilty (these two are known as 'lay people' as they are not qualified lawyers). Sentencing will also depend on which court is used and which offence is charged. Finally, the area of law may involve a precedent being set in one of the higher courts (this is where a new legal principle is created).

The above examples apply to all areas so are not repeated in every Chapter. In the 'links to the non-substantive law', I have added a little, but reminded you to look back at this diagram and these examples.

A final few things before you start the book.

It is important to try to learn plenty of cases as these help to show you how the law works in practice. If you have trouble remembering them then do the best you can, but be sure that you at least know the 'key cases' well.

Criminal cases are usually in the form *R v the defendant (D)*. It is acceptable to use just the name so if the case is **R v Miller** I have called it **Miller**. If another form is used, e.g., **DPP v Miller** I have used the full title, as you may want to look up the case for further information.

Civil cases are between the *claimant* (C) and the *defendant* (D), although you will still see the use of the old word '*plaintiff*' in cases before 1999, when it changed to claimant.

There is a list of some common abbreviations in the appendix at the end of the book.

Part 1: Criminal law for Year 1 A-level and AS (7161)

Chapter 1 covers the rule of law and some general principles of law. The rule of law only comes in to Paper 1 for AS (and Paper 3 for A-level). Other parts of the English legal system are specific to particular examination papers (see examination practice in the summary after Part 1 and at the end of the book).

Chapters 2 and 3 cover the basic requirements for criminal liability which are needed for the offences you study in both Year 1 and Year2.

The rest of Part 1 covers five different non-fatal offences against the person (also needed for both Year 1 and Year2). These are:

- **Assault** – where D puts someone in fear of harm
- **Battery** – where D uses force on someone
- **Actual bodily harm (ABH)** – when either of the above causes an injury which isn't serious
- **Grievous bodily harm (GBH) or wounding** – where someone suffers serious harm or a cut
- **Grievous bodily harm or wounding with intent** – where someone suffers serious harm or a cut which D intended

These offences are commonly called 'the assaults'. However, they are separate and distinct offences, with different rules on each.

Example

Jane threatens Jenny and then pushes her. Jenny is scared and runs away. She trips and grazes her knee. Frightening Jenny is assault, pushing her is battery. Jenny grazed her knee which is actual bodily harm. If she is seriously hurt or cut badly it will be grievous bodily harm or wounding. If Jane *intended* to harm Jenny seriously, it would be grievous bodily harm or wounding with intent.

There is some evaluation of these offences in the Chapters covering them. You will need more depth for the A-level in Year 2 so further discussion of the problems and proposals for reform are contained in 'The Bridge' at the end of Part 1.

Chapter 1: The Nature of Law and the Rule of law

This Chapter covers the nature and rule of law. You may already have covered this part of the English legal system, but I have repeated the rule of law in full, and the rest briefly, as you will now need to think about these in relation to the criminal law.

The nature of law

The nature of law is essentially that it is based on rules. Legal liability occurs when the rules have been broken. In order to understand the nature of law we need to know a bit more about where the law comes from, what distinguishes a legal rule from other rules (or norms) of behaviour, how a person may become liable in law and what differences there are between civil and criminal liability.

Sources of Law

We are governed by rules imposed by the state. This includes the courts, which produce common law through cases heard in court, and Parliament which produces statute law. Some (not many) laws come from custom, i.e., they have been going on for so long they are accepted as law even though not set out in a case or statute. These are all sources of law. Other sources of law today include European law and Human rights law.

All these areas are covered elsewhere in the course under the English legal system.

Legal rules and criminal liability

Social rules are often referred to as norms. A norm can be described as the expected standard of behaviour within a society. However both legal rules (law) and social rules (morals) are called norms by academics and lawyers. That is why it is important to be able to differentiate between law and morals (see Nature of law below). It is possible to say all rules are norms, but social norms are not enforced in law whereas legal norms are.

There is no agreed definition of law. Essentially, it is a matter of rules, but so is much a life. Therefore, a distinction needs to be made between enforceable legal rules and other norms of behaviour. There are many rules governing our lives but not all are enforceable. There may be rules governing how you behave in school or college, and there will be rules at home too. None of these rules has the force of law. A teacher or parent may punish (sanction) you for breaking these rules but there will be no such sanctions from a court of law.

Law is based on liability. A person is legally liable when accountable in law for something done/not done. There are two types of liability, criminal and civil, and both are based on the principle of individuals being responsible for their conduct.

- Criminal liability is based on an individual's responsibility to the state and society as a whole
- Civil liability is based on an individual's responsibility to other individuals

The main differences between criminal and civil liability are seen in the *consequences* not the deed. Harming someone is against the criminal law, but the victim (V) may want to sue in civil law to claim compensation for any injuries, thus there is both criminal and civil liability. Here is a summary of the different types of action in court:

Criminal Law

- Proceedings are initiated by the Crown (Crown Prosecution Service)
- Proceedings are paid for by the State
- Cases commence in the Magistrates' Court
- Serious crimes are heard in the Crown Court
- The accused is prosecuted
- The burden of proof is on the prosecution
- The standard of proof is beyond reasonable doubt
- The primary purpose is punishment
- The case is in the form of R v Smith (R stands for Regina i.e., the Crown)

Civil Law

- Proceedings are initiated by the individual (the claimant)
- Proceedings are paid for by the parties (usually the loser)
- Cases commence in the County Court or High Court depending on the amount claimed
- The defendant is sued
- The burden of proof is on the Claimant
- The standard of proof is the balance of probabilities
- The primary purpose is compensation, called damages
- The case is in the form of Smith v Brown (i.e., the parties to the dispute)

As this book deals with the criminal law a little more on the background of criminal liability is needed. There is no exact definition of a crime, but there are some fundamental principles which are accepted as being part of the nature of criminal law. The criminal law **prohibits** certain actions and **punishes** those who commit them.

The theory and nature of law for A-level

The basic elements of criminal liability are **guilty conduct** (known as *actus reus*) and **guilty mind** (known as *mens rea*). These general elements of liability are dealt with in the next two Chapters. When making rules of criminal law certain principles are upheld. One principle is that the law, especially criminal law, must be certain and the rules clearly defined. This is a requirement of both the rule of law (AS) and justice (A level). It is often referred to as 'fair labelling' and you will come to see that there are several offences that are not sufficiently clearly defined, in particular the non-fatal offences against the person we cover in Part 1. The main basis for criminalising behaviour is harm. This is not only harm to a person but also harm to property, hence laws **prohibiting** violence and theft. The law expects people to be responsible for their actions, so **punishes** those who break the law if found to be at **fault**. This is the principle of individual autonomy. Individuals are deemed responsible for their own behaviour and this justifies imposing punishment on them for breaking the rules. There are different levels of fault in criminal law, and these are covered in Chapter 3. Whatever the level of fault (*mens rea*), it is generally accepted that it should correspond with the conduct (*actus reus*) so that a person should only be criminally liable where the *mens rea* was for the offence actually committed. This principle is called the correspondence principle but you will come to see that it is not always followed in practice. Where there is no accordance, or correspondence, between the *actus reus* and *mens rea* it is known as constructive liability and you will see examples of this with the substantive law as it applies to murder, manslaughter and two of the non-fatal offences against the person. Finally, it is generally accepted that the law should not be retrospective; it should apply to the future and not the past. This is the case with statute law passed by Parliament as that will prohibit behaviour from the time the Act becomes law. However, with the common law, which comes from judgments in cases, this is not always true because if the decision has changed the law, the person in court maybe guilty of something that was not previously illegal (an example is the case of **R v R** discussed in detail in 'The bridge' as you won't need to discuss legal theory or concepts of law for AS level).

Note: There are still a few Latin terms used in law. Don't worry, they seem scary at first but you will be using them so often they will soon seem familiar.

The nature of law not only covers what law is and where it comes from, as well as the differences between civil and criminal law, but also includes how law operates in society, involving different theories (or concepts) of law which are studied for the full A-level. These are covered in depth in my book 'The Nature of Law for AQA and Eduqas A Level', as legal theory is a subject in its own right. The book also contains links to the legal system and the substantive law e.g., tort, crime, contract and human rights. The concepts of law need to be related to all your other areas of study (i.e., they are synoptic) including what you study in Year 1, and not only to the substantive law but also to the legal system. The new A-level requires that you can use the substantive law to illustrate the concepts, and can discuss the concepts in the context of the substantive law. It is therefore a good idea to think about them, at least briefly, as you work through the rest of your studies, so I have included a short introduction here. There is a little more detail in 'The Bridge' between Parts 1 and 2 of this book to prepare you for Year 2.

As well as legal principles the other concepts are law and morals, law and justice, balancing competing interests and fault. These will not be tested at AS but for the A-level you will need to apply these theories to the areas of law studied in Year 1.

We have discussed the main criminal theory and principles above. Here is a very brief explanation of each of the others so that you can consider how they might apply in practice as you work through your course. Thus, if you see a case which you think was decided unfairly you can ask yourself whether the law is achieving justice, or whether the level of fault involved was properly reflected in the decision. This is just a taster; for examples which relate to the criminal law studied in Year 1, and more on these concepts, see 'The Bridge' between Parts 1 and 2. For the rest of the course (Part 2 of this book) examples are given in each Chapter under the heading 'Links to the non-substantive law'. These illustrate how the law works in practice in relation to such concepts as justice, morals, fault, and balancing competing interests. You will then have a store of cases you already know to use as examples in a question on any of these concepts in the A-level examination at the end of your course. I have not done this for Part 1 because if you are planning to stop at the AS you don't need to study these concepts.

Balancing competing interests – the law must balance different interests (or rights) between individuals (private interests), and between an individual and the state or society (the public interest), in order to achieve justice.

Fault – both civil and criminal liability is based (usually) on fault, or to put it another way, a person is not liable unless blameworthy. Fault is an indicator of blame; therefore it justifies the imposition of liability. Fault is especially important in criminal law as the law should only punish those who are blameworthy, and the higher the level of fault the harsher the sentence.

Morals – as noted when looking at rules, the law only punishes someone for breaking legal rules, not social (or moral) ones. However, legal rules sometimes overlap with social rules and morality. This is what law and morality is about: how far social and legal rules overlap and whether the law should be involved in moral issues. Sometimes the law has to get involved because a moral issue comes up in court (examples are whether life support can be withdrawn from a patient in a coma and whether an anorexic teenager could be force-fed against her wishes).

Justice – justice is in the very nature of law, so there are many examples throughout this book of whether the legal rules on a specific area achieve justice. These are mostly in Part 2, but Part 1 includes the rule of law (see below) part of which is fairness and equality. Fairness and equality are also in the nature of justice, at least to most people. One view of justice (called positivism) is that justice depends on legal rules. A law that is made properly using the correct procedures will be a just law whether or not it is moral. Another view of justice (called natural law) is that it is based on moral rules, so if a law is not moral it is not a true law. This shows the overlap between justice and morality.

Note that these concepts are not all on all papers (see the examination practice sections for a table of what goes where in each paper as regards the non-substantive law). For criminal law, you need fault and justice, so concentrate on these, and as you work through this book ask yourself the following questions.

- Is the legal system just (procedural justice)?
- Is a particular law just (substantive justice)?
- What is the fault element here?
- Is the level of fault reflected in the judge's decision or sentence?

Linking the concepts with the law

Although only fault and justice are specifically assigned to the criminal law paper, AQA have confirmed that "where appropriate, irrespective of the Paper to which a Nature of Law/ELS topic is assigned, examples may be drawn from the substantive law in other Papers". For the nature of law, this means that although fault and justice are assigned to the criminal law paper, you can also use examples from tort, contract and/or human rights to illustrate these concepts. Similarly, law and morals is with tort on Paper 2 but there are many criminal cases which illustrate morality, e.g. euthanasia ('mercy killing') cases, which come into murder, so you could use these cases when discussing law and morality on the tort paper. It is anyway a good idea to have a basic idea of each of the concepts as not only is there an overlap, but it will also give you a better understanding of how the legal theories can be related to the law in practice. The overlap can be seen in the case example in Task 1. The interests of the people involved (to do what they wanted in private) were balanced against the public interest (in being protected from violence). The public interest was seen as more important so they were found guilty (thus enforcing morality). The fault element was high because serious harm was intended, so the law decided they should be punished even though they consented to being harmed. The decision was partly based on morality as some of the judges thought society itself was harmed by allowing such behaviour, even in private. Under the natural law view of justice the decision was correct as the behaviour was arguably immoral. Under the positivist view of justice that would not matter: a positivist would agree with the decision being based on the legal rule not to cause serious harm intentionally. This was an appeal case heard in the House of Lords by five judges. The decision was a 3-2 majority. You can see that even the judges in the case disagreed on what justice was and whether it was achieved.

This first task gives you an idea of how you might think about these concepts as you read a particular case.

Task 1

In **Brown 1994**, serious injuries had occurred during consensual sado-masochistic sex in private. This was a criminal case and those involved were convicted of grievous bodily harm. They were all adults and no-one was forced to participate, but the court decided that the defence of consent could not be applied to serious harm where it was intentional. One judge said that the public should be protected from violence and that society itself was harmed by such behaviour, even if it happened in private. Another judge said it was not for the courts to protect people from themselves.

Do you think the decision achieved justice?

What interests were balanced?

What role did fault play in the case?

What role did morality play?

The rule of law

When rules of law and procedure are formulated they should conform to the rule of law. This involves equality, clarity and fairness.

- **The law should apply to everyone equally and no-one should be above the law.**
- **The law must be clear so that people know the rules (then if the rules are broken it will be fair to punish those at fault).**
- **The law must be accessible so that if a person is accused of a crime it is only fair that access to justice and legal advice is possible.**

This is a simplified description of the rule of law, and it applies not only to Paper 1 at AS but also to Paper 3 for the A-level, so needs further discussion.

The Rule of Law

The **Constitutional Reform Act 2005** refers to the rule of law, and the Lord Chancellor's oath requires the Lord Chancellor to respect the rule of law, but there is no agreed definition of it. An early view of the rule of law is that formulated by Dr Thomas Fuller in 1733: "Be you ever so high, the law is above you". This view has continued for centuries. In **Evans v AG 2015**, the SC ruled that correspondence between Prince Charles and government ministers should be made public under the **Freedom of Information Act** and said it was "fundamental to the rule of law" that decisions and actions of the executive are subject to review in a court of law.

The rule of law was popularised by A. V. Dicey (a constitutional lawyer) the following century who, in summary, said "everyone, whatever his rank, is subject to the ordinary law of the land". A little more recently, Lord Bingham said "If you maltreat a penguin in the London zoo, you do not escape prosecution because you are the Archbishop of Canterbury". So, an important part of the rule of law is that everyone is subject to it, with no exceptions. There is more to it than that, and opinions differ on what it means in the modern sense. Although the rule of law is a somewhat abstract notion, to try to explain it today a good place to start is with Lord Bingham's 2014 lecture on the subject, taken from his book 'The Rule of Law'. The core principle is as above, that no-one is above the law, including those who make it. He notes that the rule of law has evolved and continues to do so, and sets out eight sub-rules which he feels describe the rule of law in its current form. These are:

Law must be accessible. This means that if people are bound by the law they must be able to know what the law is.

Questions of legal rights and liabilities should be resolved by application of the law and not be a matter of discretion. This does not mean there is absolutely no discretion. A judge must exercise a certain amount of discretion when deciding on an appropriate sentence or remedy – the point is that any such discretion is limited by law, e.g., statutes or earlier decisions.

The law should apply equally to all. This is accepted by most people as being part of any rule of law but Lord Bingham points out that in practice it is not always apparent. An example is the various **Terrorism Acts** where non-nationals suspected of terrorism are subject to being locked up without trial, but nationals are not – even though they pose the same threat. It is arguable that anyone subject to national laws should be entitled to the law's protection. Even where the law appears to apply equally it may not in practice. It is true that the Archbishop of Canterbury is not above the law – but if he does mistreat a penguin he can probably afford a decent lawyer to help his case! The **Legal Aid, Sentencing and Punishment of Offenders Act 2012 (LASPO)**, has severely reduced access to justice and legal aid, especially in civil cases.

The law should adequately protect fundamental human rights. This is perhaps a more recent addition to the concept of the rule of law. The preamble to the **Universal Declaration of Human Rights** says that if people are not to be compelled to rebel against tyranny and oppression that "human rights should be protected by the rule of law".

The state must meet its obligations under international law. Thus an act by a state that is unlawful would be against the rule of law. He referred to the war against Iraq and whilst not saying whether or not he believed it to be illegal, he did say that if it *was* illegal then it would be against the rule of law "if this sub-rule is sound".

Means must be provided for resolving civil disputes. He says that if people are bound by the law they should receive its benefits and should be able to go to court to have their rights and liberties determined "in the last resort". He does not rule out less formal methods of resolving disputes but sees access to the courts as a "basic right" adding that legal advice should be affordable and available without excessive delay. Where the first sub-rule requires law to be accessible in the sense of clarity, this sub-rule requires accessibility in terms of cost. It has been said that justice is open to all "like the Ritz hotel" – meaning that everyone may be entitled to it but many are unable to use it in practice due to lack of money. Going back to the mistreatment of penguins, the Archbishop is more likely to be able to afford to go to the Ritz and to gain access to justice than the average person on the street is, especially since **LASPO**.

All public officials must exercise their power reasonably and not exceed its limits. As with the second rule, this rule is against the arbitrary use of power. An example of its application is that everyone has the right to apply for judicial review of a decision made by public officers and government ministers – a judge cannot overturn such a decision, but can rule that it is unreasonable.

Adjudicative procedures must be fair. This means open court hearings, the right to be heard, the right to know what the charges and evidence against you are, that the decision maker is independent and impartial, and that in criminal cases D is innocent until guilt is proved. Fairness would also cover access to justice in both the earlier senses of clarity and cost.

Lord Bingham sees the rule of law as depending on an unspoken bargain between the individual and the state. The citizen sacrifices some freedom by accepting legal constraints on certain activities, and the state sacrifices some power by recognising it cannot do all that it has the power to do. He concludes that this means those who maintain and protect the rule of law are "guardians of an all but sacred flame which animates and enlightens the society in which we live".

To sum up the rule of law:

No-one is above the law

Everyone is subject to the law, not the arbitrary exercise of power

The law must encompass clarity, access to justice, fairness and an independent and impartial judiciary

The law must apply equally

In Lord Bingham's view, the rule of law should also protect human rights and comply with international obligations if it is to apply to a modern state with national and international commitments. Bear that in mind if you will be studying human rights for Paper 3.

As you study the law try to consider whether the rule of law is being upheld.

Task 2

Explain what Lord Bingham meant when he said "If you maltreat a penguin in the London zoo, you do not escape prosecution because you are the Archbishop of Canterbury". Add a comment of your own as to whether you agree that this should be part of the rule of law.

Self-test questions

1. State two sources of law
2. State three differences between civil and criminal law
3. What is the core principle of the rule of law?
4. What is the legal term for guilty conduct?
5. What is the legal term for a guilty mind?

Chapter 2: Actus reus: *Conduct, circumstances, consequences and causation*

"... there was gross and criminal negligence, as the man was paid to keep the gate shut and protect the public ... a man might incur criminal liability from a duty arising out of a contract". Wright J

By the end of this Chapter, you should be able to:

- **Explain *actus reus* in relation to conduct, omissions and circumstances**
- **Explain how *actus reus* may involve consequences**
- **Illustrate how causation is proved by reference to cases**
- **Identify possible criticisms for an evaluation of the law**

There are two elements which need to be proved for most offences. These are known by the Latin terms *actus reus* and *mens rea*. *Mens rea* involves the state of mind of D (the defendant) at the time of the offence and we will deal with this in Chapter 3. First we will look at *actus reus* which involves everything else (other than the mental element), which makes up the crime.

These two Chapters are important because these basic requirements for criminal liability are needed for the other offences you will study.

It is very important to identify each element of the *actus reus* of a crime because there can be no crime unless the *actus reus* is complete. This does not necessarily mean D will be acquitted. If part of the *actus reus* of an offence is not proved then *that* offence is not committed, but there may well be a connected offence or an attempt.

Although in simple terms *actus reus* means a guilty act or wrongful conduct, there is more to it than this. It may include:

- conduct (which is voluntary)
- circumstances
- a consequence (which is caused by D's conduct)

Conduct

Conduct can consist of an act, an omission, or a state of affairs. An **act** is usually straightforward, e.g., hitting someone. As a rule, the conduct must be voluntary. This is seen in **Leicester v Pearson 1952** where a car driver was prosecuted for failing to give precedence to a pedestrian on a zebra crossing. It was shown that his car had been pushed onto the crossing by another car hitting him from behind. He was acquitted. He had not acted voluntarily. An **omission** is a failure to act. In criminal law, this will not usually make you guilty unless you have a duty to act in the first place. An example is failing to look after your child. A **state of affairs** is where you can commit an offence just by being in a certain state, e.g., 'being *drunk* in charge of a motor vehicle'. In these cases the conduct may not be voluntary.

Acts and omissions

In **Fagan v Metropolitan Police Commissioner 1969**, D accidentally drove onto a police officer's foot whilst parking. He didn't move his car when asked; in fact, he used some fairly colourful language which I will not repeat here. He was promptly arrested for, and convicted of, assaulting a police officer in the execution of his duty. He argued that there was no *mens rea* at the time of the act (driving onto his foot) and that the refusal to move was only an omission, not an act. The court held that there was a *continuing act* which started with the driving onto the police officer's foot and continued up to the refusal to move. Thus, not moving when asked to was part of the original act rather than an omission. At this time, he did have *mens rea*. Having decided that this type of assault could not be committed by omission, the CA used the idea of a continuing act to overcome the problem. This case also reaffirms the point that *actus reus* and *mens rea* must be contemporaneous (i.e., coincide or happen at the same time).

A case illustrating the distinction between an act and an omission is **Airedale NHS Trust v Bland 1993**. Tony Bland, who was 17, had been badly injured in the Hillsborough football stadium disaster. He was in what is called a persistent vegetative state and had no hope of recovery. The family and doctors wanted to stop treatment, including artificial feeding. The HL confirmed a court order allowing this. They drew a distinction between a positive act that killed (such as administering a lethal injection) which could never be lawful, and an omission to act which allowed someone to die (e.g., not providing life-saving treatment).

The cases of **Diane Pretty** and **Ms B** in **2002** also illustrate this distinction. In the first, Mrs Pretty wanted her husband to help her commit suicide and took her case to the HL and then the European Court of Human Rights. She wanted a court order that he would not be prosecuted for assisting her suicide. She failed, as this would be a positive act. In the latter case, Ms B wanted treatment discontinued and succeeded in obtaining a court order to allow this, even though it meant she would die. In both cases the women were terminally ill. There have been many other cases since these as the euthanasia issue is a controversial one. These are outside the scope of this book but illustrate law and morals and balancing interests.

So, there is generally no criminal liability for *not* doing something. However, exceptions occur when there is a duty to act. A duty can occur when:

- Parliament has expressly provided for it by statute
- there is a contractual duty
- a relationship of responsibility gives rise to a common law duty
- D has created a dangerous situation.

In these cases, an omission to act is enough.

Example

You see someone drowning and you are a good swimmer, but leave the person to die. You are not guilty of any crime. However, as I said above, there are exceptions. I will come back to this as we look at the exceptions.

Statutory duty to act

An example is the **Road Traffic Act 1988**, which makes it an offence for a driver involved in a road accident to fail to stop and give a name and address when asked, or to fail to report the accident to the police. There is a duty to stop, and to report the accident, so failing to do so (an omission) is part of the *actus reus* of each of these offences. The **Wireless Telegraphy Act 1949** makes broadcasting without a licence illegal, thus in **Blake 1997**, a disc jockey was convicted under this **Act** for failing to get a licence. The same would apply to failing to have a TV licence.

Contractual duty to act

In **Pittwood 1902**, D was employed as a gatekeeper by a railway company. His job was to keep the gate at the crossing shut whenever a train passed. One day he forgot to close the gate. A hay cart crossed the track and was hit by an oncoming train. One person was killed and another seriously injured. D was under a contractual duty of employment to keep the gates to the crossing shut and to safeguard people using the crossing. His failure to act was in breach of his contractual duty and so amounted to the *actus reus* of manslaughter. The quote at the beginning came from this case.

In my example, if you were a lifeguard you would have a contractual duty to act if you saw someone drowning so could be liable.

Similar to this is a duty where you hold a public office. Thus in **Dytham 1979**, a police officer who failed to act when he saw D kicking someone to death was liable. Here though, he was not guilty of homicide, only of misconduct in a public office.

Relationship of responsibility

In **Stone and Dobinson 1977**, a couple had a relative (Fanny) come and live with them. She was anorexic, and often took to her bed for days at a time, refusing food and any other form of assistance. Her condition seriously deteriorated and after inadequate efforts to obtain medical assistance, she was found dead in her bed. The court held that Stone and Dobinson had undertaken the duty of caring for her and they had been grossly negligent in their failure to fulfil their duty. This failure had caused Fanny's death and so they were guilty of manslaughter.

In my example, if you were the parent of the swimmer you would have a duty to act so could be liable. You would also have a duty to act if you had taken on responsibility for them, as in **Dobinson**.

Creating a dangerous situation

In **Miller 1983**, D was squatting in an unoccupied house. One night he fell asleep whilst smoking. When he awoke he realised he'd set fire to the mattress but did nothing to extinguish it, he merely moved to another room. The house caught fire and damage was caused. He was convicted of arson under **s 1 Criminal Damage Act 1971**. The HL upheld his conviction on the basis that if a defendant has unintentionally caused an event, and then realises what has happened, he has a duty to take appropriate action.

In my example, if you pushed the person in, you created the dangerous situation so have a duty to take appropriate action. Again, you could be liable.

Task 3

Compare **Fagan** and **Miller**. Could Miller have been found guilty on the 'continuing act' theory?

State of affairs

A few crimes can be committed without any apparent voluntary act by the accused. In **Larsonneur 1933**, a Frenchwoman was deported against her will from Ireland and brought to England by the police. She was convicted under the **Aliens Order 1920** of being found in the UK without permission. The state of affairs amounting to the *actus reus* was 'being found', so as soon as she landed in the UK without the required permission she committed the offence. This law has since been repealed but a similar situation is seen in **Winzar v Chief Constable of Kent 1983**. A drunk was told to leave a hospital and didn't. He was removed by the police who put him in their car, which was parked on the highway. The police then arrested him for being found drunk on the highway, for which he was later convicted. The state of 'being found' was again enough. So, we can see that 'state of affairs' crimes can occur where something which is normally legal may not be so in certain circumstances. Being drunk is legal, but being drunk 'on the highway' or drunk 'in charge of a motor vehicle' (a state of affairs), is not.

Evaluation pointer

Think about whether there should be liability for omissions. Use the cases above to support your arguments. There is no 'right' answer. It can be argued that there is a moral duty to act if it will save a life. Consider whether there should also be a legal duty. Do you think the court made the right decision in **Airedale NHS Trust v Bland 1993**? It can be said that turning off the machine was an act, but the court viewed it as an omission. On the other hand, in **Fagan v Metropolitan Police**

Commissioner 1969, it could be said there was only an omission but the court found a 'continuing act'.

In addition, the 'state of affairs' cases can be criticised. One of the arguments for imposing liability without having to prove fault is that it saves lengthy investigations and court time, but is it fair to D? Should someone be convicted just for being in the wrong place at the wrong time as in **Winzar v Chief Constable of Kent 1983** and **Larsonneur 1933**? Compare these cases to **Leicester v Pearson 1952.**

Circumstances

Many crimes are committed only if the conduct is carried out in particular circumstances. The *actus reus* of theft is the appropriation (taking) of property belonging to another. 'Appropriation' is the conduct, that it is 'property' and 'belongs to another' are both circumstances. *All* these must be proved or it is not theft. Many of the offences against the person have the word 'unlawful' in their definition. If, for example, D acted in self-defence then in these circumstances the act is not unlawful. The *actus reus* is not satisfied.

Task 4 (there is no answer guide for this)

Make a separate folder for the more detailed material you need for the evaluation part of extended writing questions. As you read cases start to question whether the law achieves justice and add your thoughts to the folder. Look out for articles from newspapers or law journals on any of the issues you are discussing. Cut them out and put them in the folder, adding a few of your own comments.

Consequences and causation

Crimes where a particular consequence is part of the *actus reus* are called **result crimes**. Murder is an example. For a murder conviction, death must result from D's act. Homicide is the unlawful killing of a human being. The *actus reus* involves not just killing (conduct) but also that it is unlawful and of a human being (circumstances) and that death occurs (the consequence).

As well as the consequence itself, it must be proved that D's act *caused* this consequence. Many of the cases on causation involve a homicide because it is a result crime. However, even though the principle may come from a murder case it will apply to a case of ABH as that is also a result crime (the assault must cause the bodily harm). The prosecution must prove causation both **factually** and **legally**.

Factual causation

Factual causation is traditionally referred to as the *'sine qua non'* rule. This phrase is defined in Chambers as 'an indispensable condition'. It means D's action must be a *'sine qua non'* or an 'indispensable condition' of the result. More simply put, the result would not have occurred without D's action. It is more commonly called the 'but for' test. The prosecution must show that 'but for' D's conduct, the victim (V) would not have died (or been injured).

Key case

In **White 1910**, D put cyanide in a drink intending to kill his mother, who was found dead shortly afterwards with the drink 3 parts full. In fact, the mother had died of a heart attack unconnected with the poison. The son was found not guilty of murder. He had the *mens rea* (he intended to kill her) but not the *actus reus* (his act didn't cause her death). He didn't get away with it altogether though; he was guilty of attempted murder.

Principle: If the result would have occurred regardless of D's act then D's act did not cause that result.

White illustrates the situation where D's act has *not* factually caused death. Any of the following cases on legal causation could also be used for illustrating causation in fact. As you read them, ask the question: 'but for D's act would V have died / been injured?' If the answer is 'no' then causation in fact is shown. Causation in fact can be very wide.

Example

I ask a college student to stay on for half an hour to finish a project. She therefore misses her bus and walks home. On the way, she is attacked and injured. It can be argued that 'but for' my asking her to stay late she would not have been attacked and so I am liable for her injury. To avoid such a wide liability the courts have built up some rules on how far someone should be liable for the consequences of their actions. This is causation in law.

Legal causation

This is based on what is called the 'chain of causation'. It means proving an unbroken link, or chain, between D's action and the result, for example, death in homicide cases. When something has occurred after D's original act, then it may be argued that the chain of causation is broken. We will look at some cases to explain how this works, but in summary; the chain of causation will not be broken if:

- D's action makes a 'significant' contribution to the result (**Smith/Cheshire**)
- any intervening act was foreseeable (**Roberts**)
- V has a particular weakness and the result would not have occurred in a normal person. This is known as the 'thin skull' rule (**Blaue**)

In my example, I will argue that the chain has been broken by the attacker. I did not make a significant contribution to the harm, and the attack was not foreseeable. I have not legally caused the injuries.

Task 5 (the answer is included below)

Use my example above, but this time you should apply the rules to the attacker. Decide whether the attacker legally caused death in the following situations:

1. The attacker left her badly injured and lying in the road. She is run over by a car and killed.

2. The attacker left her badly injured but a passer-by sees her and calls an ambulance. She is taken to hospital and starts to recover. However, the treatment is wrong and she dies.

3. She was only slightly injured but (not a good day!) she is struck by lightning as she recovers from the attack.

We will come back to this, but first we'll look at some cases.

In **Smith1959**, a soldier stabbed in a fight was dropped twice on the way to the treatment centre and then left untreated for some time. Although the court recognised that this contributed to the death, they found Smith, who had stabbed him, guilty of murder. As Lord Parker LCJ put it, his act was "still an operating cause and a substantial cause" of the death. A case where D's act was *not* found to have caused the death in similar circumstances is **Jordan 1956**. Here the stab wounds were healing well, but the doctor gave the victim treatment which caused an allergic reaction from which he died. The doctor's act was found to have broken the chain of causation.

The main issue is not how negligent the medical treatment is, but whether D's original act is still having an effect. It was in **Smith** but not **Jordan**, as in the latter case the original wound had almost healed so D's act was no longer a significant cause of the death. This is shown clearly in the next case.

Key case

In **Cheshire 1991**, due to negligent treatment by the hospital, complications arose after an operation on the victim of a shooting. The victim subsequently died. The person accused of the murder argued that his act had not caused the death of the victim, the hospital had done so. The court rejected the argument, following **Smith**. They said that the jury should not regard hospital treatment as excluding D's responsibility unless it "was so **independent of his acts**, and in itself so **potent in causing death**, that they regard the contribution made by his acts as insignificant."

Principle: as long as D's action was a "significant and operative" cause of the death it need not be the sole cause.

This principle was followed by the CA in **Mellor 1996**. An elderly man was taken to hospital following an attack in which he suffered broken ribs and other injuries. He died from bronchial-pneumonia brought on by his injuries. The hospital had failed to give him oxygen which may have saved him, but D was found guilty.

These cases show that the courts are reluctant to allow medical treatment to break the chain of causation and thus prevent D being found guilty.

In **Pagett 1983**, D armed himself with a shotgun and took a pregnant girl hostage in a flat. Armed police called on him to come out. He eventually did so, holding the girl in front of him as a human shield. He then fired the shotgun at the police officers who returned fire, killing the girl hostage. The actions of the police did not break the chain because shooting back at D was held to be a 'natural consequence' of his having shot first. D was convicted of manslaughter.

So causation may be proved against D even though a third person was the immediate cause. In **Chua 2015**, D worked in a hospital and had contaminated saline bags with insulin. The bags were actually administered by other nurses, but this did not break the chain of causation between his actions and the subsequent deaths caused by the contaminated bags. His actions were the significant cause of death.

In some cases D may argue that the act of the victim has broken the chain.

Key Case

In **Roberts 1971**, D – in a moving car – committed an assault on a girl by trying to take off her coat. She jumped out and was injured. He was charged with actual bodily harm. The court had to decide whether the assault caused the injury, or whether her actions broke the chain of causation. It was held that only if it was something that no reasonable person could foresee would the chain of causation be broken by the victim's actions. Here this was not the case so he was liable for her injuries. This means a judge, magistrate or jury may take into account that the victim may do the wrong thing on the spur of the moment.

Principle: If the victim's act is foreseeable it will not break the chain of causation.

To help to remember this, think of an imaginary conversation between the girl, the defendant (D) and the judge.

D: It wasn't my fault she was injured, the stupid girl jumped out of the car.

The girl: I only jumped out because I was scared you were going to hurt me.

Judge: Quite right too, a reasonable reaction and quite foreseeable in the circumstances.

It was recognised in **Roberts** that the victim might do the wrong thing in the agony of the moment. In **Williams & Davis 1992** the CA said that only if V does something "so daft or unexpected" that no reasonable person could be expected to foresee it, would the chain of causation be broken. In **Corbett 1996**, the victim was trying to escape an attack by D, when he fell and was hit by a car. V died so it was a homicide case, but the same principle applies. His action came within a foreseeable range of consequences so did not break the chain.

Before looking at the final rule on causation, what did you decide in Task 5? Remember legal causation turns on how significant a contribution the attack made and whether the 'intervening act' (the car, the hospital treatment or the lightning) was foreseeable. You can therefore ask:

Whether it is foreseeable that a car will come along and hit her – yes, she is lying in the road. The chain is not broken by the car.

Whether it is foreseeable that hospital treatment may be inappropriate – yes, it happens enough for it to be foreseeable. The chain is not broken by the hospital treatment.

Whether it is foreseeable that she is struck by lightning – not likely; it is very rare. In addition, as she was only slightly injured, the attack did not make a significant contribution. The chain is broken by the lightning.

Note that in the last one this does not mean the attacker gets off. He will still be liable for the attack, but not the death.

Summary

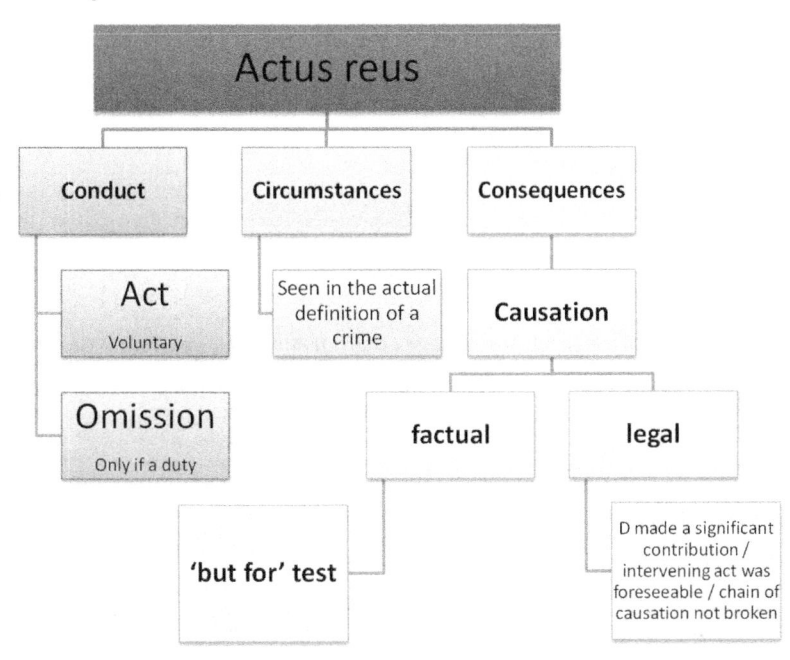

```
                        Actus reus
            ┌───────────────┼───────────────┐
         Conduct       Circumstances    Consequences
         ┌──┴──┐            │               │
         Act              Seen in the    Causation
       Voluntary        actual definition    │
                           of a crime    ┌───┴───┐
         Omission                     factual   legal
       Only if a duty
                                   'but for' test    D made a significant
                                                     contribution /
                                                     intervening act was
                                                     foreseeable / chain of
                                                     causation not broken
```

Evaluation pointer

If you were on the jury, would you know what acts should be considered 'independent' or 'potent' enough to break the causation chain? How significant is significant? What amounts to a 'daft' act by the victim? There may be a thin line between doing 'something wrong in the agony of the moment' and doing something 'daft'. This can make the decision of the jury a tough one to make.

The 'thin skull' rule

A final issue on causation is that the chain is not broken by a particular vulnerability in the victim. Lawton LJ said in **Blaue 1975**, *"those who use violence on other people must take their victims as they find them"*. Also known as the 'thin-skull rule', this appears to conflict with the 'foreseeability' rule. If a particular disability in the victim means that they are more likely to be harmed, or die, D is still liable even though it was not foreseeable.

Key case

In **Blaue 1975**, Lawton LJ went on to say, *"This in our judgement means the whole man, not just the physical man"*. The victim was stabbed repeatedly and rushed to hospital where doctors said she needed a blood transfusion to save her life. She was a Jehovah's Witness and so refused to have one. She consequently died. D was convicted of manslaughter; her refusal of treatment did not break the chain of causation because he had to take his victim as he found her. The 'disability' is more often physical (like a pre-existing medical condition such as a 'thin skull') but here it was the fact that she was a Jehovah's Witness.

Principle: Vulnerability in the victim does not break the chain of causation.

Examination pointer

In a problem question, look out for anything that D can argue broke the chain of causation. For example, D attacks someone and, as they are running away, they are hit by a car or bus. **Roberts** can be used to say that this is unlikely to break the chain. Look out for words like 'near the road' or 'in the bus station'. These suggest it is foreseeable. If V refuses treatment, you may need the 'thin-skull' rule. Here look out for the reason. If it is a completely idiotic decision, then **Blaue** may be distinguished. If it is due to religious beliefs, it will be followed.

Terminology

Make sure you understand the following terms:

- **Actus reus** – the wrongful conduct or guilty act
- **Omission** – not acting which is not usually a crime but may be if there is a duty to act
- **The chain of causation** – the chain between D's act and the result
- **The 'but for' test** – whether the result would have occurred 'but for' D's actions
- **The 'thin skull' rule** – that some kind of vulnerability in the victim will not break the chain of causation

Task 6

Draw a diagram like the summary above for your files. Add a case to each of the principles and keep it as a revision guide.

Links to the non-substantive law

For links to the English legal system, look back at the diagram and examples in the introduction to Part 1.

Self-test questions

1. What '3 Cs' may be included in the actus reus of a crime?
2. On what basis did the court find liability in **Fagan**?

3. *Give two examples of when an omission can result in criminal liability.*

4. *What is the thin skull rule?*

5. *From which case did the quote at the beginning of this Chapter come?*

Answers to tasks and self-test questions are on my website at www.drsr.org/publications/tasks. For some interactive exercises, click on 'Free Exercises'.

Chapter 3 Mens rea

"I attach great importance to the search for a direction which is both clear and simple ... I think that the **Nedrick** direction fulfils this requirement admirably." Lord Hope

By the end of this Chapter, you should be able to:

- **Explain the term *mens rea***
- **Explain how the law on *mens rea* applies in practice**
- **Identify possible criticisms for an evaluation of the law**

Mens rea basically means a guilty mind and refers to the state of mind of the accused at the time the *actus reus* is committed. Thus *mens rea* and *actus reus* must exist at the same time.

There are two **main** types of *mens rea*. These are:

- **Intention**
- **Recklessness**

Other types of *mens rea* can be seen in particular offences. **Dishonesty** comes into many of the property offence. **Gross negligence** is the *mens rea* for one type of manslaughter. These are dealt with later along with those crimes.

It is important to be able to identify both the *actus reus* and the *mens rea* of each offence when answering a problem question. Each and every part of a crime has to be proved beyond reasonable doubt.

Intention

This is the highest form of *mens rea*. For some offences, e.g., theft and murder, only intention suffices. The *mens rea* of theft is the intention to deprive someone of property permanently. If it can be shown that the property was taken absent-mindedly, D can argue that there was no *mens rea*.

Example

You borrow your friend's mobile 'phone because you have run out of credit. You forget to give it back. You have no *mens rea* so are not guilty of theft. If you borrowed it, took it home and put your own SIM card into it, this would be evidence that you intended to deprive your friend of it permanently. In these circumstances, you could be guilty of theft. Think of your own example and make a note now.

A case example is **Madeley 1990**. The host of the *Richard and Judy* television show was charged with shoplifting. He was able to show that he was suffering from stress and merely forgot to pay for the goods. The court accepted his argument and found him not guilty.

Other offences, including most of the non-fatal offences, can be committed either intentionally or recklessly. You need to know both types of *mens rea* because one of the non-fatal offences is 'wounding with intent' and this needs proof of intention; recklessness is not enough.

Although intention is the *mens rea* for 'wounding with intent' many cases you'll see here dealing with intention are homicide cases. This is because it is essentially the *mens rea* that differentiates murder from manslaughter. It is only murder if the killing is intentional. Intention can be direct or oblique (indirect). As with causation, a principle for one offence can be applied to others.

Direct Intent

Direct intent is where the result is D's aim or purpose. This is what most of us would understand by intention. If you pick up a loaded gun and fire it at someone with the aim of killing them, it can be said without any difficulty that you intended to do so. Intention was defined in **Mohan 1975** as "the decision to bring about" the result, or prohibited consequence, whether that result was desired or not. The courts have given the concept of intention a wider meaning, however. This is referred to as oblique, or indirect, intent.

Oblique intent

The consequence isn't your aim but is 'virtually certain' to occur as a result of your actions.

Example

One night, two animal rights activists set fire to a shop which sells fur coats. The shop is closed but a security guard dies in the fire. Are they guilty of murder? They do not have the *mens rea* of *direct* intent, as their purpose is to make a political point, not to kill. They may have *oblique* intent. This will depend on the evidence. We will come back to this. For now, just make a note of what you think.

The issue of intent has been problematic. **S 8 Criminal Justice Act 1967** provides that the jury *"shall not be bound in law to infer that D intended or foresaw a result of his actions by reason only of its being a natural and probable consequence of those actions"*. It also requires the jury to refer to *"all the evidence, drawing such inferences from the evidence as appear proper in the circumstances"*.

Example

Don fires a gun. The bullet kills someone. So, according to **s 8** what does the jury have to do?

The first bit means that just because it's likely to happen, it does not mean that the jury should infer that D intended it to happen. If Don fired into a crowded room, the jury may think death is a likely result, but this is *not enough by itself* to *prove* that Don intended it.

The second bit means that the jury must look at everything else. Where did it happen? What time of day was it? Did Don know there were people about? This will help the jury to decide what Don 'intended'. There is a difference between firing a gun into the air in the middle of an empty field and doing the same thing in a schoolroom. Even in the latter case, it may be that the school is closed and Don is the caretaker shooting at a rat not realising anyone is about. There is no answer which will always be right. That's what juries are for.

There has been a long line of cases on intent. Words like 'foreseeable', 'probable', 'likely' and 'natural' have all been used along the way. In **DPP v Smith 1960**, the HL had said that whether a result was probable was an objective test (what the reasonable person would "contemplate as the natural and probable result"). **S 8** makes the test subjective, whether the *defendant* saw it as probable. In **Hyam v DPP 1975**, a woman poured petrol through the letterbox of a rival and set fire to it. Two children died. She argued that she had only intended to frighten the other woman. The HL rejected her appeal but made clear the test was subjective. It was whether *she* saw the result as 'highly probable'. However, they also suggested that this was proof of intent, not just evidence of it. This point was rejected in **Moloney 1985**. It is now only a matter of evidence, not proof in itself.

In **Moloney**, D and his stepfather were having a drunken competition to see who could load and draw a shotgun the quickest. D won, and his stepfather said "I didn't think you've got the guts, but if you have, pull the trigger." D said he didn't aim the gun but just pulled the trigger. His murder conviction was quashed. The judge had directed the jury that they could find intent if D foresaw the result as 'probable' and the HL said that this was not enough; it needed to be a certainty. Lord Bridge gave an explanation of intent in terms of 'moral certainty'. However, in his later summing up he said that a consequence was 'virtually certain' if it was a 'natural consequence' (and with no mention of the word probable as required by **s 8**). This is not the same thing at all. Many 'natural' consequences are far from certain. Death from a lightning strike is a natural consequence of a storm, but not very likely – let alone certain!

In **Hancock and Shankland 1986**, two striking miners had pushed concrete blocks off a bridge to prevent a miner going to work. They said they only intended to scare him, but the driver of the taxi in which he was travelling was killed. Their conviction for murder was quashed. Both the CA and HL held that 'natural consequence' was misleading and that even awareness of the consequence as 'virtually certain' was only evidence and not proof of intent.

The law on oblique intent was clarified somewhat by the HL in **Woollin 1998**, which confirmed the direction given by the CA in **Nedrick 1986**.

The two key cases: Nedrick 1986 and Woollin 1998

In **Nedrick**, D poured paraffin through V's letterbox, circumstances not unlike those in **Hyam**, and set it alight. He said he only intended to scare her, but her child died in the resulting fire. He was convicted of murder and appealed based on lack of *mens rea*. The CA quashed his conviction because the jury had not been properly directed on intent. A conviction for manslaughter was substituted. In relation to oblique intent in a murder trial, the CA provided the following standard direction for the jury. Lord Lane said,

> *"The jury should be directed that they are not entitled to infer the necessary intention unless they feel sure that death or serious bodily harm was a **virtual certainty** (barring some unforeseen intervention) as a result of the defendant's actions and that **the defendant appreciated** that such was the case ... The decision is one for the jury to be reached on a consideration of all the evidence."*

The opening quote comes from the HL in **Woollin**. A father was convicted of murder after throwing his baby son across the room in a fit of temper. He argued that he had thrown the baby towards his pram but had not intended to kill him. His conviction was again substituted for one of manslaughter, this time by the HL. They confirmed the **Nedrick** direction.

Principle: The two questions the jury must consider as evidence of intent are:

+ was death or serious bodily harm a virtual certainty?

+ did the defendant appreciate that such was the case?

If the answer to both these questions is 'yes' then the jury may find intent. Although the HL used the word 'find' instead of 'infer', this seems of little import.

One other point. In some appeal cases, you may feel that the jury would have found intent. You could well be right. Many appeals are allowed because the jury was misdirected, not necessarily because intent could not be proved. The jury may have found sufficient evidence of intent, but were not directed correctly on the law.

Back to our example

If the defence can show that the two activists thought the shop was empty then the jury is unlikely to be convinced they appreciated that anyone's death or serious injury was a virtual certainty. They could be convicted of manslaughter but not murder. If the prosecution can prove that they knew there was a guard on duty this will be evidence for the jury that they did appreciate that death or serious injury was a virtual certainty, so a conviction for murder is possible.

I have made both **Nedrick** and **Woollin** 'Key cases' because the law was *established* by the CA in **Nedrick**, but *confirmed* by the HL in **Woollin**. A precedent carries greater weight once the HL has approved it. In addition, the **Nedrick** test has not been followed consistently. In **Walker and Hayles 1990**, although the CA held the test to be correct, they said that the use of the phrase 'a very high degree of probability' sufficed. More confusion! In **Woollin** itself, there was some confusion in the CA as to the application of the test (perhaps caused by the **Walker** decision). The Law Commission produced a report and **Draft Code**, in which it gave a definition of intent, between the cases of **Nedrick** and **Woollin**. There was therefore some doubt as to whether, if a case reached the HL, the LC's definition would be preferred to the **Nedrick** one. Apparently not.

Evaluation pointer: Intention

The **Draft Code** definition is that D acts intentionally with respect to a result *"when he acts either in order to bring it about or being aware that it will occur in the ordinary course of events"*. In **Woollin**, Lord Steyn referred to the **Draft Code** but thought the **Nedrick** test was "very similar". It is arguable that the HL should have adopted this if they thought it so similar. It seems quite clear and would become the law if the **Code** were ever adopted.

The test was followed again in **Matthews and Alleyne 2003**.

Key case

In **Matthews and Alleyne**, the Ds had thrown V from a bridge into a river. He drowned. There was evidence that he had told them he couldn't swim. They appealed against their conviction for murder. The CA rejected their appeal but again said that foresight of death as a virtual certainty does not automatically prove intent, it is merely evidence (often very strong evidence) for the jury. I have made this a key case because, unlike **Nedrick** and **Woollin**, the murder conviction was upheld by the CA.

In **Stringer 2008**, D appealed against his convictions for both murder and arson with intent to endanger life. A fire had been started at the bottom of the stairs in his house, where several of his family were sleeping. His brother died. He had denied starting the fire. At the time he was 14 and had a low IQ. The CA accepted that when directing the jury on the question of intent based on **Woollin**, the judge did not make clear the distinction between the two parts of the test (the inevitability of death or injury, and D's appreciation of it). However, on the facts, there could be only one answer to the question whether it was a virtual certainty that somebody would suffer death or serious injury from a fire in these circumstances. As to the second part of the test, even taking account of his age and low IQ the judge said that,

> "the inference that he must have appreciated it on that morning was also overwhelming. The jury's conclusion that [he] had the necessary intent was bound to follow".

So firstly, death or serious injury was a virtual certainty, and secondly, he appreciated that this was the case. He therefore had indirect intent. These are murder cases but the same principle applies to the non-fatal offences, in particular assault occasioning actual bodily harm. The only difference is that instead of serious injury or death being a virtual certainty, it will be a question of whether the assault or battery was a virtual certainty.

Examination pointer

When applying the law on intent you need only use **Nedrick** and **Woollin**, and only then in cases of oblique intent, not where it is direct. This was made clear in **Woollin**. D's knowledge will be an important factor. Look carefully at the facts for information such as 'they knew that ...' or 'unknown to them ...'. These comments will help you to apply the test as in my example. Secondly, if the offence can be committed recklessly you don't need to discuss intent at all. You can say that recklessness (see next) is enough and go on to apply the rules on that.

Summary of the development of the law on intent

Case	Development	Probable, possible or certain?	Objective / subjective Proof or evidence
DPP v Smith 1960	HL held that the *mens rea* for murder is intention to kill or cause grievous bodily harm	Foresight of death or serious injury as a natural and probable result	Objective (what the 'reasonable man or woman' would contemplate)
Hyam 1974 (similar facts to **Nedrick**)	Changed to a subjective test by HL	Foresight of death or serious injury as highly probable	Noted that s8 had amended this to subjective It proved intent (this seems to contradict s8 which refers to evidence)
Moloney 1985	HL disapproved **Hyam** Foreseeing death as 'probable' was not proof of intent	Foresight of death or serious injury as a moral certainty or natural consequence	Foresight was *evidence* of intent rather than *proof* of intent
Hancock and Shankland 1986	**Moloney** guidelines were followed but HL held that 'natural consequence' was misleading	The greater the probability the more likely it was foreseen and thus intended	Evidence
Nedrick 1986	CA provided a new test	Death or serious injury was a virtual certainty and D appreciated this	Evidence from which the jury can 'infer' intent
Walker and Hayles 1990	CA followed **Nedrick** but added	very high degree of probability sufficed	Evidence from which the jury can 'infer' intent
Woollin 1998	HL confirmed **Nedrick** test	Death or serious injury was a virtual certainty and D appreciated this	Evidence from which jury can 'find' intent
Matthews and Alleyne 2003 / Stringer 2008	Applied **Nedrick** test	Death or serious injury was a virtual certainty and D appreciated this	Evidence of intent is not proof of intent

Recklessness

There were two types of recklessness. Subjective recklessness is used for most crimes as an alternative *mens rea* to intent. Objective recklessness was used for criminal damage until 2003, but is now abolished. Subjective means looking at what was in the *defendant's* mind. Objective means looking at what the *reasonable person* would think. Although this no longer applies, you need to know a little about it for possible use in an extended writing question on the developments.

Key case

Cunningham 1957 provides the test for subjective recklessness. D ripped a gas meter from a basement wall in order to steal the money in the meter. Gas escaped and seeped through to an adjoining property where an occupant was overcome by the fumes. D was charged with maliciously administering a noxious substance, and argued that he did not realise the risk of gas escaping. The CA quashed his conviction having interpreted 'maliciously' to mean with subjective recklessness. The prosecution had failed to prove that D was aware that his actions might cause harm.

Principle: The test for subjective recklessness is that:

D is aware of the existence of a risk (of the consequence occurring) and deliberately goes ahead and takes that risk.

Objective recklessness was defined in **Caldwell 1982**. D, whilst drunk, set fire to a chair in the basement of the hotel where he worked. He was charged with arson (a type of criminal damage) endangering life. He argued that in his drunken state he had not thought about the fact that there could be people in the hotel. In the HL Lord Diplock extended the meaning of recklessness to include the situation where either

D saw a risk and ignored it (as in Cunningham, subjective recklessness) *or*

D gave no thought to a risk which was obvious to a reasonable person (a new meaning, objective recklessness)

In **Gemmell and Richards 2003**, the HL confirmed that recklessness is subjective and that the **Caldwell** test was wrong. Overruling its previous decision in **Caldwell**, the HL said that the *defendant* had to have recognised that there was some kind of risk.

Key case

In **Gemmell and Richards 2003**, two boys aged 11 and 13 set light to some papers outside the back of a shop. Several premises were badly damaged. They were convicted of arson on the basis of **Caldwell**, i.e., that the risk of damage was obvious to a reasonable person (in other words, objective recklessness). Their ages were therefore not taken into account. They appealed. The CA cannot overrule a decision of the HL and D's argument under the Human Rights Act also failed. They appealed further to the HL, which used the **1966 Practice Statement** to overrule its previous decision and quash the conviction.

Principle: The *mens rea* for criminal damage is now subjective (**Cunningham**) recklessness.

Thus, to prove recklessness it must be shown that *D is aware of a risk, but deliberately goes ahead and takes it.*

Evaluation pointer

Consider whether **Caldwell** or **Gemmell** is to be preferred. The latter seems to ensure greater fairness as it means D must recognise the risk of the result and if so then that shows a level of fault which should rightly be punished. However, **Caldwell** can be supported on the basis that being drunk shouldn't mean you get away with a crime. There were other cases that followed it which are harder to justify though.

In **Elliott 1983**, a 14-year old girl, who was in a special-needs class at school, set fire to a shed not realising the risk of lighting white spirit. The magistrates acquitted her. However, the prosecution successfully appealed on the basis of **Caldwell**. A reasonable person would have seen the risk that she took, so she had sufficient *mens rea*. This case shows the difficulties of applying the objective test to a child, or a person who lacks the capacity of a 'reasonable person'. However, **Gemmell** solves this problem.

Examination pointer

For a problem question involving recklessness, you only need to discuss subjective (**Cunningham**) recklessness. This is now the law as stated by the HL in **Gemmell**. A second point is that you do not need to discuss intent where the offence allows for a *mens rea* of recklessness, intent is hard to prove and unnecessary in such cases.

Task 7 (there is no answer guide for this)

Draw up a diagram with three columns. Use the first to list out all the key cases you have seen so far, use the second column for the facts and the third for the principle. Keep the diagram as a guide for revision. It might look nice on the bedroom wall.

Transferred Malice

Mens rea can be transferred from the intended victim to the actual victim. This means that if you intend to hit Steve but miss and hit Joe you cannot say "but I didn't intend to hit Joe so I had no *mens rea*". In **Latimer 1886**, D aimed a blow at X with his belt but missed and seriously wounded V. He had the intent (*mens rea*) to hit X, and this intent was transferred to the wounding (*actus reus*) of V. Thus, he had both the *mens rea* and the *actus reus* of wounding. Although usually referred to as 'transferred intent' it applies to *mens rea* generally, to both intention and recklessness. The *actus reus* and *mens rea* must be for the *same* crime.

Example

I throw a brick at someone but it misses and breaks a window. I had *mens rea* for an assault and *actus reus* for criminal damage. This *mens rea* can't be transferred. I am not guilty of either crime. If I throw the brick at someone but it hits someone else then this *mens rea* can be transferred. I had *mens rea* and *actus reus* for the *same* offence.

Coincidence of actus reus and mens rea

We saw in **Fagan v Metropolitan Police Commissioner 1969** that *actus reus* and *mens rea* must coincide, but that the court may view the *actus reus* as **continuing**. A similar reasoning can be seen in **Thabo Meli 1954**. Planning to kill him, the Ds attacked a man and then rolled what they thought was his dead body over a cliff, to make it look like an accident. He was only unconscious at this point, and the actual cause of death was exposure. The Ds were convicted of murder and argued that there were two separate acts. The first act (the attack) was accompanied by *mens rea* but was not the cause of death (so no *actus reus*). The second act (pushing him over the cliff) was the cause of death, but was not accompanied by *mens rea*. The *mens rea* of murder is intention to kill or seriously injure. They said there could be no such intention if they thought that the man was already dead. The court said that it was "impossible to divide up what was really one **series of acts** in this way", and refused their appeal.

Terminology

Make sure you understand the following terms:

- **Mens rea** – the 'guilty mind', which can be intent or subjective recklessness
- **Intention** – D's aim or purpose (direct intent) or knowledge that the result was a virtual certainty (indirect intent)
- **Subjective recklessness** – where D sees a risk but goes ahead and takes it
- **Transferred malice** – the *mens rea* can be transferred from the intended V to the actual V

- Coincidence of *actus reus* and *mens rea* – also called the contemporaneity rule. It means that *actus reus* and *mens rea* must exist at the same time

Summary

Level of *mens rea*	Explanation	Cases	Example crimes
• Direct Intention	• D's aim or purpose, a decision to bring about the result	• Mohan 1975	• Murder, theft, grievous bodily harm and wounding with intent
• Indirect Intention	• Result is a virtual certainty and D appreciates this	• Nedrick 1986 CA • Woollin 1998 HL	• Murder, theft, grievous bodily harm and wounding with intent
• Subjective Recklessness	• D recognises a risk and goes on to take it	• Cunningham 1957	• All other assaults, criminal damage

Links to the non-substantive law

For links to the English legal system, look back at the diagram and examples in the introduction to Part 1. In particular in this Chapter we have seen a precedent set in **Gemmell and Richards 2003**, where the HL used the 1966 Practice Statement to change the law on recklessness.

Self-test questions

1. From which case did the quote at the beginning of this Chapter come?
2. What are the two types of intent?
3. What is the **Nedrick** test for oblique intent?
4. Is recklessness now a subjective or objective test and in which case was this decided?
5. What is the principle in **Latimer**?

Chapter 4 Strict liability

"... there has for centuries been a presumption that Parliament did not intend to make criminals of persons who were in no way blameworthy in what they did. That means that whenever a section is silent as to mens rea *there is a presumption that, in order to give effect to the will of Parliament, we must read in words appropriate to require* mens rea" Lord Reid

By the end of this Chapter, you should be able to:

- **Explain the rules on strict liability**
- **Show how the law has developed by reference to cases**
- **Identify the arguments for and against strict liability, in order to attempt an evaluation**

As we have seen, most crimes require both *mens rea* and *actus reus*. Thus, even if D has carried out a criminal act, there will usually be no liability unless it happened with *mens rea*, in the sense of fault or blameworthiness. However, some crimes do not require *mens rea* in any form. These are called **strict liability** crimes. In these crimes, only the *actus reus* must be proved.

Some crimes do not require either *actus reus* or *mens rea*. Crimes which involve a 'state of affairs' can be committed without any apparent voluntary act by D. This is called absolute liability. It does not occur often so we will deal with it briefly first then look at strict liability in more detail.

As we saw, *actus reus* must be voluntary, so it is a defence if the offence was not committed voluntarily. In **Leicester v Pearson 1952**, the driver was acquitted of failing to give precedence to a pedestrian on a zebra crossing because his car had been pushed onto it by another car hitting him from behind. However, there are exceptions here too. Crimes of **absolute liability** arise where there is no defence to D's action.

Absolute liability: State of affairs crimes

As we saw in Chapter 2, a few crimes can be committed without any apparent voluntary act by the accused. In **Larsonneur 1933**, a Frenchwoman was deported against her will from Ireland and brought to England by the police. She was convicted under the **Aliens Order 1920** of being found in the UK without permission. The state of affairs amounting to the *actus reus* was 'being found', so as soon as she landed in the UK without the required permission she committed the offence, even though she had no choice. This particular law has since been repealed but a similar situation is seen in **Winzar v Chief Constable of Kent 1983**. A drunk was told to leave a hospital and didn't. He was removed by the police who put him in their car, which was parked on the highway. The police then arrested him for being found drunk on the highway, for which he was later convicted. As in **Larsonneur 1933**, the state of 'being found' in the circumstances was enough. So, we can see that 'state of affairs' crimes can occur where something which is normally legal may not be so in certain circumstances. Being drunk is legal, but being drunk 'on the highway' or drunk 'in charge of a motor vehicle', (a state of affairs) is not.

Statutory nature of strict liability

Strict liability most often applies to regulatory offences, i.e., offences that are not truly criminal in nature, such as traffic offences and offences covering areas of social concern or public health, such as the sale of food and alcohol, pollution and protection of the environment. These offences are usually governed by statute and the statute regulates how people must behave in certain circumstances. The statute will impose certain requirements on the relevant people and if these requirements are not satisfied, an offence will be committed. The **Health and Safety at Work Act 1974** is a good example. It imposes requirements on an employer to ensure a safe environment, competent staff and safe equipment. Other statutes cover trading standards and the sale of goods. Although these statutes are often seen as dealing with civil issues, because the person affected can sue for damages, they also create criminal offences. An employer or shopkeeper can be prosecuted as well as sued.

Example

In **Meah v Roberts 1977,** two children were served lemonade that had caustic soda in it. D was not responsible for it being there, but was found guilty under the **Food and Drug Act 1955**, even though not at fault herself because it had got into the bottle by accident.

Even though most such crimes are statutory, the courts must interpret the statutes, so case law is still important, especially if the Act is not clear on whether the offence requires *mens rea* or is a strict liability offence.

Interpretation by the courts

In **Harrow LBC v Shah 1999**, a newsagent was convicted for selling a lottery ticket to a person under 16 even though the staff had been told to ask for proof of age if there was any doubt, and the member of staff who actually sold the ticket believed the boy was over 16. It was held that the offence under the **National Lottery Regulations 1994** was one of strict liability, so there was no need to prove an intent, or even recklessness, as regards the age of the buyer of the ticket. The act of selling it to someone under 16 was enough.

Some statutes specifically provide a defence to strict liability crimes where D can prove that all due care was taken. This is known as the 'due diligence' defence. An example is the **Licensing Act 2003** which provides a defence to various offences under the **Act**, such as selling alcohol to young people, if D "exercised all due diligence to avoid committing the offence".

However, the courts have been reluctant to develop this approach so it only applies where the statute specifically allows for it. Thus the court found the newsagent guilty in **Shah**, even though he had taken care, as the **National Lottery Regulations** had no such provision. The Law Commission (in their 2010 report on the issue) has suggested that the due diligence defence should apply in all cases.

In **Smedley's v Breed 1974**, a caterpillar was found in a can of peas. Although the manufacturers had supplied millions of cans of peas (all without caterpillars!) they were convicted, as in **Meah v Roberts**, under the **Food and Drug Act 1955** for selling food that was unfit for human consumption.

Most strict liability crimes are fairly minor, and not usually seen as truly criminal. Someone convicted may have broken the law but there is little social stigma attached to the act, even though illegal. In 'real' crimes there is more controversy about finding someone guilty without fault, and this can be seen in **Sweet v Parsley 1970**.

Key case

In **Sweet v Parsley**, a woman let rooms to students. The police raided the premises and found cannabis. She was charged with being *"concerned in the management of premises used for the purpose of smoking cannabis"* under the **Dangerous Drugs Act 1965**. She was found guilty even though not at fault – she was completely unaware of the cannabis smoking. The HL eventually acquitted her and established the rule that strict liability could only be imposed where the Act specifically made the offence one of strict liability. In all other cases, a need for *mens rea* would be presumed.

Principle: If the Act is silent on the issue of *mens rea*, it will be interpreted so that D must either intend or be reckless regarding the criminal act.

In **K 2001,** D (who was aged 26) had sexual activity with a girl of 14 and was charged with indecent assault. He said he believed she was over 16. The HL accepted that he did not have *mens rea* and said the offence was not one of strict liability, so he was not guilty. This case indicated that the old case of **Prince 1875**, where D had been convicted of taking a girl under the age of 16 out of the possession of her parents, was wrong. She had told him she was 18 and, as she looked much older than she actually was, he believed her. D was convicted even though he had acted without *mens rea*. Lord Steyn described the decision in **Prince** as "a relic from an age dead and gone". The HL confirmed that, as stated in **Sweet v Parsley**, there was an overriding presumption of statutory interpretation that *mens rea* was needed unless there were express indications to the contrary in the statute. The presumption of *mens rea* is particularly strong in serious offences.

However in **G 2008**, in similar circumstances, a conviction was upheld. Here the charge was rape. A boy of fifteen had sexual intercourse with a girl of 12 without her consent but believing her to be 15. He was charged with rape of a child under 13 and the CA upheld his conviction on the basis that Parliament clearly intended the offence to be one of strict liability as regards age. There was a defence available where the child was over 13 and the fact that this was in the Act made it clear that the defence *only* applied in the case of older children.

In **Taylor 2016**, D took a car without consent and collided with a scooter. The scooter rider later died and D was charged with aggravated vehicle taking (**Theft Act s 12A**) and with causing a death while uninsured (**Road Traffic Act 1988**). As regards causing a death while uninsured, the prosecution had accepted that the decision in **Hughes 2013** applied, where the SC had held that there must be some element of fault in the driving which contributed to the death, so D was found not guilty under the **RTA**. He was convicted under the **Theft Act** and appealed. Aggravated vehicle taking includes taking a vehicle and then either driving dangerously or causing injury 'owing to the driving'. The prosecution argued that *mens rea* was only needed as regards the taking of the vehicle and nothing more. The SC held that having *mens rea* for the first offence could not equate to having it for the more serious offence of causing the death. The SC pointed out that this was not a regulatory offence, referring to **Sweet v Parsley**. Lord Sumption said that there must be some element of fault in the driving which contributed to the death. Here there was no evidence that D was driving dangerously and the fact that he had taken the car without consent was not enough; that did not cause the death.

social utility (usefulness) and public policy

One of the main reasons for imposing strict liability is that it is beneficial to society as a whole because it makes people more careful and protects people from harm. An example is **Meah v Roberts** above. Thus, offences covering areas of social concern such as the sale of food and drink, pollution and the protection of the environment are strict liability offences and this can be justified by the nature of the offence. The decision in **Shah** could be justified on the basis that underage gambling is a matter of social concern.

In **Alphacell v Woodward 1972**, the HL held that the offence of causing polluted matter to enter a river was a strict liability offence because pollution was a matter of the "utmost public importance".

The rules on strict liability were set out in **Gammon (Hong Kong) Ltd v AG of HK 1985**.

Key case

In **Gammon**, builders were held liable for carrying out building works in a way likely to cause damage, where they had not followed the original plans exactly. Safety regulations had prohibited 'substantial changes' and the builders argued that they hadn't known the changes they made *were* substantial. The offence was said to be one of strict liability because it was aimed at protecting public safety. In this case Lord Scarman laid down guidelines for the courts when considering whether an offence was one of strict liability. These include:

there is a presumption that *mens rea* is required

it is particularly strong if the offence is 'truly' criminal

it can only be displaced if the statute clearly states or implies this (e.g., with words such as 'knowingly' or 'maliciously')

it can only be displaced if the statute deals with an issue of social concern and public safety is an issue

A related issue to social utility is that of public policy. This means a government policy that provides a law for the well-being of society as a whole. The last point in **Gammon** is based on policy. It would be against public policy for people to be unsafe. Therefore, any law involving safety is more likely to be accepted by the courts as a strict liability offence.

The approach in **Gammon** was followed in **Blake 1997**. D was a disc jockey who was convicted under the **Wireless Telegraphy Act 1949** for broadcasting without a licence. D was in his flat at the time of the broadcast and argued that he thought he was making tapes and not transmitting. The CA felt that as unlicensed transmissions could interfere with the emergency services and air traffic control, the issue was one of public safety. On this basis, the offence could be classed as one of strict liability.

In **Jackson 2006**, the CA held that flying an aircraft at a height lower that 100 feet was a strict liability offence under the **Air Force Act 1955**. The Judge referred to both **Sweet v Parsley** and **Gammon** and ruled that there was no wording in the **Air Force Act** which required proof that D knew that he was flying below the permitted height. This meant the statute created an offence of strict liability. D's argument that the prosecution needed to prove at least recklessness was rejected. The creation of the offence was to protect the public and the public interest overrode the need to prove *mens rea*.

Examination pointer

In a question on strict liability you should not only be able to discuss what it is and when it applies, but also to provide an evaluation. There are several arguments for and against imposing strict liability and the following section will give you some ideas. Try to develop your own arguments too; you will sound more confident if you do. Also remember that liability is usually based on blameworthiness, or fault and that strict liability is an exception to this.

Arguments for and against imposing strict liability

There is never going to be a right answer as to whether the imposition of strict liability is a good thing or not. There will be valid arguments on both sides and views may change depending on the circumstances.

Example

It has been snowing and there are piles of snow at the side of the road. I manage to park my car and go shopping. When I come back, I have a parking ticket. It turns out I have parked on a double yellow line, but I couldn't see it. It would be very hard to prove I *knew* I had parked on a yellow line in the snow, so had *mens rea*. It would take up a lot of court time for what is only a minor matter. It can therefore be argued that strict liability is right as a small fine can be issued without a waste of time and taxpayers' money. On the other hand, it seems unfair because I did not know I was doing anything wrong because I could not see the yellow lines. There will be people on both sides of this argument and no-one will be either right or wrong.

The Law Commission suggested in a 2010 report that Parliament should state more clearly whether an offence was one of strict liability or not, which seems a sensible way forward but has not yet been seen in practice.

Arguments against:

- it is unfair to convict D of a criminal offence without proving *mens rea*

- it leads to the punishment of people who have taken all possible precautions
- it also means such people have a criminal record
- imposing a requirement of negligence would be fairer to D, but is a low level of fault so would still protect the public by making D careful

Arguments for:
- it makes people more careful
- it protects the public
- most such offences are minor and carry no social stigma
- proving *mens rea* is hard in many minor offences so time and money is saved
- the judge can address the issue of fault when sentencing

Examination pointer

I said that when discussing the reasons behind the concept of strict liability it is a good idea to look at it from both sides, i.e. provide a balanced argument. However, it is always important to read the question carefully – if you are only asked to discuss one or the other keep just to that.

Task 8

Choose one argument for and one against strict liability and develop them. Use a case for each to support your views and keep this for revision.

Briefly explain whether you think strict liability should, or should not, be imposed in the following situations.

- polluting the river
- jumping a traffic light
- murder
- selling food which is not fit for human consumption
- selling alcohol to a 15-year old

Summary

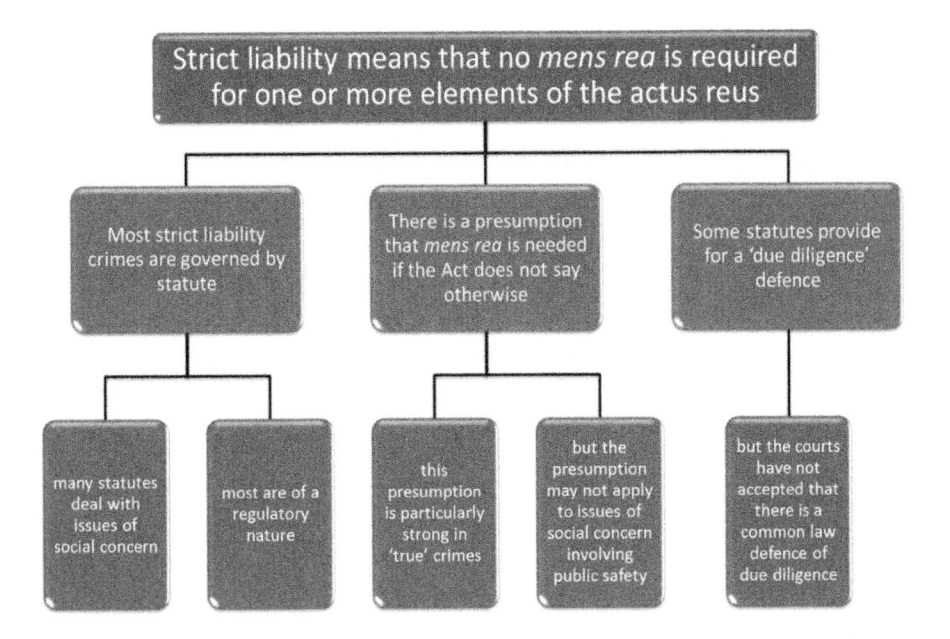

```
┌─────────────────────────────────────────────────────────┐
│ Strict liability means that no mens rea is required     │
│ for one or more elements of the actus reus              │
└─────────────────────────────────────────────────────────┘
         │                      │                      │
┌────────────────────┐ ┌──────────────────┐ ┌──────────────────┐
│ Most strict        │ │ There is a       │ │ Some statutes    │
│ liability crimes   │ │ presumption that │ │ provide for a    │
│ are governed by    │ │ mens rea is      │ │ 'due diligence'  │
│ statute            │ │ needed if the    │ │ defence          │
│                    │ │ Act does not say │ │                  │
│                    │ │ otherwise        │ │                  │
└────────────────────┘ └──────────────────┘ └──────────────────┘
     │         │            │         │            │
┌─────────┐ ┌────────┐ ┌─────────┐ ┌─────────┐ ┌──────────┐
│ many    │ │ most   │ │ this    │ │ but the │ │ but the  │
│ statutes│ │ are of │ │ presump-│ │ presump-│ │ courts   │
│ deal    │ │ a reg- │ │ tion is │ │ tion may│ │ have not │
│ with    │ │ ulatory│ │ partic- │ │ not     │ │ accepted │
│ issues  │ │ nature │ │ ularly  │ │ apply to│ │ that     │
│ of      │ │        │ │ strong  │ │ issues  │ │ there is │
│ social  │ │        │ │ in      │ │ of      │ │ a common │
│ concern │ │        │ │ 'true'  │ │ social  │ │ law      │
│         │ │        │ │ crimes  │ │ concern │ │ defence  │
│         │ │        │ │         │ │ involv- │ │ of due   │
│         │ │        │ │         │ │ ing     │ │ diligence│
│         │ │        │ │         │ │ public  │ │          │
│         │ │        │ │         │ │ safety  │ │          │
└─────────┘ └────────┘ └─────────┘ └─────────┘ └──────────┘
```

Task 9 – terminology

Make sure you understand the following terms. Add a short description to each one.

- **Strict liability**
- **Absolute liability**
- **Statutory nature**
- **Social utility**
- **Public policy**
- **Regulatory offences**

Links to the non-substantive law

For links to the English legal system, look back at the diagram and examples in the introduction to Part 1.

Self-test questions

1. State three areas of social concern where strict liability applies
2. Which case established that there is a presumption of mens rea in most criminal offences where the Act is silent on the matter?

3. *In which case were the guidelines set out for imposing strict liability where the Act is silent?*
4. *State three reasons for imposing strict liability*
5. *State three reasons for not imposing strict liability*

Answers to tasks and self-test questions are on my website at www.drsr.org/publications/tasks. For some interactive exercises, click on 'Free Exercises'.

Chapter 5 Common assault: Assault and Battery

"There could be no dispute that if you touch a person's clothes while he is wearing them that is equivalent to touching him." **R v Thomas 1985**

By the end of this Chapter, you should be able to:

- Explain the *actus reus* and *mens rea* of assault and battery
- Explain the differences between them
- Explain how the law applies in practice by reference to cases
- Identify possible criticisms for an evaluation of the law

Common assault includes two separate offences, assault and battery. It is called common assault because it comes from the common law. This means that assault and battery are not defined in any statute so the rules come from cases. The **Criminal Justice Act 1988 s 39** classifies them as summary offences (triable only in the magistrates' court) so for convenience they are charged under this section.

Examination pointer

It is better not to say they are *offences* under **s 39 Criminal Justice Act**. They are common law offences *charged* under the **Act**. Think of common assault as an umbrella under which the two crimes of assault and battery sit. They frequently occur together. If you need to discuss both, then refer to common assault and then describe assault and battery in turn.

Assault and battery are also trespass to the person which is a civil matter, a tort. Here we are only dealing with *criminal* assault. The definitions as developed by case law are currently:

Assault: to cause someone to apprehend immediate and unlawful personal violence

Battery: the unlawful application of force to another

Example

Fred raises his fist and threatens Simon with a punch on the nose. This is an assault because Simon 'apprehends', or fears, violence. If Fred then follows up the threat there is both an assault and a battery. It may also be actual bodily harm, but we'll come to that later.

We will look at each offence in turn.

Assault

The definition of assault is "an act by which a person **intentionally or recklessly causes another to apprehend immediate and unlawful violence**". This definition was used by the CA in **Ireland 1996** (discussed below) and confirmed by the HL the following year, in the twin appeals of **Ireland & Burstow 1997**.

Actus reus

The *actus reus* is to:

- cause the victim to apprehend
- immediate and unlawful violence

Cause the victim to apprehend

Apprehend means to become aware of or look forward to. Here it is not look forward to in the positive sense but with a sense of fear. It is the effect on the victim that is important with assault. Assault is not the actual violence but the *threat* of it, so as long as V expects violence to take place, that is enough.

Example

D walks into a bank pointing a banana concealed in a bag and saying, "I have a gun. Give me the money or I'll shoot you." The cashier is very frightened and does as D says. This is an assault. The fact that there is no possibility of carrying out the threat doesn't matter. V is in fear of immediate violence.

D walks into a bank pointing a real gun and saying, "Give me the money or I'll shoot." The cashier knows him from college and she thinks he is doing it as a joke. This is unlikely to be assault. V doesn't believe that any violence is about to take place.

Whether it amounts to assault therefore depends on whether or not V *thinks* that violence is about to take place.

Can words alone constitute an assault?

Early cases indicated that words would not amount to assault unless accompanied by some threatening gesture (like raising your fist). In **Meade and Belt 1823**, it was said that "no words or singing are equivalent to an assault". This has changed over the years and in **Wilson 1955**, the words "get out the knives" was said to be enough for assault. Also in **Constanza 1997**, a case of stalking, the CA held that words alone could amount to an assault. Even silence is now capable of amounting to an assault. In **Smith v Chief Superintendent of Woking Police Station 1983**, a 'peeping Tom' assaulted a woman by looking at her through her bedroom window at night. He had caused her to be frightened.

Evaluation pointer

It is the effect on the victim that is important, thus it seems right that words – or even silence – should amount to assault if they put the victim in fear of harm. The law has arguably become more satisfactory over the years, at least on this point.

Key case

In **Ireland**, D had repeatedly made silent telephone calls, accompanied by heavy breathing, to three women who then suffered psychiatric illness. In the appeal to the HL in 1997, Lord Steyn confirmed that words would be enough for assault, saying,

> "The proposition that a gesture may amount to an assault, but that words can never suffice, is unrealistic and indefensible. A thing said is also a thing done. There is no reason why something said should be incapable of causing an apprehension of immediate personal violence, e.g., a man accosting a woman in a dark alley saying 'come with me or I will stab you.' I would, therefore, reject the proposition that an assault can never be committed by words".

Words may prevent an assault

If D accompanies the threat with words which indicate that no violence will take place then there is no assault. An example of this is seen in a very old case. In **Turbeville v Savage 1669**, D was having an argument with V and placed his hand on the hilt of his sword. This would indicate an assault. He then said "If it were not assize time, I would not take such language from you". There was held to be no assault. The statement was held to indicate that he would *not* assault V because it was assize time and the judges were in town.

Example

You say to John "I would hit you if it were not your birthday." This indicates you won't do so (assuming it is his birthday!). No assault has taken place.

immediate and unlawful violence

The threat must be of 'immediate' violence. This means if you threaten someone just as you are about to get on a train it won't be enough. You can't carry out your threat 'immediately'. The term is widely interpreted though. In **Smith v Chief Superintendent of Woking Police Station**, V was scared by D looking at her through her bedroom window at night. She was frightened of what he might do next. The CA held this was sufficient.

In **Ireland 1996**, D argued that the 'immediacy' requirement was lacking. The CA held it was satisfied because by putting himself in contact with the victims D had caused them to be in immediate fear.

Evaluation pointer

Is immediate fear the same thing as fear of immediate harm? The CA in **Ireland** seemed to think so. The appeal to the HL did not focus on this issue so it remains unclear. If D phones V and says, "I have planted a bomb in your house. It is set to go off in 5 minutes." there is no problem. Both the fear and the harm are immediate. However, if D says "I have planted a bomb in your house. It is set to go off in a week." then it is a different matter. V may be in immediate fear, but is not in fear of immediate harm.

On a positive note, the courts appear to be reacting to the reality of the times. In **Ireland**, the CA said, "*We must apply the law to the conditions as they are in the 20th century*".

It is now the 21st century and the law will hopefully be applied taking into account the latest methods of communication which are much more 'immediate'.

Note that in many of these cases some actual harm was also caused. This means they can come under the statutory offence of an assault occasioning actual bodily harm under **s 47 Offences Against the Persons Act 1861** as happened in **Roberts 1971**. They are discussed here as well as the next Chapter because for **s 47** to be satisfied an assault or battery must take place first.

Evaluation pointer

A good argument that words should suffice is that they can sometimes be just as threatening as a gesture. As in the 'bomb' example I used earlier. Also in a society that has a sophisticated communications network the immediacy issue is more easily satisfied.

Mens rea

In **Savage1991**, Lord Ackner said, "... the mental element of assault is an intention to cause the victim to apprehend unlawful and immediate violence or recklessness whether such an apprehension is caused". That recklessness for all assaults is **Cunningham** (subjective) recklessness was confirmed in the joint appeals of **Savage & Parmenter 1992**.

Applying the mens rea rules to assault

For **direct intent**, the prosecution must prove that it was D's aim or purpose to cause the victim to apprehend unlawful and immediate violence.

For **indirect intent**, it must be proved that it was a virtual certainty that V would apprehend immediate and unlawful violence and that D appreciated this.

For **recklessness**, it must be proved that D recognises a risk that V would apprehend immediate and unlawful violence but goes ahead and takes that risk.

Battery

Battery is the unlawful application of force to another. As noted earlier it often follows an assault. Assault and battery therefore go together in many, but not all, cases.

Example

In my earlier example of the punch on the nose, there would be both. Simon saw the punch coming, so he was in fear of harm. If Fred hit Simon from behind this would only be a battery. No assault would have occurred because Simon was not in fear.

Actus reus

The *actus reus* is the unlawful application of force to another. It can be slight because the law sees people's bodies as inviolate. Lane LCJ said in **Faulkner and Talbot 1981**, that it was "any intentional touching of another person without the consent of that person and without lawful excuse. It need not necessarily be hostile, or rude, or aggressive, as some earlier cases seemed to indicate".

In **Thomas 1985**, the court said, "if you touch a person's clothes whilst he is wearing them that is equivalent to touching him".

In 2011, the TV presenter Fiona Bruce was sprayed with some aerosol string while she was filming an episode of Antiques Roadshow. The Ds were charged with common assault, specifically battery, for applying unlawful force.

Unlawful

Part of the *actus reus* is that the force must be unlawful. In **Collins v Wilcock 1984**, a police constable who took hold of a woman's arm was acting unlawfully so his actions amounted to battery. If there had been a lawful arrest this would not have been the case.

Consent may make the application of force lawful. Consent may be implied, e.g., most sports contacts are not battery because there is implied consent to touching.

Consent

Consent is also a defence, but for our purposes it is part of the *actus reus* of common assault (assault and battery). If consent is shown then the threat or act is not unlawful, so the *actus reus* is not complete. Consent can be express or implied.

In **AG's Reference (No 6 of 1980) 1981**, a fight between two youths resulted in one of them suffering a bloody nose. The other was charged with assault occasioning actual bodily harm. The CA held that consent did not apply in that case (mainly because it was a fight in public), but listed some circumstances where it could. These included properly conducted games and sports, and reasonable surgical interference. In circumstances like these consent may be implied even if not expressly given.

There is implied consent to harm in most contact sports. Where D's conduct was not within the rules of the game, the position was unclear, but was clarified in **Barnes 2004**. D had injured another player during a late tackle in a football match. His conviction was quashed and the CA held that criminal cases should be reserved for times when the conduct was *"sufficiently grave to be categorised as criminal"*. It now seems that consent can make the act lawful in most sporting cases – but it would not apply if a player punched the referee for making a bad decision!

Case law has long viewed 'manly sports' and 'manly diversions' as lawful activities. In **Jones 1988**, a group of boys tossed two other boys 10 feet into the air resulting in injuries. This seems more than 'properly conducted games and sports' but it was accepted that there was implied consent to such 'rough horseplay'.

It is generally accepted that consent must be real. Thus, consent by a child or consent induced by fraud may not be valid, even if expressly given. In **Burrell and Harmer 1967**, a 12- and 13-year-old were not deemed to have consented to actual bodily harm caused by tattooing.

Self-defence also makes a battery lawful. This is discussed further in Chapter 17 because, unlike consent, it can also apply to the fatal offences.

Application of force

There is a requirement that force is applied. Battery cannot be caused by an omission; there must be an act. This was confirmed in **Fagan v Metropolitan Police Commissioner 1969**. D argued that not moving off the police officer's foot was an omission not an act. The court confirmed that battery could not be committed by omission, but found him guilty on the basis that there was a continuing act. The *actus reus* was the driving onto the police officer's foot and staying there.

Direct or indirect force

Some early cases suggest that the force had to be direct but this is unlikely to be the case now. In **DPP v K 1990**, a schoolboy put acid in a hot air drier. Later another pupil used the drier and was badly scarred by the acid. This was held to be a battery. The case raised another issue. The boy had been using the acid in an experiment in class and was merely trying to hide it. He did not have *mens rea* when he put it in the machine, but he did have *mens rea* when he failed to do anything about it. We saw above that a battery could not be committed by omission. In **DPP v K**, omitting to rectify what he had done was held to be enough though.

In **Haystead 2000**, the harm appeared to be indirect. Here, D punched his girlfriend who was holding her baby. She dropped the baby resulting in the baby hitting his head on the floor. The defendant was convicted of battery on the baby.

Evaluation pointer

Although in **Haystead**, it seemed to be indirect force it may just be a widening of the meaning of direct. The court held that direct could include *via* another person or a weapon. Thus setting a dog on someone can be seen as direct force. This is reasonable, as it is unlikely to be argued that throwing a brick at someone was not direct and there is little real difference.

As a recap let's have a few more examples.

Examples

Matt threatens to hit Leon, who is scared. This is an assault because Leon 'apprehends', or fears, immediate violence.

Matt threatens to hit Leon but Leon thinks he is joking. Leon is not in fear of violence so part of the *actus reus* is missing and there is no assault.

Matt threatens to hit Leon if he ever sees him in the area again. Even if Leon is in fear of violence, he is not in fear of *immediate* violence. Again, part of the *actus reus* is missing, so there is no assault.

Matt hits Leon. This is battery as Matt has used unlawful force (there is no need for any injury or harm to result).

Matt taps Leon on the shoulder to attract his attention. Even though he has applied force, it is *lawful* force, because there is implied consent to this type of touching. Part of the *actus reus* is missing, so there is no battery.

Matt threatens to hit Leon and then does so. Here there is both an assault and a battery.

Matt hits Leon from behind. Here there is a battery but no assault because Leon cannot be in fear of violence if he doesn't see it coming.

Mens rea

As with assault, the *mens rea* is intent or recklessness. The *mens rea* of battery is intent or recklessness to cause unlawful force (**Venna 1976**).

Here it is as to whether force is applied.

Task 10

Look back at the application of the rules on intent and recklessness to an assault. Apply the same rules for a case of battery.

Terminology

Make sure you understand the following terms:

- **Common assault – means an assault or a battery**
- **Apprehend – means to fear**
- **Consent – may make a battery lawful**

Summary

Assault *Actus reus* to cause the victim to apprehend immediate and unlawful personal violence Words may be enough, or even silence	What is the effect on the victim? Ireland Wilson/Ireland
Mens rea	intent to cause the victim to apprehend immediate and unlawful personal violence or being subjectively reckless as to this
Battery *Actus reus* unlawful application of force to another Can include touching V's clothes May include indirect force	Collins v Wilcock Thomas DPP v K
Mens rea	intent to apply unlawful force or being subjectively reckless as to this

Links to the non-substantive law

For links to the English legal system, look back at the diagram and examples in the introduction to Part 1. Now we are looking at specific offences bear in mind this can affect where a case is heard and other matters involving the English legal system. Assault and battery are summary offences. This means it must be the magistrates' court, which has limited powers of sentencing. Another link is to law reform, as all the non-fatal offences have been the subject of proposals for reform by the Law Commission. Remember also that any cases establishing new principles are indicative of the development of the law and can be related to many areas of law-making.

Self-test questions

1. What is the current definition of assault?
2. Can words alone constitute an assault? Use a case to support your answer.
3. What is the mens rea for assault?
4. Does a battery have to be hostile? Use a case to support your answer.
5. What two defences may make a battery lawful?

Answers to tasks and self-test questions are on my website at www.drsr.org/publications/tasks. For some interactive exercises, click on 'Free Exercises'.

Chapter 6 Assault occasioning actual bodily harm (ABH) under s 47 of the Offences against the Person Act 1861

"It has been recognised for many centuries that putting a person in fear may amount to an assault. The early cases predate the invention of the telephone. We must apply the law to the conditions as they are in the 20th century". Swinton LJ

By the end of this Chapter, you should be able to:

- **Explain the *actus reus* of ABH as an assault or battery which causes harm**
- **Explain the *mens rea* of ABH**
- **Explain how the law applies in practice by reference to cases**
- **Identify possible criticisms for an evaluation of the law**

This offence comes under **s 47 Offences against the Persons Act 1861**. It is commonly known as ABH. **S 47** provides:

*"whosoever shall be convicted on indictment of any **assault occasioning actual bodily harm** shall be liable to imprisonment for not more than five years"*

Until 1984, it was thought that the Act merely provided for a greater penalty where an assault resulted in harm being caused. It is now clear that a new offence was created (**Courtie 1984**). In fact, in **Savage1991**, Lord Ackner indicated that it created two offences, an assault occasioning ABH and a battery occasioning ABH.

The offence has the *actus reus* and *mens rea* of assault or battery plus the further *actus reus* of some harm being caused. Let's look at this in more detail.

Actus reus

There are three parts to this.

- **assault** – the conduct, an assault or battery
- **occasioning** – a matter of causation
- **actual bodily harm** – the consequence

Assault

The offence is an *assault* occasioning actual bodily harm. Assault, as we saw, covers both assault and battery. This is seen in **Savage1991**.

Key case

In **Savage**, a girl threw a glass of beer over another girl. As she did so, she let go of the glass which broke, resulting in a cut to the other girl's wrist. The throwing of the beer was enough for a battery. Lord Ackner said, *"It is of course common ground that Mrs Savage committed an assault upon Miss Beal when she threw the contents of her glass of beer over her."* In referring to assault, he is describing a battery, confirming that the word assault in **s 47** includes both assault and battery.

There was no proof she intended to throw the glass and she said it was an accident. However, she did intend to throw the beer. The throwing of the beer was enough for the *actus reus* of battery. She intended to do this, so there was *mens rea* too. Once battery was proved, for her to be convicted under **s 47** the prosecution merely had to show this had 'occasioned' (caused) the harm.

Principle: *Mens rea* is needed only as regards the assault or battery, not the harm.

So, 'assault' for **s 47** requires the *actus reus* and *mens rea* of an assault or a battery. This will include each and every part, so, e.g., if there is consent to the battery it will be lawful and so cannot amount to ABH.

In **Wilson 1996**, a husband branded his initials on his wife's buttocks. It was done at her request but she needed medical attention and he was charged with ABH. The CA accepted that she had consented to the harm so he was not guilty.

In **R v R 1991**, a man was convicted of ABH and rape. He appealed, arguing that both the rape and the ABH were lawful. This was on the basis that although separated he was married to the woman, and there was an old common law tradition that a woman consented to sex by marrying. The CA found him guilty and the HL followed the CA's reasoning and confirmed there was no longer immunity based on consent for a man who assaulted and raped his wife

Occasioning

Occasioning means bringing about, or causing. **S 47** is a result crime so the prosecution must show that the assault or battery caused the result (actual bodily harm). D's actions must make a significant contribution to the harm and the chain of causation must not be broken.

Task 11

Look back at Chapter 2 on *actus reus* and causation. Read **Roberts** to remind you of the facts. The question was whether the battery by D caused the harm. Why did the action by the victim not break the chain of causation? What type of action might do so?

In **Savage**, the HL said that once the assault was established, the only remaining question was whether the victim's conduct was the natural consequence of that assault. According to Lord Ackner,

> "the word 'occasioning' raised solely a question of causation, an objective question which does not involve inquiring into the accused's state of mind".

Occasioning therefore relates to *actus reus* not *mens rea*. There is no need to intend any harm at all.

Examination pointer

Causation is a common issue in a problem question where a result crime like ABH is involved. If harm has occurred, you may need to discuss all three of these offences. You will certainly have to discuss two of them because **s 47** cannot happen without one of the others. You will need to define and explain assault and/or battery. Then define harm. Finally show that the assault (or battery) caused the harm. Use a case like **Roberts** or **Savage** to explain this and apply it to the facts given. If those facts remind you of a more relevant case, use that instead.

Finally, you will need to explain *mens rea*, but only regarding the assault. We'll come back to this.

Actual bodily harm

In **Miller 1954**, actual bodily harm was held to be any hurt or injury calculated to "interfere with health or comfort", which could include mental discomfort. In **Chan-Fook 1994**, the CA qualified this a little. Psychiatric injury was enough but not "mere emotions" such as fear, distress or panic. Really trivial or insignificant harm is excluded. Some type of identifiable medical condition will be needed, but it is clear that harm is not confined to physical injury.

In **DPP v Ross Smith 2006**, the QBD held that cutting someone's hair without consent amounted to assault occasioning actual bodily harm. At trial, the magistrates had accepted that as the victim had suffered no physical or psychological harm the offence was not proved. The QBD disagreed. Referring to **Chan-Fook** and **Burstow**, it was held that 'harm' included hurt or damage and 'actual' meant merely that it was not trivial harm. 'Bodily' harm applied to all parts of the body, of which hair was a part, and her hair had been cut so there was 'bodily harm'. The court also held that pain was not a necessary requirement of actual bodily harm.

Note that this case is actually **DPP v Smith 2006** but you will see reference to either Ross or Michael (his first two names) in most textbooks as Smith is a common name.

Key case

In **Ireland 1996**, silent 'phone calls which caused psychiatric harm came under **s 47**. D's argument was that there was no assault because there was no fear of 'immediate' harm. If there was no assault, there could be no assault occasioning actual bodily harm. The argument failed as the court found sufficient 'immediacy' in a telephone call. The CA also relied on **Chan-Fook** to confirm that psychiatric harm was enough for 'bodily harm'. The opening quote came from the CA and was approved in the HL.

Principles: Silence can amount to assault; harm includes psychiatric harm and immediacy is wide-ranging.

Mens rea

The *mens rea* is intent or recklessness.

D need not intend, or be reckless as to, any harm, only the assault or battery. This was held to be the case by the CA in **Roberts 1971**. D argued that he did not intend to cause harm and nor was he reckless. He was found guilty because he had the *mens rea* and the *actus reus* for the battery, plus harm had been caused. This was enough for **s 47**. Despite this seemingly clear principle of law, there was conflict in several cases over the next 20 years.

Key case

The issue was finally put beyond doubt by the HL in the joint appeals of **Savage & Parmenter 1992**. These two cases had been decided differently in the lower courts. The principle of **Roberts** had been followed in **Savage** but not in **Parmenter**.

In **Savage & Parmenter**, the HL held **Roberts** to be the correct law. The throwing of the beer with intent to do so was enough for a battery. The question for the court was whether a further mental state had to be established in relation to the bodily harm element of the **s 47** offence. Lord Ackner said, *"Clearly the section, by its terms, expressly imposes no such requirement"*.

This means that if D has *mens rea* for the assault and additionally harm occurs, it can amount to the more serious charge under **s 47**. Think about it as an equation:

Assault (AR + MR of assault or battery) + occasions (AR, causation) + harm (AR consequence) = **s 47**

Example

Sandra shouts threateningly at Tara. Tara is scared that Sandra will hit her. She jumps back and hits her head causing severe bruising. This will be enough for a charge under **s 47**. There is the *actus reus* of an assault (Tara is in fear of immediate violence) plus *mens rea* (Sandra intends to frighten her) and this assault occasioned (caused – jumping back and falling is foreseeable, as in **Roberts**) actual bodily harm (severe bruising).

So, the *mens rea* for **s 47** is intent or subjective recklessness as to the assault only, not the harm. The prosecution will have to show one of the following:

- **Direct intent:** causing fear of violence or the application of force is D's aim or purpose.
- **Indirect intent:** D appreciates that it is virtually certain that the V will fear violence, or D appreciates that the application of force is virtually certain.
- **Subjective recklessness:** D is aware of the risk of V being in fear, or is aware of the risk of force being applied, and goes ahead anyway.

Terminology

Make sure you understand the following terms:

- **Occasioning** – means causing
- **Actual bodily harm** – is some type of hurt that is more than trivial and can be physical or psychiatric

Evaluation pointer

One problem with **s 47** is that the *mens rea* does not match the *actus reus*. For the *actus reus* of **s 47** you need ABH to have occurred, the *mens rea* is only for assault or battery though (**Roberts, Savage**). This is confusing, and arguably unfair. Should D be guilty of causing ABH where there was only intent to scare someone? On the other hand, should D get away with harming someone when the attempt to scare them caused harm?

Summary of s 47

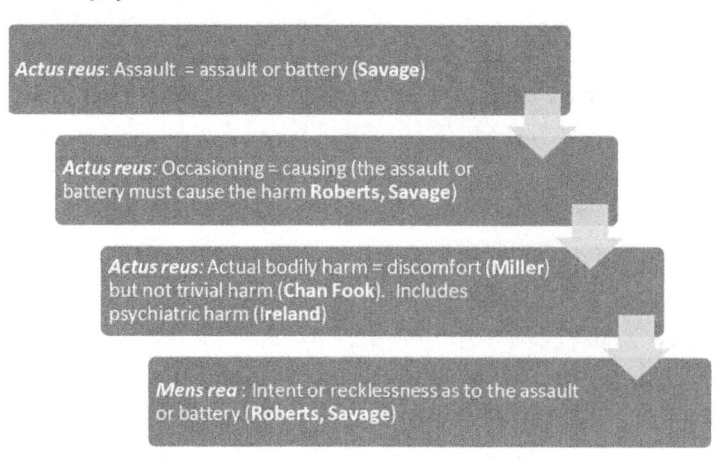

- **Actus reus**: Assault = assault or battery (**Savage**)
- **Actus reus**: Occasioning = causing (the assault or battery must cause the harm **Roberts, Savage**)
- **Actus reus**: Actual bodily harm = discomfort (**Miller**) but not trivial harm (**Chan Fook**). Includes psychiatric harm (**Ireland**)
- **Mens rea**: Intent or recklessness as to the assault or battery (**Roberts, Savage**)

Links to the non-substantive law

For links to the English legal system, look back at the diagram and examples in the introduction to Part 1. Now we are looking at specific offences, bear in mind this can affect where a case is heard and other matters involving the English legal system. ABH is a triable either-way offence so can be tried in either the magistrates' court or Crown Court. The maximum sentence is 5 years but magistrates have limited powers so if the harm is not minor, or there are several aggravating factors, the case may be sent to the Crown Court. D may also choose the Crown Court. The case will then be heard by a jury, which may have its advantages depending on the facts of the case. The jury applies the standards of the average person to these facts, so if D feels the circumstances will be viewed sympathetically it might be wise to opt for jury trial in the Crown Court. **R v R** is an example of a persuasive precedent as the HL followed the CA. It is also an example of the law needing to respond to changing circumstances. Society no longer regarded such behaviour as acceptable and the courts followed this line of thinking. Another link is to law reform, as all the non-fatal offences have been the subject of proposals for reform by the Law Commission. These are covered in more detail in the summary and the Bridge at the end of Part 1. Statutory interpretation is also relevant as judges must try to interpret words that may be used differently today. It will be hard to use the literal rule, but just as hard to try to find the intentions or purpose of Members of Parliament in 1861.

Self-test questions

1. From which case did the opening quote come?
2. What are the three parts to the actus reus?
3. For which part of this is mens rea needed?
4. According to **Roberts**, what sort of action by V could break the chain of causation?
5. In which case did the HL finally confirm that the principle in **Roberts** was correct?

Answers to tasks and self-test questions are on my website at www.drsr.org/publications/tasks. For some interactive exercises, click on 'Free Exercises'.

Chapter 7 Grievous bodily harm (GBH) and wounding under s 20 and s 18 of the Offences against the Person Act 1861

"In the context of a criminal act therefore the words 'cause' and 'inflict' may be taken to be interchangeable." Lord Hope

By the end of this Chapter, you should be able to:

- **Explain the *actus reus* of wounding and GBH in s 20 and s 18**
- **Explain the difference in the *mens rea* between the two sections**
- **Explain how the law applies in practice by reference to cases**
- **Identify possible criticisms and explain the proposed reforms for all the non-fatal offences**

Section 20 makes it an offence to:

"unlawfully and maliciously wound or inflict any grievous bodily harm upon any other person, either with or without any weapon or instrument"

Section 18 makes it an offence to:

"unlawfully and maliciously by any means whatsoever wound or cause any grievous bodily harm to any person with intent to do some grievous bodily harm to any person"

These two offences are commonly called malicious wounding (**s 20**) and wounding with intent (**s 18**). However, there are actually two separate offences under each section.

- unlawfully and maliciously wounding
- unlawfully and maliciously inflicting / causing grievous bodily harm

There is very little difference in the *actus reus*; each needs **either** a wound **or** serious injury. We will deal with the two sections together for *actus reus* and then look at the different *mens rea* for each.

Actus reus for s 18 and s 20

There are four matters to consider.

- unlawfully
- wound
- inflict / cause
- grievous bodily harm

We'll take these in turn. I have left out 'malicious' for the moment as this has been treated as relating to *mens rea*.

Unlawfully

If the act is done lawfully, no offence has occurred. Thus if D has acted in self-defence this makes it lawful, so part of the *actus reus* is missing. Consent may also make it lawful, but is not usually applicable to serious harm, only ABH, as discussed earlier.

In **Brown 1994**, the House of Lords decided that consent of the victim could no longer be a defence if serious harm was *intended*. This can be compared with **Wilson 1996** where a man branded his initials on his wife's buttocks and it was accepted that the wife consented to ABH. In **Dica 2004**, D had consensual sex with two women knowing he was HIV positive. They both became infected with HIV and he was convicted under **s 20** with recklessly inflicting grievous bodily harm. On appeal, the CA confirmed the point in **Brown** that consent was not a defence to *intentional* harm. However, as the charge was *recklessly* inflicting grievous bodily harm, they held that the issue of consent should not have been withdrawn from the jury. A retrial was ordered at which he was found guilty under **s 20**. In **Golding 2014**, a man infected his girlfriend with herpes and admitted recklessly inflicting GBH because he knew he was infected prior to having sex with her.

Wound

Key case

In **C v Eisenhower 1983**, a wound was defined as being "any puncture of the skin". The case involved a child firing an air gun. The pellet hit V in the eye but did not break the skin. It was held that internal bleeding caused by the rupture of an internal organ was not a wound. Therefore, something that does not break the skin, such as an abrasion, bruise or burn would not amount to a wound.

Principle: Wound means a cut in the whole skin.

Examination pointer

You can see in **Eisenhower** that D was not guilty because the skin wasn't broken. This shows the importance of bringing the right charge because if the prosecution had charged him with GBH he could have been guilty, as the harm was serious. Remember this when applying the law in an examination scenario; you will be given the facts and will be expected to choose the appropriate offence.

Inflict and cause – is there a difference?

The *actus reus* of **s 20** is to unlawfully and maliciously wound or *'inflict'* grievous bodily harm. The *actus reus* of **s 18** is to unlawfully and maliciously wound or *'cause'* grievous bodily harm. In **Clarence 1888**, the word 'inflict' was held to mean that a prior assault was required, as for **s 47**. Other cases seem to have ignored this requirement. In **Wilson 1984**, the HL held that a person could be charged under **s 20** without an assault. They relied on the Australian case of **Salisbury 1976** where it was said that 'inflict' does not imply assault is needed. However it was said that the word 'inflict' did mean that *direct* application of force was needed. It was therefore narrower than the word 'cause'.

Evaluation pointer

This uncertainty has been clarified. Both **Salisbury** and **Wilson** were approved by the HL in **Ireland & Burstow 1997**. In the CA Lord Bingham had said it would be *"an affront to common sense"* to distinguish between the two offences in this way. The HL confirmed that liability for GBH could occur without the application of direct or indirect force, and rejected the argument that 'inflict' was narrower than 'cause'. Lord Hope made the statement in the opening quote, that the words 'cause' and 'inflict' may be taken to be interchangeable. **Clarence** was referred to as a "troublesome authority". In **Dica**, the CA again confirmed that there was no requirement of assault for a charge under **s 20**. This seems sensible as there is no requirement, as in **s 47**, that an assault causes, inflicts or occasions the harm – only that D does.

A factor worth noting (as it was by the HL) is that the **1861 Act** consolidated several different Acts. Therefore, the difference in the two sections is not as significant as it would be had they been written at the same time.

One criticism is that if there is no requirement of assault in **s 20** then it is hard to justify convicting D of *assault* occasioning actual bodily harm as an alternative, as was confirmed again in **Savage & Parmenter 1992**.

Grievous bodily harm

This is commonly called GBH. In **Smith 1961**, grievous was interpreted by the HL to mean 'really serious'. In **Saunders 1985**, the CA held that the word 'really' was unnecessary. Thus, GBH includes *any* serious harm. In **Burstow 1996**, a campaign of harassment by D, which led to V suffering severe depressive illness, was charged under **s 20**. In the joint appeals to the HL in **Ireland & Burstow 1997**, the HL confirmed that psychiatric harm could come under **s 47, s 18** or **s 20**.

Serious harm is usually required, but note should be taken of **Bollom 2004**. A baby suffered bruising to several parts of her body and her mother's partner was charged with GBH. Although the CA substituted the conviction for one of ABH, it was made clear that bruising could amount to GBH if the victim was a young child. This means the age of the victim may be relevant in deciding the appropriate charge. Presumably, this argument could also be applied to an old or vulnerable person.

A wound may occur without GBH. Conversely, GBH may occur without a wound.

Example

Let's reconsider two cases we saw when looking at **s 47**.

In **Savage**, the glass broke and cut the other girl. This is technically a wound as the skin has been broken. She could have been charged with wounding under **s 20**. It would not be 'serious' harm though so no charge of inflicting GBH would succeed.

In the joint appeals of **Ireland & Burstow**, the HL said psychiatric harm could amount to GBH. This type of harm could not be a wound though.

Examination pointer

Look for clues in the scenario. If it refers to a cut then discuss wounding under either **s 18** or **s 20**. If it is only a small cut you could discuss **s 47**. If a serious internal injury is mentioned then discuss GBH. In all cases, the prosecution must establish a chain of causation. D's act must make a *significant contribution* to the wound or harm (see Chapter 2).

S 20 refers to "with or without any weapon or instrument". **S 18** refers to "by any means whatsoever". Remember these offences came from different Acts and were not written at the same time. It doesn't matter *how* D inflicts or causes the harm. However, the use of a weapon may help in establishing intent to cause serious harm, and so point you at **s 18**.

Mens rea

It is important to be able to identify the different *mens rea* in **s 18** and **s 20**. There are two differences: the type of *mens rea* and the type of harm that the *mens rea* relates to.

Both sections contain the word 'maliciously'. This does not mean spite or ill will, as we might view the word. As regards **s 20**, the CA interpreted it in **Cunningham 1957** as meaning intent or subjective recklessness (see Chapter 3). For **s 18**, it would appear that the word 'maliciously' is unnecessary. In **Mowatt 1968**, the judge said, *"In s 18 the word 'maliciously' adds nothing"*.

Mens rea *for s 20*

As noted above this is intent or subjective recklessness. However, D need not intend or recognise the risk of serious harm. Intending or seeing the risk (*mens rea*) of *some* harm is enough as long as the result (*actus reus*) is serious harm. This was confirmed by the CA in **Mowatt** and later approved by the HL in **Savage & Parmenter 1992**.

Key case

In **Parmenter** D threw his baby into the air and caused GBH when he caught it. His argument that he lacked *mens rea* succeeded. He had not seen the risk of *any* injury (he'd done it before several times with older children) so he was not guilty.

Principle: The *mens rea* for **s 20** is intent or recklessness to inflict some harm, not serious harm.

It is only necessary to prove that D foresaw some harm *might* occur. It is not necessary to prove that D foresaw that some harm *would* occur. This point was confirmed in **DPP v A 2000**. Here a 13-year-old boy shot his friend whilst they were playing with two air pistols. His argument that he lacked *mens rea* was rejected. The case is similar to **C v Eisenhower 1983**.

In **Jones v First-Tier Tribunal 2011**, the CA held that for a charge of GBH there was no need to prove that the action was hostile. D had run in front of a lorry and the driver was injured. D argued he had no *mens rea* as he had only intended to harm himself, not anyone else. The CA held that it was foreseeable that harm could be caused to the driver of the lorry; therefore, the *mens rea* of recklessness could be proved for the **s 20** offence. In **Jones v FTT 2013**, the SC allowed D's appeal. The SC noted that the CA had decided that anyone running into a busy road must have at least seen the risk of some harm and, referring to **Parmenter,** held this was sufficient *mens rea* for **s 20**. However, the SC said that the question of whether D *himself* foresaw harm was a matter for the tribunal and not an appeal court, and reinstated the tribunal's decision

Evaluation pointer

S 18 and **s 20** involve *either* GBH *or* wounding. The first has been interpreted as 'really serious' harm (**Smith**), however wounding has been interpreted as an 'open cut' (**Eisenhower**), which could be quite trivial. The prosecution failed to prove D had inflicted a wound in **Eisenhower** because there was no open cut and thus no 'wound'. This case highlights the need to get the charge right. A charge of GBH could have succeeded. Another issue is that, as for **s 47**, the *mens rea* does not match the *actus reus*. For **s 20**, you need serious harm to have occurred, but the *mens rea* is only for *some* harm (**Mowatt**).

Application of mens rea for s 20

- Direct intent: It is D's aim to cause *some harm*
- Indirect intent: *Some harm* is a virtual certainty and D appreciates this
- Subjective recklessness: D recognises the risk of *some harm* and goes ahead anyway

Mens rea *for s 18*

The *mens rea* for **s 18** is specific intent, i.e., intent only. It was confirmed in **Belfon 1976**, where D had slashed someone with a razor, that recklessness was not enough, there must be intent to cause serious harm. **S 18** says *"with intent to do some grievous bodily harm"*. It was confirmed in **Parmenter** that for **s 18** D must intend *serious harm*. This is the vital difference and makes **s 18** much more serious, leading to a possible maximum life sentence. **S 20** carries a maximum of 5 years. In **Mair 2016**, the killer of the MP Jo Cox knifed a man who had tried to intervene when he saw the attack, causing serious injuries. He was found guilty under **s 18** (and of the murder). He was sentenced to life imprisonment for both offences.

In **Press & another 2013**, two soldiers were convicted of GBH under **s 18 OAPA** after attacking another two men at a burger stall. The CA confirmed that if D has taken alcohol (or drugs) the jury should ignore the alcohol and consider whether the act was accompanied by the required intent even in drink. The fact that the defendant was intoxicated does not constitute a defence. If intent had not been proved they would still have been guilty under **s 20** as they were at least reckless. **S 20** is a basic intent crime and voluntary intoxication is never a defence to a basic intent crime (one where recklessness suffices for *mens rea* – see under defences).

A further difference with **s 18** *mens rea* is that it includes intent to resist or prevent a lawful arrest. The problem with this is that it is added as an alternative to intent to cause GBH, so has been interpreted as meaning that if the situation is resisting or preventing an arrest, intent is only needed for that, not the harm. This is seen in **Morrison 1989** where D dived through a window resisting arrest and a police officer was badly cut. The CA upheld his conviction and held that it was enough that he intended resisting arrest. Regarding GBH, the word 'malicious' suggested that intent OR recklessness was enough, and he had been reckless.

Evaluation pointer

If **s 18** requires serious harm in both *actus reus* and *mens rea*, then arguably so should **s 20**. There is still a difference in the *mens rea* because **s 18** requires intent to be proved.

Another issue is sentencing. The maximum sentences for **s 20** and **s 18** are very different. The maximum for **s 20** is the same as **s 47**, i.e., 5 years. This seems strange. Life for **s 18** can be justified in that intent seriously to injure is also the *mens rea* for murder. Which charge is brought will depend on the chance factor of whether the victim dies or not. The same sentence for **s 47** and **s 20** is harder to justify. In **Parmenter**, the CA. noted there was an overlap between **s 47** and **s 20** but indicated that **s 20** was a more serious offence. The Law Commission proposes a maximum of 5 years for **s 47**, as now, but a maximum 7 years for **s 20**. This seems more realistic – but the reforms may be a long way off becoming reality.

A further recommendation by the Law Commission is that **s 18** would be 'intentional serious injury' and **s 20** would be 'reckless serious injury'. This would clear up the problem of the *mens rea*. It is arguably unfair to charge someone with GBH when the *mens rea* was only for some harm. A final criticism of the current law is that there are two different offences in each section. This makes four offences in all, which is unnecessarily complicated

The Commission notes that the Act is widely recognised as being outdated and that it uses archaic language. It also says that the structure of the Act is unsatisfactory; because there is no clear hierarchy of offences and the differences between **sections 18, 20** and **47** are not clearly spelt out.

Reforms are further discussed, along with the latest report from 2015, in the summary which follows this Chapter.

Application of mens rea for s 18

- **Direct intent:** It is D's aim or purpose to cause *grievous bodily harm*
- **Indirect intent:** *Grievous bodily harm* is a virtual certainty and D appreciates this

Which charge?

It was confirmed in **Savage 1991** that a jury could bring in **s 20** as an alternative verdict when someone is charged under **s 18** and **s 47** as an alternative to **s 20**.

If not, the conviction may be changed on appeal.

In **Bollom 2004**, the conviction for GBH under **s 20** was reduced by the CA to ABH under **s 47**.

Alternatively, D may put in a plea before or during the trial.

In **Topp 2011**, (unreported) a woman bit her boyfriend's testicles. He needed several stitches and she was charged with wounding with intent under **s 18**. Prior to the trial, she pleaded guilty to **s 20**, arguing she did not intend serious harm. The prosecution accepted the alternative plea.

Sometimes both charges are brought so the prosecution can be more confident of getting a conviction.

In **Hargreaves 2010**, D was in a taxi with her boyfriend and another man, all of whom had been drinking. She was in the back and was having an argument with her boyfriend, who was sitting in the front. He turned towards her and she kicked out at him, ramming a stiletto heel through his eye and into his brain. She was charged with both grievous bodily harm with intent under **s 18**, and an alternative charge of inflicting grievous bodily harm under **s 20**. (There would have been a conviction under **s 20** but she said that she had kicked out at him as she believed he was going to attack her, and pleaded self-defence. The defence succeeded so she was acquitted of both offences.)

Task 12

Mick threw a brick at Steve as he was riding down a country lane on his bicycle. The brick missed but Steve fell off his bike onto a sharp stone, causing a deep cut which needed several stitches. Explain the most appropriate offence and then apply the law to justify it.

Examination pointer

All this means you may need to discuss all three statutory offences. Explain the *actus reus* of either GBH or wounding as appropriate, using cases in support. Note carefully the difference in the *mens rea* as this may help you to decide which section is most appropriate. Thus if you go for **s 18**, explain and apply the law (with cases) but then say that if the prosecution can't prove intent to cause GBH then D may be convicted of **s 20** instead. If you go for **s 20**, you can then discuss **s 47** if you feel the harm may not be serious enough.

Terminology

Make sure you understand the following terms:

- **Grievous bodily harm** – means serious harm
- **Wounding** – means cutting through the skin

Summary

Actus reus	
Inflict or cause	Mean the same thing (Ireland)
Wound	Open cut (Eisenhower)
Grievous bodily harm	Serious harm (Smith/Saunders)
Mens rea	
S 20 Intent or recklessness	To cause some harm (Mowatt)
S 18 Intent only	To cause serious harm (Parmenter)

Links to the non-substantive law

For links to the English legal system, look back at the diagram and examples in the introduction to Part 1. Now we are looking at specific offences, bear in mind this can affect where a case is heard and other matters involving the English legal system. GBH under **s 20** is a triable either-way offence so can be tried in either the magistrates' court or Crown Court. The maximum sentence is 5 years but magistrates have limited powers so the case may be sent to the Crown Court because serious harm will have been suffered. Anyway, D can choose the Crown Court where the case will be heard by a jury, which may have its advantages in some cases. **S 18** is an indictable offence with a maximum sentence of life imprisonment so must be heard in the Crown Court. Another link is to law reform, as all the non-fatal offences have been the subject of proposals for reform by the Law Commission. These are covered in more detail in the summary following this Chapter. Statutory interpretation is also relevant as judges must try to interpret words that may be used differently today. It will be hard to use the literal rule, but just as hard to try to find the intentions or purpose of Members of Parliament in 1861.

Self-test questions

1. *How has 'wound' been interpreted?*
2. *How has 'grievous bodily harm' been interpreted?*
3. *Which cases can you use to support your answers to the above questions?*
4. *What is the difference in the mens rea between **s 20** and **s 18**?*
5. *What are the maximum sentences for **s 20** and **s 18** respectively?*

Answers to tasks and self-test questions are on my website at www.drsr.org/publications/tasks. For some interactive exercises, click on 'Free Exercises'.

Summary and examination practice: Non-fatal offences against the person

The offences of assault and battery come from the common law, the others from the **Offences against the Person Act 1861**. Make sure you know the section numbers for these. Also, note the date of the Act. It is very old and is in need of reform. Reforms have been suggested but not implemented (this is discussed in 'The Bridge' under criticisms and reforms for evaluation purposes).

Note in particular these statutory offences where the *mens rea* doesn't match the *actus reus*. Make sure you understand the *mens rea* for each offence.

Examination pointer

You need to be accurate when discussing the *actus reus* and *mens rea* of these offences, so make sure you learn the definitions. Assault and battery are common law offences so it is cases which provide both the definitions and the principles of law. For ABH, GBH and wounding the law comes from a statute, (the **Offences against the Person Act 1861**), but as you know statutes have to be interpreted by judges. For these offences you need to learn the definitions **and section numbers** from the statute, and then make sure you know the cases which establish the various principles of law.

Assault

Actus reus: to cause the victim to apprehend *immediate* and unlawful personal violence – **Ireland**

Mens rea: intent or subjective recklessness to cause fear of harm – **Savage**

Battery

Actus reus: unlawful application of force to another – **Collins v Wilcock**

Mens rea: intent or subjective recklessness to apply force – **Venna**

Assault occasioning actual bodily harm under s 47 OAPA 1861

Actus reus: An assault (or battery) which causes harm – **Chan Fook**

Mens rea: intent or subjective recklessness for the assault or battery only – **Savage**

Malicious Wounding under s 20 OAPA 1861

Actus reus: unlawful and malicious wounding or inflicting grievous bodily harm – **C v Eisenhower / Saunders**

Mens rea: intent or subjective recklessness to inflict *some* harm – **Mowatt**

Wounding with intent under s 18 OAPA 1861

Actus reus: unlawful and malicious wounding or causing grievous bodily harm **C v Eisenhower / Saunders**

Mens rea – intent (only) to cause grievous bodily harm – **Parmenter**

Task 13

Match the principle to the case

Cases:

- Wilson 1955
- Ireland 1996

- C v Eisenhower 1983
- Miller 1954
- Haystead 2000
- Smith1961
- Chan-Fook 1994

Principles:

- Silence may be enough for an assault
- Grievous means really serious harm
- Words may be enough for an assault
- A battery can be via another person
- Actual bodily harm is anything that causes personal discomfort
- Mere emotions such as fear, distress or panic are not enough for actual bodily harm
- Wound means an open cut

Problems and proposals for reform of the non-fatal offences

The **Act** is very complicated and was written in 1861, so much of the language is obscure. Lawyers and juries have struggled to understand the complexities of the different offences. The courts also have difficulty interpreting words such as 'occasioning', 'actual bodily harm', 'grievous' and 'maliciously' as they are not used in the same sense today.

Assault and battery are outside the **Act**. Clarity would require all the offences to be together in one place. However, an alternative argument is that the common law can keep them up to date, as in **Ireland**.

The main problem is that the *actus reus* and *mens rea* do not always match, so that D can be liable for a result without intending or being reckless as to that result. This applies to **s 20** and **s 47**. This lack of correspondence between *actus reus* and *mens rea* is known as 'constructive liability'. It is called constructive liability because liability is constructed from the *actus reus* of one offence and the *mens rea* of another e.g., liability for assault occasioning actual bodily harm under **s 47** is constructed from the *actus reus* of **s 47** plus the *mens rea* of assault.

The Law Commission has produced proposals for reform over a very long period of time. In 1998 the government produced its own Bill incorporating most of the LC's recommended changes, but to date Parliament has not found time to debate the issues.

From the outset, the LC has pointed out that the Act is outdated and uses archaic language. Also that there is a lack of a clear hierarchy and the offences are not classified in a coherent way. In 2014, the LC readdressed the issue and issued a consultation paper (a scoping paper), which noted that the frequent changes in the law had left it in an incoherent and confusing state. A report followed and was published in November 2015 (Report No. 361). The 2015 proposals are based on the 1998 Draft Bill.

The table which follow shows the proposals from the 1998 Bill. The offences are redefined and in all of them the *mens rea* matches the *actus reus*.

Name of proposed offence	Explanation of proposed offence	Current offence
Intentional serious injury	Clause 1: intentionally causing serious injury	S 18
Reckless serious injury	Clause 2: recklessly causing serious injury	S 20
Intentional or reckless injury	Clause 3: intentionally or recklessly causing injury	S 47
Assault	Clause 4: intentionally or recklessly applying force to or causing an impact on the body of another; or intentionally or recklessly causing another to believe force is imminent	Common assault (assault and battery)

There are some minor amendments to the 1998 draft bill in the 2015 report. The first three offences (intentionally causing serious injury, recklessly causing serious injury and intentionally or recklessly causing injury) would be as above. Assault would also be as above, but renamed as 'physical assault' (currently battery) and 'threatened assault' or 'assault by threats' (currently assault).

The only real difference is the proposal of a new offence of causing minor injuries. This would fall between intentionally or recklessly causing injury and assault so would span Clauses 3 and 4 from the Draft Bill. It would include cases where the assault (whether physical or threatened) causes some injury, however minor but would not require *mens rea* for the injury, as for **s 47** now. However, it would be triable only in the magistrates' court, with a maximum sentence of 12 months.

All the above could be discussed when looking at law reform and the work of the Law Commission, and statutory interpretation is also relevant.

There is more on the problems and proposals for reform in 'The Bridge' as A-level students need a little more depth.

The AS examination (7161)

Remember, if you plan to do the A-level there is no need to take an external examination at the end of Year 1 and it won't count towards the A-level. However, if, you are not 100% sure about doing the full A-Level you should do it, then you will have a law qualification for AS.

All papers are a mix of multiple-choice, short answer and extended writing questions. The English legal system (non-substantive law) comes into both papers (see the table below for what is examined on each paper), the difference being the core substantive law. Each paper represents 50% of the AS examination.

Paper 1: The English legal system (40 marks) plus criminal law (40 marks)

Paper 2: The English legal system (40 marks) plus tort (40 marks)

About the examination

The assessment objectives (AOs)

These apply to all A-level courses and all examination boards. The examination will test you in the following ways.

AO1 tests your knowledge and understanding of the English legal system and legal rules and principles (23-25%)

AO2 tests your ability to apply legal rules and principles to given scenarios in order to present a legal argument using appropriate terminology (12.5-14.5%)

AO3 tests your ability to evaluate and analyse the legal rules, principles and concepts (11.5-13.5%)

The percentages total 50% for each of the two papers so together total 100% of the AS examination. You should be aware of these weightings so that you plan your time accordingly. A01 accounts for nearly half the marks. The other two are reasonably even.

There is a complete Chapter on examination practice and guidance for the A-level at the end of this book. For specimen papers and mark schemes visit the AQA site at www.aqa.org.uk. The following table relates to the AS examination.

For teachers: Please visit my website at www.drsr.org for a teacher's guide on the changes to the specifications and examinations.

The English legal system: What goes where for AS 7161?

Paper 1 Crime	Paper 2 Tort
The nature of law (legal and other rules, civil & criminal distinctions and sources)	The nature of law (legal and other rules, civil & criminal distinctions and sources)
The rule of law	Parliamentary law-making
Precedent	Delegated legislation
Law Reform (including Law Commission proposals and reforms)	The Law Commission as an influence on law-making
Criminal courts and process (including appeals and sentencing)	Statutory interpretation
Lay people	The European Union
Legal personnel	Civil courts and process (including appeals)
Judges and their role in criminal courts	Alternative dispute resolution
Independence of the judiciary	Judges and their role in civil courts
Access to justice and funding in the criminal system	Access to justice and funding in the civil system

Types of question and apportionment of marks

For each paper, there are:

5 multiple-choice questions on the substantive law and 5 on the English legal system at 1 mark each (total 10 marks).

2 short-answer questions (1 on substantive law and 1 on the English legal system) at 3 marks each (total 6 marks).

2 mixed questions covering BOTH the substantive law and the English legal system at 12 marks each (total 24 marks)

2 extended writing questions (1 on substantive law and 1 on the English legal system) at 20 marks each (total 40 marks).

Overall totals are 40 marks for the substantive law and 40 for ELS making a total for each paper of 80 marks.

Extended writing questions can be on the application or evaluation of the law, or a mix of both of these. They require that you provide "an extended answer which shows a clear logical and sustained line of reasoning leading to a valid conclusion".

The diagram below gives a brief idea about how the two mixed questions might work (repeated from the introduction). You would need to explain and apply the law on ABH and then explain the law on one of the other matters as appropriate, depending on the question asked. You would need to expand on these depending on the given facts; this is just a brief example to show how they can link to a question on ABH.

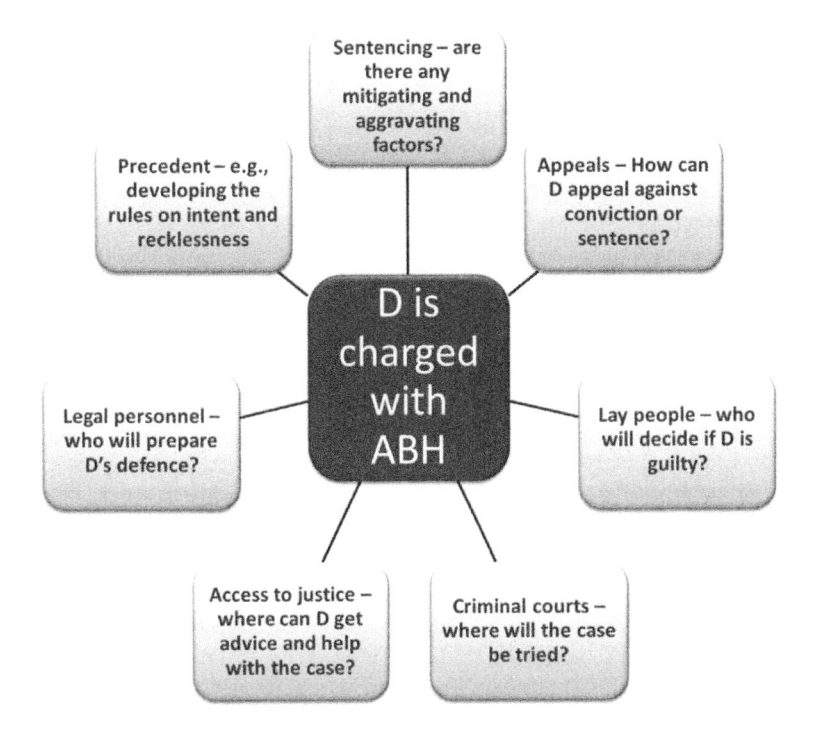

D is charged with ABH

- Sentencing – are there any mitigating and aggravating factors?
- Precedent – e.g., developing the rules on intent and recklessness
- Appeals – How can D appeal against conviction or sentence?
- Legal personnel – who will prepare D's defence?
- Lay people – who will decide if D is guilty?
- Access to justice – where can D get advice and help with the case?
- Criminal courts – where will the case be tried?

Examination guidance

Application advice

Read the scenarios carefully to make sure you understand the questions.

Sometimes you will be directed to a specific offence and sometimes not. It may be necessary to discuss more than one as there is an overlap, however, if you are told to discuss a particular offence you cannot get marks for discussing any other offence(s).

S 18 and **s 20** clearly overlap, so unless directed to one or the other you may need to discuss both. There is also a close connection to attempted murder, as it is sometimes a matter of chance that V did not die, for example due to prompt medical treatment. In **R v Z 2017** (unreported), a Year 10 schoolgirl thought a school friend had been involved in some online bullying she had suffered. Telling her that she had a present for her she arranged a meeting, and while the girl shut her eyes and waited for the present Z stabbed her. Fortunately, the girl sensed something was wrong and opened her eyes, therefore managing to avoid a fatal wound. The knife went through her school blazer and shirt but only a short way into her body. Although not a deep cut there was a wound and Z admitted wounding under **s 20**. She intended at least serious harm so it could certainly be **s 18**. In the actual case the jury found that Z had sufficient *mens rea* for murder. As the girl had only survived because she jumped back Z was convicted of attempted murder.

Always read the questions carefully so you know which offence(s) to discuss.

Try to summarise the facts in a few words. This is valuable when time is short. The principle of the case is the important part, although you may need to discuss the facts briefly to show why you have chosen that particular case.

Example

> In **Roberts 1971 and Pagett 1983**, the principle was that a foreseeable act will not break the chain of causation. If the scenario involves someone being injured when running away from the threat of an attack, **Roberts** is the most appropriate case. You don't need all the facts but should refer to the fact that she tried to escape an attack, and this was foreseeable. The principle of the case was based on this, i.e., a foreseeable act does not break the chain of causation. This case therefore supports a conclusion that the chain wasn't broken so D is guilty for the injury caused.

If you can't remember the name of a case that is relevant don't leave it out but refer to it in a general way, e.g., 'in one decided case....' or 'in a similar case....'

You need to use *current* and *relevant* legal rules, which come from statutes or cases. **Key cases** highlight cases which are particularly important. Also use the **examination pointers** plus the **diagrams** or **summaries** at the end of each Chapter as a guide. An answer should be rounded off with a conclusion as to liability. This need not be a firm conclusion; it may not be clear-cut, especially where a jury may be making the decision. You should never start an answer with "D will be guilty of ...." What you need to do is to:

Identify the appropriate area of law – this will tell the examiner you have understood the focus of the scenario and will shape your answer.

Apply the relevant rules in a logical way to the facts– this will be the substance of your answer. Define the offence(s) then take each part of the *actus reus* and *mens rea* in turn. Do this for each offence if there is more than one. If you do this logically you won't leave anything out. If the area is covered by a statute, quote the law from that statute accurately and with section numbers if possible.

Add a little more detail if there is a particular issue shown by the facts – there will often be something particular to focus on so look for clues in the given facts to see if you need more on anything, e.g., causation.

Support your application with relevant cases – only use cases which are relevant to the particular scenario, and only state those facts that are essential to show the examiner why you have chosen that case e.g., because the facts are similar.

Conclude in a way that is sustainable and supported by what you have said and the cases you used – it is useful to look back at the question at this point. If it says "Advise Mary ...", then make sure that your answer does so. In your conclusion you should pull together the different strands of your answer and then say that based on that application "I would advise Mary that ...".

Try to refer to the facts of a scenario as often as you can when applying the law. This indicates that you are answering the specific question and have a sound enough knowledge to know which cases are relevant to the particular facts. It also helps to keep you focused.

Evaluation advice

Essays require more discussion and evaluation of the law or legal issues. The **key criticisms** in the summaries are designed to help with this, along with the **evaluation pointers**.

In an essay question, you may need to form an opinion or weigh up arguments about a particular area of law or legal procedure. Try to balance any arguments by referring to more than one viewpoint. Also round off your answer with a short concluding paragraph, preferably referring back to the question. This shows the examiner you are addressing the specific question and not one you would have preferred to have been asked.

As with application of the law, you should try to take a logical approach. The beginning should introduce the subject matter, the central part should explain/analyse/consider advantages and disadvantages of it as appropriate, and the conclusion should bring the various strands of argument together with reference to the question set.

The mixed questions

As mentioned in the introduction, there are two mixed questions. The '**links to non-substantive law**' should help you to see how a particular area of law connects to the English legal system. The law spans various areas of process, procedure, rights and remedies as well as substantive laws such as crime and tort. These all interconnect and you will need to show you understand this connection between the substantive and non-substantive law.

Some questions may have a clear link, e.g., a scenario involving several mitigating or aggravating factors linked to a question on sentencing. Others may not, but there will always be some type of link so try to connect the two parts, e.g., if asked to explain if Tom is liable for an offence and also whether juries are a good method of trial you would first need to apply the law you have learnt on the offence to whatever Tom has done. Depending on the exact information given in the question you can then discuss juries reasonably separately, but you can tie the two together with occasional references to Tom and to the role of a jury in relation to his particular offence, and maybe whether it would be to Tom's advantage or not to opt for trial by jury. There are two mixed questions on each paper. The mixed question will cover both application and evaluation so …

... here's a summary:

Application question

Identify the appropriate area of law
- Show the examiner you have understood the focus of the scenario

Apply the relevant rules in a logical way
- Define the offence(s)
- Take each part of the actus reus and mens rea in turn
- Do this for each offence if there is more than one

Add more detail
- look for clues in the given facts to see if you need more on anything, e.g., causation

Support your application with relevant cases
- only use cases which are relevant to the particular scenario
- only state those facts that are essential to show the examiner why you have chosen that case

Conclude
- Look back at the question
- If it says "Advise Mary ...", then make sure that you do
- Pull together the different strands

Evaluation question

Introduce the subject matter
- Identify the area of law
- State the main issue(s)

Explain, Analyse, Consider
- Advantages
- Disadvantages
- Either: take all the advantages and then all the disadvantages (AAA + DDD)
- Or: take advantages and disadvantages one at a time (A-D + A-D + A-D etc.)

Conclude
- Bring the various strands of argument together
- Refer to the question set

Examination paper for AS

Although this book covers criminal law, I have included the English legal system in this paper because that is what you will get in the real examination.

Task 14

For the AS examination the marks are evenly distributed between the English legal system and criminal law. There are 80 marks in total and a time of 1½ hours.

Answer all questions

Tick the correct answer for multiple choice questions

[1] Which **one** of the following statements best describes liability for an omission? **1 mark**

A A person can never be liable for an omission

B A person can only be liable for an omission if there is a duty to act

C A person can always be liable for an omission

D A person can only be liable for an omission if there is a family relationship

[2] Which **one** of the following statements best defines the *mens rea* of an offence under **s 47 Offences against the Person Act**? **1 mark**

A Intent to cause harm

B Intent or recklessness to cause harm

C Intent or recklessness to use or threaten force

D Intent to use or threaten force

[3] John says to Jack "If the teacher wasn't here I'd punch you". What, if any, offence has John committed? **1 mark**

A Assault and battery

B Assault

C Battery

D None of the above

[4] Which **one** of the following statements best defines the *actus reus* of an offence under **s 18 Offences against the Person Act** 1861? **1 mark**

A Wounding and causing grievous bodily harm

B Wounding

C Grievous bodily harm

D Wounding or causing grievous bodily harm

[5] Which **one** of the following statements best defines strict liability? **1 mark**

A Liability without *mens rea*

B Liability without *actus reus*

C Liability without either *actus reus* or *mens rea*

D Liability with both *actus reus* and *mens rea*

[6] Which **one** of the following is **not** a lawyer? **1 mark**

A A legal executive

B A magistrate

C A barrister

D A solicitor

[7] Assuming Susie is charged with wounding contrary to **s 18** of the **Offences against the Person Act 1861** which court will hear the case? **1 mark**

A The magistrates' court

B The High court

C The Crown Court

D The magistrates' court or the Crown Court

[8] Which **one** of the following statements is most accurate in relation to appeals from the magistrates' court? **1 mark**

A Most appeals go to the Court of Appeal

B All appeals go to the Crown Court

C Most appeals go to the Crown Court

D All appeals go to the Court of Appeal

[9] Which **one** of the following statements is **false**? **1 mark**

A Bail will be granted if there is no real prospect of a custody sentence

B Bail need not be granted if there are substantial grounds that D may engage in conduct that might cause physical or mental injury or harm

C Bail will not usually be granted where the offence occurred whilst D was on bail for another offence

D Bail is never granted in a murder case

[10] Which **one** of the following institutions oversees legal aid provision? **1 mark**

A The Legal Aid Agency

B The Legal Aid Board

C The Legal Services Commission

D The Legal Aid Commission

[11]

Explain what is meant by the term 'duty solicitor' and explain when a person charged with an offence might be entitled to free advice **3 marks**

[12]

Rob is employed as a lifeguard at the local swimming pool. After a night out with friends he is tired and doesn't notice that a child has fallen into the pool and is in difficulties. Outline how an omission can form part of the *actus reus* of a crime. Briefly discuss whether Rob's failure to act might form the basis of criminal liability if the child drowns. **3 marks**

[13] Rafael was lying in wait for Mike because he was angry and wanted to scare him. As Mike went past he jumped out waving a knife and shouting racial abuse. Mike ran away and tripped over, suffering cuts and bruises to his arms and face. Outline what is meant by actual bodily harm under **s 47** of the **Offences against the Person Act 1861**. Briefly discuss whether Rafael is liable for Mike's injuries. Explain what is meant by mitigating and aggravating factors. Assuming Rafael is convicted explain which factors may be taken into account and discuss how these can affect his sentence

12 marks

[14]

Kylie is trying to study for her university exams while looking after 5-year old Mal for the evening. The child is misbehaving and really annoying her. Eventually she loses her temper and slaps Mal across the back of the legs causing bruises and swelling. Advise Kylie as to her liability under **s 20** of the **Offences against the Person Act 1861**.

Discuss the advantages and disadvantages of a jury trial in determining Kylie's liability.

12 marks

[15] **In this question you are expected to provide an extended answer which shows a clear, logical and sustained line of reasoning leading to a valid conclusion.**

Don, Frank, Sergei and Tom are at a disco. Frank has an argument with Sergei. He pulls out a knife and stabs Sergei in the arm. Sergei is taken to hospital where he has to have several stitches.

Meanwhile, Don sees Tom dancing with his girlfriend, he grabs Tom's jacket and pulls him off the dance floor. Tom lands on a table laden with drinks and cuts his hand slightly on some broken glass.

Discuss the criminal liability of both Frank and Don under the **Offences against the Person Act 1861**.

20 marks

[16] 'Stare decisis' means stand by things decided. Using case examples, explain how far this rule of precedent means judges in the Court of Appeal and Supreme Court must follow earlier decisions, and discuss why they might not want to do so.

20 marks

END OF QUESTIONS

Total: 80 marks

Answers to tasks and self-test questions are on my website at www.drsr.org/publications/tasks. For some interactive exercises, click on 'Free Exercises'.

The Bridge

This section contains an evaluation of the law so far, along with examples of the role the law plays in society from the areas already covered. You will need to be able to evaluate the law, and discuss the role law plays in relation to what you have learned for the A-level criminal law examination. I have included proposals for reform because although law reform is not linked to criminal law for the A-level (only AS), the issues with the non-fatal offences clearly suggest that justice is not being achieved and fault is an issue with several of the offences where *mens rea* does not match *actus reus*. It is also relevant to matters such as the thin-skull rule (**Blaue**) and voluntariness of conduct (**Leicester v Pearson**).

In Part 2 of this book, examples of the nature of law appear at the end of every Chapter so you can think about these as you go through each area. As before, look for the heading 'Links to the non-substantive law' which I have now split into the English legal system (ELS) and the nature of law. In these boxes the links to the nature of law specifically relate to the concepts of law and justice and fault which need to be linked to crime for the A-level examination. However, if appropriate, you can use criminal cases in a discussion of the concepts which appear on other papers (morals and balancing competing interests). Therefore, if one of these is particularly relevant I have mentioned it.

Evaluation of the non-fatal offences against the person and proposals for reform

In Chapter 1 we looked at the main principles of criminal law which included the correspondence principle and fair labelling. The criticisms in the summary plus the following problems can all be related to these principles. We have seen many problems whilst looking at the individual offences and it is in clear the **Offences against the Person Act 1861** is in need of reform. There are also more general issues:

Language: the **Act** is very complicated and was written in 1861, so much of the language is obscure. Lawyers and juries have struggled to understand the complexities of the different offences. The courts also have difficulty interpreting words such as 'occasioning', 'actual bodily harm', 'grievous' and 'maliciously' as they are not used in the same sense today. This can result in conflicting case law and injustice. The word 'bodily' in **s 47** indicates some kind of physical harm but has been interpreted to include psychiatric harm. This may make sense but the statute should be able to be applied by the judges without having to stretch the language. The word 'maliciously' has been interpreted as meaning recklessly (**Savage & Parmenter 1992**). However, it appears in **s 18** as well as **s 20** and the *mens rea* for **s 18** is intent only. In **Parmenter,** the judge had difficulty explaining 'maliciously' to the jury. He said that it meant that it was enough that D *should have foreseen* that some harm might occur. This sounds very like objective rather than subjective recklessness. In fact, on appeal, this was said to be a misdirection. It highlights the fact that these words need to be clearly explained. If the law lacks clarity then it does not achieve justice. It is also hard for the courts to interpret the words and meaning in such an old Act with obscure language.

Common law: assault and battery are outside the **Act**. Clarity (and therefore justice) would require all the offences to be together in one place. However, an alternative argument is that the common law can keep them up to date. This happened in **Ireland,** where it was recognised that an assault could be via a telephone. It is also confusing that assault means two things. It is used to cover the two offences of assault and battery (as seen in **s 47** which refers to an assault but means assault and battery) and the actual offence of causing someone to apprehend violence.

Proposals for reform have been produced and Bills put before Parliament over a long period, but to date Parliament has not found time to debate the issues – see below under proposed reforms

Task 15

Look back at the **Evaluation pointer** boxes in Part 1. Write some notes on these with case examples. Add your own thoughts. Then read through the reforms. Ask yourself whether the proposed reforms would solve any of the problems you have identified.

Keep these notes for revision and as a guide to an evaluation question.

So, there are plenty of problems. What is being done about them?

Background of proposed reforms

The Law Commission has been considering codification of the criminal law for some time. This was a huge task and so it was decided it would be better to work on a series of self-contained bills to deal with different parts of the criminal law. In 1993, the Commission produced a report (**No 218**) and draft Bill on the non-fatal offences against the person. This never received parliamentary time but in 1998, the government produced its own Bill incorporating most of the recommended changes, but again little happened. In 2014, the Commission readdressed the issue and issued a consultation paper (a scoping paper), which noted that the frequent changes in the law had left it in an incoherent and confusing state. A report followed and was published in November 2015. The 2015 proposals are based on the 1998 Draft Bill.

From the outset, the LC has pointed out that:

- The Act is outdated and uses archaic language

- There is a lack of a clear hierarchy and the offences are not classified in a coherent way. They are not classified in order of seriousness, so that **s 20** and **s 47** differ in the seriousness of harm but not in the maximum sentence. The Law Commission proposes a maximum of 5 years for **s 47**, as now, but a maximum 7 years for **s 20**. **S 18** would still carry a maximum of life.

- The Act does not actually accord with current practice. This means that although a minor wound may legally be a wound it is likely to be charged under **s 47**. Similarly, a minor injury is legally **s 47** but usually charged as an assault (battery).

- As regards *mens rea*, the mental element is not clearly defined and the word malicious comes into both **s 20** and **s 18**. In the first case, it is not explained and in the second case, it 'adds nothing'. In **Mowatt 1968**, the judge said "In **s 18** the word 'maliciously' adds nothing".

The main problem is that the *actus reus* and *mens rea* do not always match, so that D can be liable for a result without intending or being reckless as to that result. This applies to **s 20** and **s 47**. This lack of correspondence between *actus reus* and *mens rea* is known as 'constructive liability'. It is called constructive liability because liability is constructed from the *actus reus* of one offence and the *mens rea* of another e.g., liability for assault occasioning actual bodily harm under **s 47** is constructed from the *actus reus* of **s 47** plus the *mens rea* of assault. (Constructive liability is also seen in murder and 'constructive' manslaughter). Any law which allows someone to be guilty of a more serious offence when the fault element was for a lesser offence can be said to be unjust.

The Law Commission Report (No 361) 2015

The 2015 report makes the same points and it is also clear the LC would uphold the 'correspondence principle' and would abolish constructive liability for the non-fatal offences.

The LC points out that there are four different ways of committing the offence under **s 18** and suggests that resisting arrest should be a separate offence and not included in **s 18**.

The LC also refers to the problem caused by the different words of 'cause' and 'inflict' in **s 18** and **20**. The intention is to restructure the law and modernise and simplify the language. The LC suggests basing the reforms on the 1998 draft bill with some amendments.

The table which follow shows the proposals from the 1998 Bill. The offences are redefined and in all of them the *mens rea* matches the *actus reus*.

Name of proposed offence	Explanation of proposed offence	Current offence
Intentional serious injury	Clause 1: intentionally causing serious injury	S 18
Reckless serious injury	Clause 2: recklessly causing serious injury	S 20
Intentional or reckless injury	Clause 3: intentionally or recklessly causing injury	S 47
Assault	Clause 4: intentionally or recklessly applying force to or causing an impact on the body of another; or intentionally or recklessly causing another to believe force is imminent	Common assault (assault and battery)

In each case, the word 'cause' is used. The Bill also defines injury to include both physical and psychiatric harm.

Injury would include mental as well as physical harm, as long as it is a recognised psychiatric condition and also include disease. Note that there is no need for a prior assault for any of these offences (as there is currently for **s 47**). Nor is there a mention of the word 'wound'. The LC felt that wounding does not need to be a separate category as it can be an injury or a serious injury depending on the facts. As regards transmitting a disease it was felt this could come within causing injury (serious or otherwise) but if it could not then there should be a separate review of this area.

The 2015 proposals

The 2015 proposals are still based on the 1998 Bill, but with some minor amendments. The first three offences (intentionally causing serious injury, recklessly causing serious injury and intentionally or recklessly causing injury) would be as above. Assault would also be as above, but renamed as 'physical assault' (currently battery) and 'threatened assault' or 'assault by threats' (currently assault).

The only real difference is the proposal of a new offence of causing minor injuries. This would fall between intentionally or recklessly causing injury and assault so would span Clauses 3 and 4 from the Draft Bill. It would include cases where the assault (whether physical or threatened) causes some injury, however minor but would not require *mens rea* for the injury, as for **s 47** now. However, it would be triable only in the magistrates' court, with a maximum sentence of 12 months.

Note that statutory interpretation is included as a non-substantive matter on Paper 1 at A-level, that means you could link it to the **Offences against the Person Act** as well as the Acts you will cover in Part 2.

Links to the non-substantive law

For AS, you only needed to link the substantive criminal law to the English legal system, for A-level you still need to do that but you also need to link it to the nature of law, particularly in relation to fault and justice. I gave you a brief introduction to the nature of law concepts in Part 1 because you will need to do this for the Part 1 subjects too, just not for the AS examination. Here is a bit more detail.

The nature of law (concepts)

The word law in phrases such as criminal law, human rights law, contract law etc., refers to the substance of the law (hence these topics are called substantive law). The word law in a wider sense is a more elusive concept, as it relates to the nature rather than the substance of law. It involves consideration of what academics and judges think the nature of law is (and what it should be). This in itself involves consideration of theories of law, such as law and justice, law and morality, the role of law in balancing competing interests and the role of law in punishing (criminal liability) or compensating (civil liability) based on fault. When considering the nature of law you need to look at the rest of your course from a different perspective. The examples given at the end of each Chapter should help you use cases and procedures you know to illustrate a discussion of any of these concepts. As a reminder, I repeat here what I said in Chapter 1.

Although only fault and justice are specifically assigned to the criminal law paper (along with the principles of criminal liability discussed in Chapter 1), AQA have confirmed that "where appropriate, irrespective of the Paper to which a Nature of Law/ELS topic is assigned, examples may be drawn from the substantive law in other Papers". For the nature of law this means that although fault and justice are assigned to the criminal law paper, you can also use examples from tort, contract and/or human rights to illustrate these concepts. Similarly, law and morals is with tort on Paper 2 but there are many criminal cases which illustrate morality, e.g. euthanasia cases, which come into murder. You could therefore use these cases when discussing law and morality on the tort paper (unless you have been specifically asked to discuss civil cases only).

The law plays a role in society by regulating behaviour and establishing social control. It punishes those convicted of a crime and compensates the victims of any civil wrongdoing. It also facilitates (e.g., by giving powers to form contracts or get married) and protects (e.g., by laws against theft and violence, and consumer protection laws). The law plays an important role in society not only in providing **justice** but also in **balancing competing interests** (both public and private) in order to do so. It sometimes involves enforcing **moral** as well as legal rules, and legal liability usually relies on **fault**, e.g., one role of the criminal law is to punish those found to be at fault, or blameworthy. These are all concepts of law, or legal theories.

Most people recognise the role of law in punishing offenders who are found to be at fault in criminal cases, but the law has a less obvious role in many other areas. The following are all real cases and provide examples of the role that the law plays in society in relation to the above concepts. This covers a range so that you can get an idea of how the law in practice relates to the different theories. However, for the purposes of the final examination fault and justice come into Paper 1, fault, balancing competing interests and law and morality come into Paper 2, and balancing competing interests, justice, and law and morality come into Paper 3. I have included a little on law and morality and balancing competing interests in the table below even though not specifically with Paper 1 because as stated above, you can use case examples from any substantive areas where appropriate. It also helps show you how to relate the substantive law in practice to the nature of law in theory, and there is an overlap between these concepts.

Case	Brief facts	The nature and role of law
Brown 1994 (See Chapter 7)	A criminal case where serious injuries had occurred during consensual sado-masochistic sex in private. Those involved were convicted of grievous bodily harm. A controversial case because they were all adults and no-one was forced.	In balancing the interests the law included the public interest (what was best for society) and also thought the moral wrong should be punished (society needs protecting from violent behaviour, even in private).
Re A 2001	A hospital sought a court order to allow an operation on Siamese twins to separate them. The result would be that one twin would die but without the operation they both would.	In granting the order the law had balanced many different interests. This not only included the people concerned but the public interest. The morality of the action also affected the decision in court. This shows the difficulty for the courts as society is divided on such issues.
Miller v Jackson 1977	A woman wanted the court to award an injunction to stop cricket being played nearby because she often had cricket balls landing in her garden.	In balancing the interests the court included the public interest and thought society would not be best served by granting an injunction to stop the cricket. The injunction was refused.
Murray v Express Newspapers 2008	The author of the Harry Potter books, JK Rowling, brought a case on behalf of her young son against a photographic agency for publishing secretly taken photographs of him.	The court had to balance the interests of the agency in freedom of expression against the child's right to privacy. The balance came down in favour of the child's right, but the court made clear each case would depend on its own facts and the decision could be different with an adult. This shows that in balancing interests the law is also protecting the vulnerable (the child).
Gemmell & Richards 2003 (See Chapter 3)	Two boys set light to some papers outside the back of a shop. Several premises were badly damaged. They were convicted of recklessly causing criminal damage by fire (arson) because the risk of damage was obvious to a reasonable person. Their ages were therefore not taken into account.	In order to achieve justice the HL overruled an earlier law and decided a person required a greater level of fault in order to be guilty of a crime. Thus to prove recklessness it must be shown that D is aware of a risk, but deliberately goes ahead and takes it. This shows the importance of proving fault in criminal law.

Some knowledge of these concepts is needed for you to understand how the links to the non-substantive law given in each Chapter apply, so here is a brief description of each with a couple of views and/or comments as a taster, using cases from the table above.

Balancing competing Interests

If one person has a right (an 'interest') this often conflicts with the rights of another person, as in the **Murray** case in the table. In order to decide whose rights are to be enforced the courts must balance the competing interests to arrive at a decision. The balance is not only between private interests (as in **Murray**) but may be between public and private (as in **Miller v Jackson**). There may be several interests to balance, as in **Re A**, and the court may find the balancing act difficult – but that is part of the role of law, to consider difficult issues and make a decision as to what the legal position should be.

One view (that of Roscoe Pound) regarding competing interests is that law is an engineering tool which can be used to balance the different interests in society to achieve social control. However he believed that public interests should not be balanced against private ones because the public interest will always prevail, a case example is **Miller v Jackson**. When you look at the cases in each Chapter consider what the interests involved are and how they conflict. Then consider whether the law achieved an appropriate balance (and therefore justice).

Fault

The meaning of fault in most cases is a sense of blameworthiness. The level of blame, or fault, is different in criminal and civil law. Criminal law usually requires a fairly high level of fault before someone is found guilty of a crime, this is that they acted with either intention or recklessness (you saw an example of the latter in **Gemmell** above). For civil law the most common type of fault is negligence, which is a lower level of fault.

In both crime and tort there may be strict liability. This means liability without proof of fault, which can seem unjust.

Some argue that strict liability is unfair, especially in criminal law, but others see it as necessary, especially in matters of social concern, because it protects the public. When you look at cases consider not only the meaning of fault, but the importance of fault and whether the law set the level of fault appropriately, as in **Gemmell** where the HL decided the level had been set too low and changed the law.

Law and morals

Both law and morals involve rules. As noted earlier, although they share many characteristics, there is a distinction between social rules and legal rules. The courts enforce the law, but not social rules. An important question is whether moral issues should be a matter for society alone, or whether the law should promote and/or enforce morality. A law which makes immoral behaviour illegal is promoting morality, engineering the way society behaves. If the law makes a decision in court based on morality it is enforcing morality, as in **Brown 1994**. There has been much debate on this subject and there are opposing views. Here are simplified versions of three:

Professor Hart says that law and morals are separate and the law should not be used to enforce morality. If a law is made using the proper procedures, it is a valid law even if immoral, and so it must be obeyed. This is positivism.

Lord Devlin said that law and morals are related and immoral acts, even in private, should be punished. Also, even if made using the proper procedures, if a law is immoral it is not a valid law and need not be obeyed. This is natural law.

John Stuart Mill said that the law shouldn't normally be used to enforce morality but could if harm to others is involved. This is a type of positivism and also of utilitarianism (see under justice).

The decision in **Brown** was partly based on the fact that the acts were seen as immoral. Hart would see that as irrelevant, Devlin would not. Mill might go either way as harm was caused to others but it was by consent. The decision was only by a 3-2 majority so you can see that the judges disagreed on this issue too. Note the overlap with justice. The three views above are all views on what justice involves.

Consider whether the law should be involved in what is essentially a moral issue. We live in a pluralist society with diverse views, so there is no 'shared morality'. What some people see as immoral, others don't (e.g., fox-hunting and smoking). What is regarded as immoral in one society, or in one time, may not be so in another (e.g., gay marriage, abortion and adultery). This makes legal involvement in morals a tricky issue, especially in controversial areas like euthanasia and enforced feeding for anorexics.

Law and justice

One important role of the law is to achieve justice, so any of the cases in the table can be used to illustrate this concept. As you saw in Chapter 1, the rule of law requires fairness, and this is one meaning of justice, as is equality, another part of the rule of law. However, justice means different things to different people and as you can see from **Re A**, justice may be achieved for some but not all. There are different theories on what justice means and how it is achieved.

The three theories under 'law and morals' are theories of justice. Another theory of justice, called utilitarianism, is that justice is achieved when the 'greatest happiness' is achieved. A law which produces a lot of benefit would be a just law. Applying this to **Re A**, we can say that as the operation would save a life this was a big plus, so justice would be achieved by allowing it. However, if you look back to the natural law theory of justice, this is that it should have a moral content so an immoral law is not a proper law. On this view the decision in **Re A** did not achieve justice because it was immoral to operate knowing the other twin would die.

When you look at the case examples consider whether the law achieves justice, and by whose theory. You should also consider justice when studying the English legal system so that you can discuss whether the different legal institutions and procedures achieve justice.

Let's finish on this by applying all the above concepts to just one example, with a hint of the English legal system thrown in.

Example

R v R 1991, involved a man accused of raping his wife. They were separated and she had moved back in with her parents. He forced his way in to their house and assaulted her while attempting rape. At the time, rape within marriage was not against the law because a woman was deemed to have consented to sex purely by being married. The case went to the House of Lords (now the Supreme Court) on appeal.

The HL decided that rape within marriage was no longer acceptable. The judges presumably felt they achieved **justice** for the wife. Whether the man achieved justice is another matter. It is part of the concept of justice that the law is not retrospective and however wrong he may have been **morally**, at the time of the event it was not against the law. In making the decision the court had to **balance the competing interests** of D (not to be guilty of what had at the time been a legal act) against those of his wife (to have the law's protection) and the wider public interest (violence can affect society as a whole). The public interest will usually prevail and here there was the added interest of the wife. The fact that the act was accompanied by violence showed a greater degree of **fault**, which may have tipped the balance against D. He should be punished (sanctioned) for his wrongdoing. Finally, there is clearly a **moral** issue because the judges thought the law was wrong to allow an immoral act such as rape, even within marriage. However, Hart could say the decision should be based only on legal rules not morality, and that D should not have been punished for what was a legal action, even if it was immoral.

However, Devlin might agree that he should be punished because the law which allowed rape within marriage was itself immoral and so not valid.

It is also arguable that it should be an elected Parliament which should decide on whether this type of act is against the law, not unelected judges. In fact Parliament did act, after the event, and changed the law to match the decision (which was therefore an influence on Parliament).

A utilitarian would say this decision, and the later law by Parliament, achieve justice as a greater number of people benefit from the law prohibiting acts of violence, especially as (unlike **Brown 1994**) it was against the victim's wishes.

Evaluation pointer

As you saw in Part 1, an important role for the law is to uphold the rule of law. Another is to achieve justice. Both these require, among other things, equality, clarity and fairness. Any of the cases you see where the decision seems wrong on the facts, can illustrate a lack of fairness. Cases where there is inconsistency can illustrate a lack of clarity, and cases where those involved are not treated equally can illustrate a lack of equality. As you look at case examples bear this in mind. This will give you lots of material to illustrate a discussion of the role of law in achieving justice, and will help you understand how the rule of law applies. You don't need the rule of law for Paper 1 for the A-level but it comes into Paper 3, so it is a good idea to think about it at least in a general sense as you go along.

Links to the non-substantive law from Part 1

For links to the English legal system look back to the introduction to Part 1. The diagram and explanation there apply to A-level too. As in Part 1, at the end of each Chapter in Part 2 is a reminder to look back at this diagram to see what parts of the English legal system the particular topic you have just studied could link to. One difference from AS is that statutory interpretation was not included but will be for A-level. This may be relevant to how the **Offences against the Person Act** has been interpreted and how difficult that is to do.

The nature of law

Now you have had a better look at the nature of law, let's see how these concepts can link to what you studied in Part 1, with the emphasis on fault and justice.

Actus reus

There are several cases in this Chapter which can be used to illustrate the various concepts of law. Here are a few of them.

One role of law is to provide justice and to punish those at fault. 'State of affairs' cases such as **Larsonneur 1933** and **Winzar v Chief Constable of Kent 1983** seem unjust because the Ds did not act voluntarily, so were not at fault. There is not usually a legal obligation to act even though there may be a moral one, so there is not usually liability where there is an omission to act rather than an act.

However, this rule changes where there is a duty to act, as in **Pittwood 1902**, **Stone and Dobinson 1977** etc. There is also a lower degree of fault in such cases but D may be liable for a serious crime such as manslaughter, and even murder (**Gibbins & Proctor**). The role of law is to provide justice and this is arguably unjust. The thin-skull rule also seems unjust because D may be guilty because of the victim's actions, as in **Blaue 1975**.

Mens rea

Mens rea is the fault element in criminal law so the issue of fault arises in several cases. The role of law is to punish those at fault. However, D can be guilty of murder where there is no intent to kill (**Vickers/DPP v Smith**). Where the *mens rea* does not correspond with the *actus reus* this is known as constructive liability. It is not a just law. D should only be liable where the *mens rea* was for the offence actually committed – you will see more examples of this with the substantive law as it applies to murder, manslaughter and two of the non-fatal offences against the person. The role the law played in **Gemmell and Richards 2003** was a more just one. The HL confirmed that recklessness is subjective and that the **Caldwell** test was wrong. By overruling its previous decision and raising the level of fault required, the HL achieved a greater degree of justice.

Strict liability

Strict liability means liability without fault so any cases in this Chapter can be used to illustrate this concept. One role of law is to punish those at fault, so arguably there should be no liability without fault. Balancing competing interests also arises because another role of law is to balance the interests of society in being protected with those of D who should not be liable without fault, as in **Shah**. As in most cases where the public interest is balanced against a private one, the public interest prevails (**Pound**). It is questionable whether this type of liability achieves justice.

The non-fatal offences

Constructive liability, where the *mens rea* does not correspond with the *actus reus*, is not just. The level of fault in such cases is lower than it should be. This occurs with both **s 47** and **s 20**. D should only be liable where the *mens rea* was for the offence actually committed, but under **s 47** D is liable for the more serious offence of causing actual bodily harm even though the *mens rea* was only for an assault or a battery. Cases such as **Roberts 1971** and **Savage 1991** illustrate this point.

Again, for **s 20**, the level of fault required is lower than it should be as liability for grievous bodily harm or wounding only requires that D had *mens rea* for causing 'some harm', not serious harm – **Mowatt 1968** illustrates this point. The role of law is to punish those at fault and to achieve justice, and it can be said that with constructive liability the law does neither of these adequately. In **Brown 1994**, the decision was partly based on morality and arguable this is not the role of law. However, the law balanced the interests of D with those of society and the decision favoured protecting society from immoral and violent acts. The fact that the **Offences against the Person Act** is so old means that the role the law plays is a difficult one. It is hard to achieve justice when the language and meaning of an Act is obscure. In **C v Eisenhower 1983**, he was found not guilty merely because the charge was wrong and there was no wound. Justice was not achieved. Refer back to the problems and reforms in the summary for more on this.

Part 2: Criminal law for A-level 7162

We now move on to the fatal offences against the person, murder and manslaughter (forms of homicide).

Murder, somewhat surprisingly, is not a statutory offence. It comes from the common law not an Act of Parliament. Murder is killing someone with intent and carries a mandatory life sentence.

There are two specific defences to murder which, if successful, reduce it to manslaughter, and thus allow sentencing to be at the discretion of the judge. This is called voluntary manslaughter, D admits killing (hence 'voluntary') but argues there were special circumstances which mean the conviction should be for manslaughter not murder. These circumstances are loss of control (D killed in reaction to something done or said by the victim) or diminished responsibility (D was suffering from some kind of mental abnormality). So, murder and voluntary manslaughter have the same *actus reus* and *mens rea*. The difference lies only in these defences.

Example

Jane picks up a knife and stabs Jenny, who dies. Jane has the *actus reus* of murder as her act has caused Jenny's death. She also has the *mens rea* because she intended to kill, or at least seriously harm, her. Jane will be sentenced to life imprisonment.

If Jenny had taunted Jane in some way, Jane may be able to use the defence of loss of control if this is what caused her to stab Jenny. If she is suffering from some kind of mental disability at the time, Jane may argue diminished responsibility. If either defence succeeds, Jane will be convicted of manslaughter, not murder. The judge can choose the sentence.

These two defences ONLY apply to a murder charge. Other defences to murder also apply to other crimes so are dealt with under general defences.

Involuntary manslaughter is different as, unlike voluntary manslaughter, it is a separate offence. The difference between murder and involuntary manslaughter is in the *mens rea*. The *actus reus* is the same. Where D kills without the intent required for murder, manslaughter will be the appropriate charge. There are two types: gross negligence manslaughter and constructive manslaughter (also called unlawful act manslaughter).

Example

Going back to Jane. If she had stabbed Jenny in the finger but Jenny got a bad infection and later died from poor hospital treatment, Jane could say there was no intent to kill or seriously injure so it was not murder. However her act was unlawful and caused death (poor treatment is unlikely to break the chain of causation) so this will be constructive manslaughter.

If the treatment was particularly bad, the doctor could be liable for gross negligence manslaughter. This is where a person has been criminally negligent, even though not acting unlawfully.

Note that 'voluntary' and 'involuntary' are legal terms, used to distinguish between manslaughter following a murder charge, and manslaughter as a separate charge. There is no such charge as 'voluntary manslaughter' or 'involuntary manslaughter'. The first would be charged as murder, the second as manslaughter.

After these offences we look at property offences and attempt.

Theft is a big area but don't be daunted as once you have done theft you will find that you have almost all you need for robbery. The two offences are closely connected.

The terms 'theft' and 'robbery' are used rather indiscriminately by the media which can be confusing. Simply put, theft covers what most people would think of as stealing, like taking property belonging to someone else without their consent. Robbery is theft (all the *actus reus* and *mens rea*) with an added ingredient; that of using force, or a threat of force, in order to steal.

Example

I take a bicycle from outside the railway station. This is theft.

I take the bike and tell the owner I will beat him up if he tries to stop me. This is robbery.

We will look at the different ways a theft may be committed. Although my example is valid, theft is wider than just taking something and can include e.g., merely using something belonging to someone else. Robbery is fairly straightforward but you need to understand what amounts to 'force' so we will then discuss this in more detail.

The final offence is the preliminary crime of attempt. Such crimes are called *inchoate* offences. This means that they are incomplete, there is an **attempt** to commit a crime but the crime has not actually been completed. D can be convicted of the preliminary crime even if the main offence never occurs. Thus if D tries to kill someone but fails, there can be a charge of **attempted** murder. This would also apply where there is a problem with causation.

Examples

Going back to bicycles – if I approach the bicycle outside the station with a pair of wire-cutters in my hand intending to cut the chain attaching the bike to the railings I can be charged with attempted theft.

Attempt applies to all crimes. In **White 1910** (see Chapter 2), D was not guilty of his mother's murder because she died of a heart attack before the poison he gave her took effect. He had not caused her death so his conviction was for attempted murder.

The last thing to consider is the defences to the various crimes.

There are four general defences you need to study. Unlike the two special defences for murder these apply to most offences. They are insanity and automatism (most commonly seen with homicide) self-defence (most commonly seen with the non-fatal offences against the person), and intoxication, which can apply to all crimes, but rarely succeeds. The last defence is duress (most commonly seen with the property offences).

Example

If Jane hears voices in her head which tell her to kill someone and she is charged with murder, she can plead the defence of insanity. If she is concussed by a blow to the head which causes her to lose control and she kills someone, this may be automatism as she is acting 'automatically'. If she killed because she was intoxicated at the time, she would use the defence of intoxication. As you'll see, this defence rarely succeeds. If Jane believes that she is being attacked by Jenny and she hits her, she can use self-defence. This is a defence in itself, but also (as with consent) makes a battery lawful. Finally, if Jenny threatens to beat Jane up if she doesn't steal some money from her mother Jane can use the defence of duress if she is charged with theft.

This is a good area for tying in with the various concepts of law. Defences often relate to issues of fault (a defence may excuse or justify the commission of a crime) and are a way of achieving justice (by taking into account the particular circumstances).

As Year 2 covers a large area I have added summaries after the fatal offences, after the property offences and attempt, and finally after the defences.

Chapter 8 Murder

"... if at the time of death the original wound is still an operating cause and a substantial cause, then the death can properly be said to be the result of the wound, albeit that some other cause of death is also operating." Lord Parker CJ

Can you remember in which case this statement was made? If not, look back at legal causation in Chapter 2.

By the end of this Chapter, you should be able to:

- Identify the *actus reus* and mens rea of murder
- Explain how the law on causation (*actus reus*) applies in murder cases
- Explain how intent (*mens rea*) is proved by reference to cases
- Identify possible criticisms for an evaluation of the law

There are definitions of murder going back to the 18th century and beyond. The most famous is that by Sir Edward Coke: 'the unlawful killing of a reasonable creature in being under the King's peace and with malice aforethought'. However, murder is a common law offence (not covered by an Act of Parliament), so the definition has changed through case law over time (for a start we now have a Queen not a King).

Actus reus

The *actus reus* is essentially the same for both murder and manslaughter. The modern definition of murder is the "**unlawful killing of a human being under the Queen's peace**".

Unlawful

Most killing will be unlawful. However, killing in self-defence (see defences) may make the act lawful and so not murder.

Killing

People generally think of murder as involving an action (conduct) such as shooting or stabbing someone. However, murder can be committed by omission. In **Gibbins and Proctor 1918**, (a similar case to **Stone and Dobinson 1977** which was manslaughter) the D's lived together with the man's daughter. They failed to give her food and she died. The court held that where food was withheld with intent to cause grievous bodily harm then it would be murder if this caused death. The CA upheld their murder convictions.

The courts do draw a distinction between an act and an omission. In **Airedale NHS Trust v Bland 1993**, discontinuing medical treatment was treated as an omission rather than a positive action. This was a civil case so is not strictly binding on the criminal courts. It will be highly persuasive though. It can be compared to **Cox 1992**, where a doctor gave an injection to a patient begging for help to die. This is a positive act, and so amounts to murder. (On the facts, it was only attempted murder as the cause of death was not clear.) Intentionally accelerating death is still murder. Thus even if someone is going to die anyway you will be guilty of murder if you intentionally shorten their life. The only exception is what is known as the *de minimis* rule: if D's act is so small that it cannot be said to play a significant part in the death, there is no liability for murder.

Example

V is in severe pain from an incurable illness. The doctor gives her a huge overdose of painkillers in order to end her suffering. Before these take effect, V's husband gives her two more painkillers.

The doctor's act would be murder. The husband's act *could* be murder as it probably hastened the death, but the court might treat it as *'de minimis'*.

Evaluation pointer

Any intentional act which causes death will be murder. Thus 'mercy killing', or euthanasia, is murder. You might argue that you were easing the suffering of someone incurably ill, but this argument will not succeed. You may feel morally justified, but legally an intentional killing is murder and even if the person was already dying, accelerating death is still murder. The motive for a crime is rarely relevant (it is as much theft to steal a loaf of bread for a starving child as it is to steal a £5,000 music system). The motive could affect the sentence, but with murder, the judge has no choice in this.

This is why **Airedale NHS Trust v Bland 1993** went to the House of Lords. Without a court order, it could have been murder.

A related issue is the sentence for murder. One argument against a mandatory life sentence is that if the members of jury see the killing as morally justified they may be reluctant to find someone guilty of murder. They would know that it would mean a life sentence and that the judge would be unable to consider the circumstances.

Human being

This may seem obvious but questions arise about whether someone who is 'brain dead' or a foetus in the womb is a human being. In **AGs Reference (No 3 of 1994) 1997**, the HL held that a foetus was not a human being for the purpose of a murder conviction. However, there could be a chain of causation extending from the initial harm to the foetus which triggered its premature birth through to the point of death after the birth, even though the *actus reus* of murder is not complete until the time of death. Thus if the foetus is injured and dies from that injury after being born, that could amount to murder. That a foetus is not a human being was confirmed in **CICA v FTT 2014**, although in this case the latter point did not arise because it was a claim for compensation following a non-fatal offence against "a person" so once it was decided that C was not a person the claim failed.

Under the Queen's peace

This part of the *actus reus* means that killing in war is not murder. It does not apply to cases outside the actual war. In **Adebolajo 2014**, D killed an off-duty soldier and claimed he was a 'soldier of Allah' and that, as there was a war between the British army and Muslims throughout the world, the killing was not unlawful as it did not take place under the Queen's peace. His argument failed and he was convicted of murder.

Causation

Murder is a result crime so it must be proved that death resulted from D's actions. If D caused death then the charge can be murder or manslaughter depending on the *mens rea*. If D did not cause death then it can only be one of the non-fatal offences or an attempt. We have seen that the prosecution must show **factual causation**: 'but for' the defendant's conduct the victim would not have died. Also **legal causation**: that D's act was a 'significant' cause of death and there was no intervening act.

Task 16

Before going any further, look up the following cases. Make a note of the facts.

White

Roberts

Smith

Cheshire

Pagett

Now make a note of the causation issue in each. Then read on to check these principles.

OK, let's have a quick recap of the causation principles involved.

Factual causation

| R v White 1910 | 'but for' his actions would she be alive? No, she would have died anyway so he did not cause that death. |

Legal causation

R v Smith 1959	If D's act was an **operating and substantial** cause of death, there is no break in the chain of causation.
R v Cheshire 1991	Following **Smith**, if D has made a **significant contribution** to the death then hospital treatment will only break the chain of causation if it is **independent of the original act** and a potent cause in itself.
Roberts 1971 The prosecution relied on this case in **Corbett 1996**, to find that D caused the death of a victim who was hit and killed by a car when trying to escape from D's attack.	If the *victim's* act is **foreseeable**, it will not break the chain of causation, as long as it is not 'daft'.
R v Pagett 1983	If a *third party's* act is **foreseeable** it will not break the chain of causation and the police returning fire was a **natural consequence** of D's actions.

All these cases could also be used to explain factual causation. In **Pagett** you would ask 'but for' his actions would she have died? No, so he factually caused death. (Note this test is sometimes reversed but the effect is the same: 'but for' his actions would she be alive? Yes, so he caused death.)

Evaluation pointer

If V is easily scared and does something 'daft' then there is arguably a vulnerability that is no different from having a thin skull or being a Jehovah's Witness, as in **Blaue 1975**. **Blaue** itself is somewhat controversial. If the victim does not have a life-threatening injury but refuses treatment, should D be liable for the resulting death?

In **Gnango 2011**, two people had been involved in a shoot-out in a car park on a housing estate. The first man fired at D who shot back, the man then fired again and his bullet killed a woman nearby. The prosecution argued that in returning fire D had caused the other man to shoot again, so had also caused the woman's death. The SC held that, although it may have made it more likely that the man would shoot again, this was not enough. The voluntary act of the other man had broken any possible chain of causation between D's return of fire and the death. The other man alone had caused the death. This can be compared to **Pagett**, where it was found to be foreseeable that the police would return fire so the chain of causation was not broken. The main difference seems to be that in

Gnango the victim was not being held by D as a hostage, but was merely walking nearby. Additionally, in **Pagett**, D shot first which was not the case in **Gnango**.

Another case where causation was proved, even though another person was the immediate cause of death, was **Chua 2015**. Here D worked in a hospital and had contaminated saline bags with insulin knowing these would be given to patients, many of whom were elderly and vulnerable. He had enough medical knowledge to know this could cause death. The fact that the saline bags were actually administered by other nurses did not break the chain of causation. It was his actions that played the most significant role in their deaths (not all the patients died so several of the charges were for GBH instead).

The fact that there is a long gap between the intention to cause serious harm and the actual death does not matter. There used to be a rule that after a year and a day a person could not be convicted of murder. However that was abolished in 1996 because medical techniques had moved on, which meant that a person could be kept alive for much longer. In **Heath 2015**, D had caused his partner's baby serious brain damage, but due to good medical care she lived for nearly another 11 years. His actions were held to be the cause of her later death and he was convicted of her murder (previously he had been convicted of causing GBH).

Mens rea

In Coke's 18th Century definition of murder, the unlawful killing must be done with *'malice aforethought'*. This expression has been interpreted as meaning with intention.

The *mens rea* for murder is an intention to kill or seriously injure someone. In **Vickers 1957**, the CA held that the *mens rea* for murder is satisfied by either an intention to kill, or an intention to cause grievous bodily harm. This was confirmed by the HL in **DPP v Smith 1960**, where the HL said that grievous bodily harm should be given its ordinary and natural meaning, that is to say, "really serious bodily harm". In **Saunders 1985**, it was said that the word 'really' did not add anything. Thus, the *mens rea* of murder is **intent to kill or seriously injure**.

In **Sindall 2014**, D burgled a house and was attempting to drive away when the owner stopped him. He hit the owner several times with a torch he was carrying, and with his fists. The jury accepted that he did not intend to kill but found that he did intend to cause grievous bodily harm. He was therefore guilty of murder.

Intention can be direct or oblique (indirect).

Task 17

Look up the cases of **Nedrick 1986** and **Woollin 1998**. Make a note of the facts, and whether the murder charge succeeded, and why/why not.

For application of the law, it is the current law that is important. We saw that this comes from the CA in **Nedrick**. It was confirmed by the HL in **Woollin** as being the correct direction for oblique intent. There is *evidence* of intent if:

- **death or serious bodily harm was a virtual certainty as a result of the defendant's actions**
- **the defendant appreciated that such was the case**

Key cases

In **Woollin**, the jury had to consider whether D appreciated that it was a virtual certainty the baby would be killed or seriously injured by being thrown in the direction of the pram. The HL confirmed the point that this is only evidence of intention, not proof. The jury should be directed on the **Nedrick** test and told to take into account ALL the circumstances. The test was followed again in **Matthews and Alleyne 2003**. The CA confirmed the test and also that foresight of death as a virtual certainty does not automatically *prove* intent; it is merely *evidence* ("often very strong evidence") for the jury.

The CA used the test again in **Stringer 2008** (see Chapter 3 on *mens re*a). It would now appear to be the established test as **Nedrick** was over twenty years earlier.

Problems and reforms

In its 2006 report, 'Murder, manslaughter and Infanticide', the Law Commission noted that

"The law governing homicide in England and Wales is a rickety structure set upon shaky foundations. Some of its rules have remained unaltered since the seventeenth century, even though it has long been acknowledged that they are in dire need of reform".

The LC recommended a three-tier structure for homicide, which would cover

- 1st-degree murder (killing with intent to kill or with intent to cause serious harm knowing the conduct carried a serious risk of death)
- 2nd-degree murder (killing with intent to cause serious harm or where there is a defence of provocation (now loss of control) or diminished responsibility as now for voluntary manslaughter) and
- Manslaughter (killing without intent, as now for involuntary manslaughter but with *mens rea* needed for some kind of harm rather than for the unlawful act)

Only the first of these would have a mandatory life sentence. These recommendations have not been taken up.

Evaluation pointer

The *mens rea* of murder is intent to kill or seriously injure (**Smith 1960**). This means you can be guilty of murder even if you did not intend to kill. This point was confirmed in **Cunningham 1981** (not to be confused with the 1957 case of the same name on recklessness). The HL criticised the rule but has refused to overrule it in several cases, preferring to leave that to Parliament.

The Law Commission has also criticised it but no government has yet suggested amending the law. In **Attorney-General's Reference (No 3 of 1994) 1997**, the HL, although not overruling the rule, refused to apply it so as to find someone guilty of murder where there was only intent to cause serious injury, however this was a case of transferred malice so may be of limited application.

Murder is the most serious offence, so it is vital that the law is clear. Look at the development of intent in the summary below. Has it produced a clear meaning of intent? Pretend you are on a jury. Could you decide what degree of probability is virtually certain? The test for recklessness from **Cunningham 1957** is that D knowingly takes a foreseeable risk. The **Nedrick** test for intent is foresight of something as a virtual certainty. At what stage does a foreseeable risk become a certainty?

To practise for a problem question look at a case you are familiar with and apply the law you have learnt. Let's try this with **Pagett 1983**.

Summary of how to apply the rules

Facts:

1. D shot at the police whilst holding the girl in front of him.

2. The police returned fire.

3. The girl was killed.

Application with cases in support:

Actus reus

There is an unlawful killing, but did D cause it?

'But for' his action she would not have died (**White**). He factually caused death.

He also made a **'significant contribution'** (**Cheshire**) to the girl's death. The intervening act of the police shooting back was **foreseeable** and so did not break the **chain of causation** (**Roberts**). He legally caused death.

We have *actus reus* but is it murder or manslaughter?

Mens rea

Was D's **aim** to **kill or seriously injure** the girl? No, so there is no direct intent. Was death or serious injury a **'virtual certainty'** and did D **appreciate** this (**Nedrick**)? If the jury find this not to be the case there is no indirect intent. He will probably be found not guilty of murder due to lack of *mens rea*. However, if the jury believes that D intended to kill or seriously injure the police, whether directly or by appreciating it as a virtual certainty, then the principle of transferred malice means that this intent is transferred from them to the girl and he may be found guilty.

Examination pointer

Two points here. Firstly, murder is one of the few crimes where you need to discuss the *mens rea* of intent as only intent will do. If a crime can be committed recklessly, there is no need to discuss intent. Secondly, it is quite acceptable to say 'probably' in a conclusion. You can't be expected to play judge and jury. In any case you should never start with "D will be guilty (or not) of ..." – not only is it rarely that simple, you also need to decide what charge seems most appropriate, and then use the law to prove it. You could say, "D could be charged with murder, but it may be hard to prove intent so a manslaughter charge may be more appropriate". Then go on to discuss involuntary manslaughter. However, read the question carefully. If you are *only* asked to discuss murder, don't go on to manslaughter.

Intent and 'mercy killing'

In **Inglis 2010**, a mother was convicted of murder and sentenced to life imprisonment for killing her severely disabled son. There was clear intent to kill, so even though she acted in what she believed were her son's best interests the charge was murder. This can be compared with **Gilderdale 2010** heard in the same week. Here a woman killed her daughter who had a chronic illness and who had tried to commit suicide herself on several occasions. She was cleared of attempted murder by a jury (attempted murder because it could not be shown if the drugs she gave caused the death or not). Again, she intended to kill her daughter so the charge had to be murder, but the jury was clearly sympathetic.

Evaluation pointer

These cases highlight the difficulties. Mrs Gilderdale was given a 12-month conditional discharge for aiding and abetting a suicide, whereas Mrs Inglis was given a life sentence for murder, even though there was little real difference in the facts and in both cases the mothers acted in what they believed was the child's best interests. The main difference seems to have been that in **Inglis** her son was too disabled to be able to communicate his own wishes, whereas in **Gilderdale** the daughter would probably have found a way to kill herself anyway. She had expressed a desire to end her life and this was taken into account by the jury and by the judge when he said that the decision of the jury showed "*common sense, decency and humanity*".

However, the huge contrast in sentencing in these cases shows the problem of having a mandatory life sentence where the judge has no discretion. The law cannot be said to have achieved justice with two such different outcomes on similar facts.

In its 2004 report 'Partial Defences to Murder' the Law Commission said

> "the Government should undertake a public consultation on whether, and if so to what extent, the law should recognise either an offence of "mercy" killing or a partial defence of "mercy" killing".

Making it a separate offence or a partial defence (as with diminished responsibility and loss of control) would allow for discretion in sentencing and perhaps make juries more willing to convict. No Government has yet felt able to tackle these issues and the law remains unchanged.

Task 18

Practise your application of the law using my example with **Pagett** as a guide. Choose a case you know quite well and go through the stages step by step. This will produce the kind of logical structure you need for problem exam questions in other areas too. Keep it as a template for answering exam questions.

The cases leading up to **Woollin 1998** could be useful for an evaluation of murder. A summary of these follows, repeated from Chapter 3.

Summary of murder

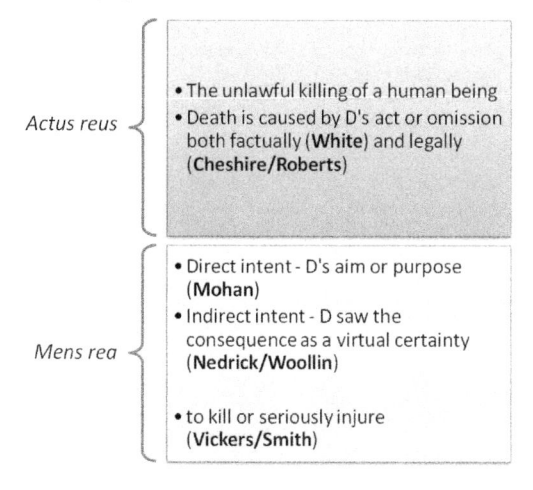

Actus reus
- The unlawful killing of a human being
- Death is caused by D's act or omission both factually (**White**) and legally (**Cheshire/Roberts**)

Mens rea
- Direct intent - D's aim or purpose (**Mohan**)
- Indirect intent - D saw the consequence as a virtual certainty (**Nedrick/Woollin**)
- to kill or seriously injure (**Vickers/Smith**)

Summary of the development of the law on intent

Case	Development	Probable, possible or certain?	Objective / subjective Proof or evidence
DPP v Smith 1960	HL held that the *mens rea* for murder is intention to kill or cause grievous bodily harm	Foresight of death or serious injury as a natural and probable result	Objective (what the 'reasonable man or woman' would contemplate)
Hyam 1974 (similar facts to **Nedrick**)	Changed to a subjective test by HL	Foresight of death or serious injury as highly probable	Noted that s8 had amended this to subjective. It proved intent (this seems to contradict s8 which refers to evidence)
Moloney 1985	HL disapproved **Hyam** Foreseeing death as 'probable' was not proof of intent	Foresight of death or serious injury as a moral certainty or natural consequence	Foresight was *evidence* of intent rather than *proof* of intent
Hancock and Shankland 1986	**Moloney** guidelines were followed but HL held that 'natural consequence' was misleading	The greater the probability the more likely it was foreseen and thus intended	Evidence
Nedrick 1986	CA provided a new test	Death or serious injury was a virtual certainty and D appreciated this	Evidence from which the jury can 'infer' intent
Walker and Hayles 1990	CA followed **Nedrick** but added	very high degree of probability sufficed	Evidence from which the jury can 'infer' intent
Woollin 1998	HL confirmed **Nedrick** test	Death or serious injury was a virtual certainty and D appreciated this	Evidence from which jury can 'find' intent
Matthews and Alleyne 2003 / Stringer 2008	Applied **Nedrick** test	Death or serious injury was a virtual certainty and D appreciated this	Evidence of intent is not proof of intent

Links to the non-substantive law

ELS: For links to the English legal system, look back at the diagram and examples in the introduction to Part 1. Now we are looking at specific offences bear in mind this can affect where a case is heard and other matters involving the English legal system. Murder is indictable so only the Crown Court can hear the case and the maximum sentence is life. A jury will decide on the facts of the case and this could have its advantages. Much will depend on the type of killing. In euthanasia cases juries have been sympathetic, as in **Gilderdale 2010**.

The nature of law: Constructive liability, where the *mens rea* does not correspond with the *actus reus*, is not just. We saw this with **s 47** and **s 20** but it occurs with murder too. D should only be liable where the *mens rea* was for the offence actually committed, especially in such a serious crime where the sentence is mandatory. The level of fault is lower in such cases too, as the *mens rea* is for a lesser crime. The role of law in euthanasia cases has not been fully consistent, as the different decisions in **Inglis** and **Gilderdale** illustrate. Justice requires clarity and fairness, and it is arguable that neither has been achieved if the law is inconsistent. On the other hand, the law was applied strictly in **Cox**, so that even though he acted in the patient's best interests he was guilty of attempted murder. Some would say that although the law was applied properly the result did not achieve justice, the patient was begging to die and the doctor helped. Others would say that any taking of life is immoral, for whatever reason. The role of law is a difficult one when there are several different opinions and different interests to take into the balance.

Self-test questions

1. What is the actus reus and mens rea of murder, and how have the courts interpreted the latter?
2. What is a result crime and what is the significance in terms of actus reus?
3. Can you explain the law on causation using two murder cases?
4. In which CA case was the 'virtual certainty' test for mens rea established, and which HL case confirmed this?
5. Have you achieved the aims not only of this Chapter, but of the Chapters on actus reus (causation) and mens rea (intent) too?

Answers to tasks and self-test questions are on my website at www.drsr.org/publications/tasks. For some interactive exercises, click on 'Free Exercises'.

Chapter 9: Voluntary manslaughter under the Coroners and Justice Act 2009 – Loss of control

"Would a sober man, in relation to that drunken observation, batter his friend over the head with a nearly two pound-weight ashtray?" Newell 1980

By the end of this Chapter, you should be able to:

- **Explain the main legal requirements in proving the s 54 defence**
- **Explain how the law on loss of control applies in practice by reference to cases**
- **Identify possible criticisms for an evaluation of the law**

The law on loss of control is found in **s 54** and **s 55** of the **Coroners and Justice Act 2009 (CJA)**, which repealed **s 3** of the **Homicide Act** and replaced the previous defence of provocation. You will see the old defence of provocation in cases prior to 2010, some of which may still have relevance.

S 54 states:

> '(1) Where a person ("D") kills or is a party to the killing of another ("V"), D is not to be convicted of murder if –
> (a) D's acts and omissions in doing or being a party to the killing resulted from D's loss of self-control,
> (b) the loss of self-control had a qualifying trigger, and
> (c) a person of D's sex and age, with a normal degree of tolerance and self-restraint and in the circumstances of D, might have reacted in the same or in a similar way to D.'

The burden of proof is on the prosecution. If D raises loss of control as a defence, then the prosecution have to prove beyond reasonable doubt – the criminal standard of proof – that the case is *not* one of loss of control. (With the alternative defence to murder of diminished responsibility, the burden is reversed and D must prove the defence.)

Examination pointer

These defences ONLY apply to a murder charge. Don't try to apply them to other crimes. Where there is a death combined with intent to kill you can deal with the murder issues and then look at these defences. If intent and causation are clear, you don't need to discuss these in detail, move quickly to the defences having briefly explained why the charge is likely to be murder. Only if the facts indicate it is necessary, for example, if there is a possible break in the chain of causation, or if intent may be hard to prove, should you discuss these in any detail. Examiners know you cannot discuss everything in the time so questions are usually set which address specific issues. Be selective!

So, for the defence to succeed there are three questions to consider:

- **Did D's act result from a loss of self-control?**
- **Did the loss of self-control have a qualifying trigger as specified in s 55?**
- **Would a person of D's sex and age have reacted in the same way in D's circumstances?**

Did D's act result from a loss of self-control?

Whether D lost self-control is initially a matter for the judge. If there is evidence of loss of control the judge will put it to the jury to decide on the facts whether in the circumstances D lost self-control and whether the killing resulted from this.

Under the old law, the loss of control had to be 'sudden and temporary'. In several cases women who had suffered years of abuse killed their partners. Accused of murder, they argued the old provocation defence. Many failed on the 'sudden and temporary' point because there was a 'cooling-off' period between the provocative conduct and the killing. **S 54(2)** states that the loss of self-control does not need to be sudden, so these cases could succeed now. However, it may be difficult to prove any loss of control after a cooling off period.

In **Thornton 1992 and 1996**, D had gone to the kitchen to calm down after a violent argument. Whilst there she picked up a knife and sharpened it. She then went to where her husband was lying on the sofa and stabbed him. The judge put the defence to the jury and it was rejected. The evidence was that she had cooled down by the time she stabbed him. In a later appeal fresh medical evidence was introduced which showed she had a personality disorder and 'battered woman syndrome'. The CA held that the jury should have been allowed to consider whether a reasonable woman with these characteristics would have acted as Mrs Thornton did. However, Lord Taylor said that the defence would fail unless the jury believed she suffered *"a sudden and temporary loss of self-control at the time of the killing"*. A retrial was ordered, and in 1996 she was convicted of manslaughter due to diminished responsibility (see next Chapter).

It is possible that she would now succeed with the loss of control defence, but unlikely. Although there is no longer a 'sudden and temporary' requirement, there must be a loss of control, and she does not appear to have lost control at all; she went into the kitchen to calm down before getting the knife. The Law Commission had advised not keeping the loss of control requirement and this is understandable considering the need to extend the defence to 'battered women' cases such as **Thornton**.

There must be loss of *control* not just *self-restraint*. In **Cocker 1989**, D had finally given way to his wife's entreaties to ease her pain and end her life. His defence failed as the evidence showed he had not lost control. This would still apply.

It has been made clear in several cases that under the new law if there is no evidence of loss of control the judge does not need to put the defence to the jury. This and the fact that the loss of control no longer had to be sudden were both confirmed in **Dawes 2013**, discussed below.

Note the words 'resulted from'. This means the killing must have been caused by the loss of self-control; this is a new requirement under the **2009 Act**.

Did the loss of self-control have a qualifying trigger?

Under **s 54(1)(b)** there must be a 'qualifying trigger'; this refers to whether something triggered D's loss of control – and what that something was. Under the old law, there was no specific restriction on what caused D to lose control.

S 55(1) of the Act sets out the qualifying triggers. The loss of control must be triggered by:

D's fear of serious violence from V against D or another identified person; or

a thing or things done or said (or both) which—

(a) constituted circumstances of an extremely grave character, and

(b) caused D to have a justifiable sense of being seriously wronged.

Or a combination of both of these

Excluded matters

First, note that some matters are specifically excluded as qualifying triggers.

S 54(4) states that the defence is not allowed if D acted in a 'considered desire for revenge'.

S 55(6) contains two other exclusions. If the fear of serious violence or the things said or done were incited by D "for the purpose of providing an excuse to use violence" or if the thing done or said constituted sexual infidelity, these are to be disregarded.

We'll look at these as we discuss the two qualifying triggers. The triggers are fear of serious violence and things done or said.

In **Sian 2016**, D had been attacked by two boys and he stabbed one of them causing fatal injuries. The prosecution accepted his plea of loss of control so the full trial did not take place, but he was found guilty of manslaughter due to loss of control. There had been ill feelings between D and V for some time and the two boys went out with the purpose of attacking and robbing D, which they did. The trigger for his loss of control was the attack which caused him to fear serious violence.

As long as there is a fear of serious violence and the loss of control resulted from this, the violence need not be directed at D. Fear of violence against D or *'another identified person'* will be enough, as in **Ward 2012**, where D lost control and killed a man who had attacked his brother at a party.

The 'things done and said' means the loss of control can be caused by both actions and words. Again, this is the same as the previous law. In **Doughty 1986**, the crying of a baby was said to amount to what was then called provocation.

It is unlikely that **Doughty** would succeed now. This is because **s 55** adds that the 'things done or said' must be 'extremely grave' and 'justifiably' cause D to feel 'seriously' wronged. The crying of a baby is unlikely to be deemed *extremely grave* nor is a jury likely to be persuaded that it caused D to have a *justifiable* sense of being *seriously* wronged.

The matters in **s 55** must be viewed objectively so it is not merely a question of whether D thought the circumstances were of an extremely grave character and so was justified in feeling grievously wronged, the judge must believe this too or the defence need not be put to the jury.

In **Parker 2012**, D had killed his wife during an argument. The evidence was that he had placed knives close to hand in preparation for the attack. However he argued that he had 'lost it' when she told him she didn't love him. This is a useful case because the judge summed up the new law for the jury:

> 'When D stabbed his wife had he lost self-control?
>
> If not then go no further. Otherwise, consider whether his loss of self-control was caused by a qualifying trigger. The qualifying triggers are things said or done by his wife which
>
> a. constitute circumstances of an extremely grave character and
>
> b. caused the defendant to have a justified sense of being seriously wronged.
>
> If neither was the case then he is guilty of murder, otherwise consider whether a man of D's age with a normal degree of tolerance and self-restraint would have reacted in the same or in a similar way to the way that the defendant reacted'.

The jury reached a verdict of murder. In dismissing D's appeal (heard with **Clinton** and **Evans**, see below) the CA held that the matters relied on by D could not reasonably be treated by any jury as circumstances of an extremely grave character which caused him to have a justifiable sense that he had been seriously wronged.

Where a defence could have failed under the sudden and temporary rule in the old law, it could now fail because acting in revenge is excluded by **s 54(4)**. An act of revenge (especially if 'considered') is likely to be after a period of time.

In **Ibrams and Gregory 1981**, the Ds and a girl had been terrorised by V. They planned to entice V to the girl's bed and then the Ds would attack him. They carried out the planned attack several days later, and killed V. At their appeal against a conviction for murder, the CA held that the defence failed because there was no sudden loss of control, the attack was planned and carried out over several days. Under **s 54(2)**, although there is no need for the loss of self-control to be sudden, any such time delay may indicate that there was no loss of control at all. It could also indicate a 'considered desire for revenge' and so be excluded by **s 54(4)**. Finally, it may fail because even if there was a loss of control at the start, it is unlikely to have caused D to kill several days later, so the killing did not 'result from' the loss of control as required by **s 54(1)**.

In **Baillie 1995**, D's son was getting drugs from a dealer who had threatened him with violence. When D found out, he drove to the dealer's house armed with a razor and a sawn-off shotgun. They had an argument and D shot the dealer as he left, killing him. The trial judge refused to allow the defence (then provocation) to be put to the jury and D appealed. The CA allowed the appeal because there was sufficient evidence for the matter to be put to the jury. This case could go either way now. There is no need for the loss of control to be sudden, but there is an element of revenge in D's act of driving to the dealer's house in response to the threat to his son. Much would depend on whether the jury saw it as a 'considered' desire for revenge. In **Baillie**, unlike in **Ibrams**, D drove to V's house whilst still angry, so any desire for revenge may not be deemed 'considered', also the killing could have 'resulted from' the loss of control as there was not a long gap between the two.

In one of three appeals heard together under the **CJA, Evans 2012**, D had killed his wife after she had goaded him. He said she had stabbed him, but it was not clear if this was the case, or whether he had done it himself. The prosecution case was that he killed her because she told him that she was going to leave him. The defence case was that she had stabbed him, and he had lost control and stabbed her. The main issue was whether he had 'acted in a considered desire for revenge'. The judge summed up the law for the jury and said:

> "If you conclude so that you are sure either that this was a considered act of revenge by the defendant or that he had not lost the ability to control himself, this defence does not apply and your verdict would be guilty of murder".

He was found guilty of murder. The CA dismissed his appeal and held that there was sufficient evidence that he had acted in revenge so the jury decision was correct. The judge had summed up both the prosecution and defence arguments as regards the possibility of it being an act of revenge, so the conviction was fair.

In **Bamford 2016**, D had been in a short relationship with another man and some months later went to try to borrow money from him. After some sexual activity D went downstairs to the kitchen and then returned to the bedroom and stabbed the man. The jury rejected the defence of loss of control as he had not reacted in a spontaneous manner to anything done or said by V and was not in fear of serious violence. The judge also noted that even if he acted because he was aggrieved at the way V had treated him sexually, the fact that he chose to return to the bedroom indicated a considered desire for revenge.

Under **s 55(6)**, if the thing 'done or said' constituted sexual infidelity it is to be disregarded. Under the old law, it would have been allowed as a cause of the loss of control. In fact, the original law was introduced to cover such cases.

In **Holley 2005**, D killed his girlfriend with an axe after she had slept with another man and had also taunted him about his lack of courage. The fact that she had slept with someone else would not be a qualifying trigger as sexual infidelity is excluded by **s 55(6)** but the taunt about his lack of courage would be 'a thing said' so would be relevant.

Key case

In the third of the three appeals heard together, **Clinton 2012**, D had killed his wife during a heated exchange and claimed both diminished responsibility and loss of control. She had told him she was having an affair and he had seen graphic pictures of her and her lover on Facebook. They also had financial difficulties and were undergoing a trial separation. The evidence was that he had planned the death having done some research on the internet. The jury rejected the diminished responsibility plea and the judge held that there was no 'qualifying trigger' as required by the

Coroners' and Justice Act, and that the wife's infidelity should be ignored as this was specifically excluded by the Act. He was convicted of murder and appealed. The CA held that the judge had misdirected herself about the possible relevance of the wife's infidelity. Under **s 54(1)(c)** regard should be had to 'the circumstances of D'. The CA said this meant all the circumstances should be taken together. In this case, the sexual infidelity was an essential part of the whole, and had had sufficient impact on D to suggest the defence should have been put to the jury. A retrial was ordered so the jury could consider how the sexual infidelity affected the gravity of the circumstances or their impact on D. Strangely, at this retrial he changed his plea to guilty and did not rely on the defence. He was given a life sentence for murder.

Principle: When considering the circumstances of D, all the circumstances should be taken together.

Clinton was followed in **Dawes 2013** where D killed a man after returning home to find his wife asleep on the sofa with him. The marriage was volatile and D had left the house in a temper after a row, and his wife did not expect him back that night. She invited the man, who was a friend, for a drink and they fell asleep after consuming a lot of vodka. D hit the man with his fists and then threw the bottle of vodka at him. The man picked up the bottle by the neck and swung it at D. D said he was afraid and so got a knife from the kitchen, the next time the man came at him with the bottle he lashed out and the knife caught the man in the neck. D said he didn't intend to cause serious harm and was acting in self-defence when he stabbed him. He did not argue loss of control as self-defence would mean acquittal if it succeeded. Anyway, he said he was more shocked than angry. The jury concluded that the violence used was excessive so self-defence could not succeed. The judge therefore went on to consider whether the partial defence of loss of control should be put to the jury. As D had said he was more shocked than angry there was little evidence of loss of control. Anyway, sexual infidelity is excluded as a trigger by **s 55(6)** and so is a situation where D has incited the violence, so the judge decided that even if he had lost control it was not due to a qualifying trigger. The CA confirmed the judge's decision not to put the defence to the jury, but only on the basis that there was little evidence of loss of control.

These cases were followed again in **Gurpinar 2015** where Lord Thomas said "*it follows from the terms of the Act (as clearly set out in both Clinton and Dawes) that if the judge considers that there is no sufficient evidence of loss of self-control (the first component) there will be no need to consider the other two components. Nor if there is insufficient evidence of the second will there be a need to address the third.*" He added that the judge must "*undertake a much more rigorous evaluation of the evidence before the defence could be left to the jury than was required under the former law*".

The loss of control defence is stricter than the provocation defence in this way.

In **Orrett Duncan 2014**, D had been threatened by a man and so when he saw him in town he went into a nearby shop and bought a sharp vegetable knife. The man ran towards him and slashed him across the face. D lost control and stabbed the man three times, killing him. The court accepted his plea of loss of control, but on a 'very narrow basis' because he had been aware that there may be trouble and so his defence could arguably have failed under **s 55(6)** on the basis that he incited the fear of violence.

However, the incitement is only to be disregarded if it is "for the purpose of providing an excuse to use violence". In **Dawes 2013**, see above, the judge considered the qualifying triggers and decided that there was none. If there was a trigger at all it was not a qualifying one because D had incited the fear of violence, and sexual infidelity is also excluded by **s 55(6)**. The CA upheld the decision not to put the defence to the jury, as there was no real evidence of loss of control. However, the CA also held that the judge was wrong to rely on the exclusion of 'incitement' as a trigger because there was no evidence D incited the violence "for the purpose of providing an excuse to use violence".

Would a person of D's sex and age have reacted in the same way in D's circumstances?

S 54(1)(c) asks whether *'a person of D's sex and age, with a normal degree of tolerance and self-restraint and in the circumstances of D, might have reacted in the same or similar way'*. This is further clarified by **s 54(3)** which allows for *'reference to all of D's circumstances other than those whose only relevance to D's conduct is that they bear on D's general capacity for tolerance or self-restraint'*. This means age and sex are relevant in deciding the level of control expected and what the 'reasonable person' would do, but the addition of 'in the circumstances' means others matters can be looked at as long as they don't relate to D's capacity for tolerance or self-restraint. A medical problem like an addiction, or a history of abuse would be a 'circumstance' but a short temper would not because this relates to D's capacity for restraint.

You should be aware of some of the older cases as these may be needed for evaluation and discussion of reforms.

The question is objective, what 'a person' would do, not what D did. The Act refers to these persons having the same age and sex as D. What other personal characteristics can be attributed to this hypothetical person had caused many problems. In **Camplin 1978**, a 15 year-old boy hit V with a chapatti pan after being homosexually assaulted and then taunted about it. V died and D was charged with murder. The HL said the question was whether a reasonable person of his *age* and *sex* would have done as he did. The **2009 Act** confirms this.

It was not fully clear from **Camplin** whether characteristics other than age and sex could be taken into account. Earlier cases centred on physical characteristics; this was later extended to mental ones. One of the reasons for ordering a retrial in **Thornton** was that this development had occurred since her original trial. In addition, the characteristics had to be both *relevant* and *permanent*. In **Newell 1980**, an alcoholic was in an emotional state and was provoked by his friend making homosexual advances. He hit him over the head with a heavy ashtray and killed him. The court held that although alcoholism was a possible characteristic it was not to be taken into account, as it wasn't related to the provocation. The fact that he was drunk and emotional wasn't attributable because this was a temporary state. The court asked the jury the question in the opening quote.

In **Morhall 1995**, glue sniffing was said by the CA not to be a characteristic to be attributed to the reasonable man but this was reversed by the HL. It was held that as D was addicted this would be attributable, in the same way that alcoholism is, but being drunk isn't. D had been taunted by V about his addiction and they got into a fight, during which he stabbed V. Here the addiction was both relevant and permanent.

In **Luc Thiet Thuan 1996**, the Privy Council took a more restrictive view. D killed his girlfriend after she teased him about his sexual prowess. There was evidence he was mentally unstable and had difficulty controlling his impulses. The Privy Council held that such mental factors could not be attributed to the reasonable man.

However, in **Smith 2000**, the HL widened the law again and held that characteristics such as jealousy and obsession should be ignored, and added 'exceptional pugnacity or excitability' but accepted that anything else was attributable. However, Lord Hobhouse produced a lengthy and reasoned argument against the decision and referred to "monsters" being produced by attributing characteristics like glue sniffing to the reasonable person.

The **Coroners and Justice Act** clarifies matters a little, as **s 54** provides that "the circumstances of D" is a reference to all of D's circumstances other than those whose only relevance to D's conduct is that they bear on D's general capacity for tolerance or self-restraint.

In **Mohammed 2005**, D found a young man in his daughter's bedroom. The man escaped but D killed his daughter with a knife. He was very strict and had a reputation for being violent and short-tempered. D was convicted of murder and appealed. The CA had to decide whether his violence and short-temper were relevant to the question of how what was then referred to as a 'reasonable man' would have reacted. Lord Justice Scott Baker said that D's temperament was not relevant and that

> "... the reasonable man is a fixed rather than a variable creature. The yardstick is a person of the age and sex of the appellant having and exercising ordinary powers of self-control."

This is similar to the **CJA**. Violence and short-temper would relate to D's capacity for self-restraint or control, so cannot be taken into account when deciding whether another person would have reacted in a similar way. It is likely that glue sniffing, taking drugs or being drunk will also be irrelevant as these affect D's capacity for tolerance and self-restraint. It is probable that (as in **Newell**) the 'particular circumstances that D was in' would need to be relevant to the loss of control, i.e., could be a reason for D's reaction. This was previously referred to as affecting the 'gravity of the provocation', i.e., the things done or said meant more to D in the particular circumstances.

Example

If Newell had been taunted about being an alcoholic he may have succeeded in the defence as that would have been one of his 'circumstances', and would have been relevant to his loss of control.

As the question of what such a person would do refers to a person 'having a normal degree of tolerance and self-restraint', it is questionable whether this defence should ever succeed. A person having a normal degree of tolerance and self-restraint would never kill.

Evaluation pointer

That this has been a problematic defence is clear. In 2003, the Law Commission said, "its defects are beyond cure by judicial development of the law". Some improvements are made in the **Coroners and Justice Act** but it is still complicated. Groups such as Justice for Women have long argued that the defence of provocation favours men as it can be used only by those strong enough to fight back. The women who suffer years of abuse and finally kill in desperation – but not in the heat of the moment – failed on the 'sudden and temporary' requirement. The removal of the need for a 'sudden and temporary' loss of control is an improvement but there must be a loss of control and the killing must result from this, so many of these cases would still not succeed. The fact that loss of control must be shown goes against the Law Commission's proposals and prevents the defence clearly extending to cases of abuse against women, who may be physically weaker and liable to even greater abuse if they lose control and fight back. Justice requires that the law should apply equally in practice as well as in theory.

Cases since the **Act**, such as **Clinton**, **Dawes** and **Gurpinar** have made clear that it is up to the judge to decide whether to put the loss of control defence before the jury and that there is no need to do this if there is no evidence for it, viewed objectively.

Intoxication and loss of control

In **Asmelash 2013**, D had been drinking with another man and got into a fight with him, during which D stabbed and killed him. He said the deceased had made him so angry that he lost control. The judge applied **s 54** of the **Coroners and Justice Act 2009** and said the jury should consider whether a person of D's sex and age with a normal degree of tolerance and self-restraint and in the same circumstances, but unaffected by alcohol, would have reacted in the same or similar way. D was convicted and appealed. The CA agreed with the judge that the consumption of alcohol should be ignored. The judges noted that in **Dowds 2012** (see next Chapter), the **CJA** was held not to change the rule that voluntary intoxication was not capable of establishing diminished responsibility. It was "inconceivable" that different criteria should apply to voluntary drunkenness depending on whether the partial defence under consideration was diminished responsibility or loss of control. This did not mean D could not use the loss of control defence; it simply means that the defence had to be approached without reference to the voluntary intoxication.

This is a complex defence so let's have a quick recap.

Would a person of D's age and sex have reacted in the same way?

The level of control expected is that of a person of the same age and sex with normal levels of self-restraint. This is an objective test.

In the circumstances of D

This is partly subjective: D's particular circumstances, such as a history of abuse or alcoholism, can be taken into account, because these will relate not to the ability to retain control but to the reason for losing it. According to **Clinton 2012**, sexual infidelity can be taken into account at this point as it will affect the gravity of the circumstances as a whole, and their impact on D.

Other than those whose only relevance to D's conduct is that they bear on D's general capacity for tolerance or self-restraint

Things that made D lose control more easily, such as being drunk or aggressive by nature, will be irrelevant.

Task 19

Go to the Law Commission's website (www.lawcom.gov.uk) and see what they say concerning murder and voluntary manslaughter - remember that it is only murder that the two partial defences apply to. Click on projects and type in murder. You will find lots of information which you can refer to in an essay on voluntary manslaughter or justice. You can see how far the **Coroners and Justice Act** took up the LC's proposals for reform. Reference to these (and quotes from the LC) will enhance an answer and show you have done some independent research.

Examination pointer

Look for clues like 'goaded by what X said' or 'in reaction to what X did'. You will not usually be expected to reach a firm conclusion because the most difficult issues are for the jury to decide. Remember to explain that there must be a qualifying trigger. State and apply the law in a logical manner and then say "D may be charged with murder, but if the jury is satisfied that a reasonable person would have done the same the defence will succeed and the conviction will be for manslaughter"

Summary of the developments for evaluation purposes

DPP v Camplin 1978	only age and sex attributable
Morhall 1993	CA said glue-sniffing was not a characteristic to be attributed to the reasonable person, but this was reversed by HL
Luc Thiet Thuan 1996	mental factors could not be attributed
Smith 2000	everything but excitability, jealousy, obsession and exceptional pugnacity could be attributed
AG v Holley 2005	the jury should not take into account D's mental state, just age and sex, but can then consider how a person would have acted in D's circumstances
S 54 & 55 Coroners and Justice Act 2009	as for Holley, as long as D's circumstances don't relate to the ability to show tolerance or self-restraint
Clinton 2012	sexual infidelity can be a 'circumstance' as long as it is part of the whole

Some matters are excluded as qualifying triggers.

S 54(4) Revenge: The defence is not allowed if D acted in a 'considered desire for revenge'. Revenge is usually carried out after a period of time so would have failed under the sudden and temporary rule in the old law, now it could fail because revenge is excluded by the **Act**.

S 55 (6) Sexual infidelity: this cannot be a qualifying trigger. Under the old law, it would have been allowed as a cause of the loss of control. However, note that the law was interpreted liberally in **Clinton 2012**, where sexual infidelity was accepted as a 'circumstance' as long as it was integral to the whole situation and not a trigger on its own.

S 55 (6) Also excluded is a situation where D incited the violence or the thing done or said (the two qualifying triggers) for the purpose of using violence. This was implicit before but is now stated in the **Act**.

Summary of the Coroners' and Justice Act 2009 for application purposes

Did D lose control s 54(1)? However the defence cannot be used where acted in a 'considered desire for revenge' s 54(4)	D must have lost self-control but this need not be sudden s 54(2), however any sign of calming down and/or planning an attack is likely to mean the defence fails
D's act must have resulted from the loss of control s 54(1)(a)	A causation issue, did the loss of control cause D to kill?
There must be a qualifying trigger 55	Did D lose control because of a fear of violence s 55(3)? Did D lose control because of things done or said s 55(4)? Or a combination of these s 55(5)
If the trigger was 'things done or said':- (this is narrower than the old law)	These 'things' must be of an 'extremely grave character' and have caused D to have a justifiable sense of being seriously wronged 55(4)(a) and (b).
Was the trigger excluded by the Act?	If D acted in a considered desire for revenge s 54(4) or the thing 'done or said' constituted sexual infidelity s 55 (6) the defence fails
A person of the same sex and age would have reacted in the same way as D in the same circumstances. The jury should ignore matters that affect the ability to retain control.	The old case law is clarified here, i.e., the jury should not take into account mental characteristics which might have made losing control more likely, like a short temper
Did D lose control s 54(1)? However the defence cannot be used where acted in a 'considered desire for revenge' s 54(4)	D must have lost self-control but this need not be sudden s 54(2), however any sign of calming down and/or planning an attack is likely to mean the defence fails

Links to the non-substantive law

ELS: For links to the English legal system, look back at the diagram and examples in the introduction to Part 1. As the charge would be murder, which is an indictable offence, the case will be tried in the Crown Court and the maximum sentence is life, as for murder. The difference with the defence succeeding is that this sentence is now discretionary so the judge can choose a sentence appropriate to the facts. A jury will decide on the facts of the case and this could have its advantages. Much will depend on the type of killing. The judge may need to interpret the **Coroners' and Justice Act**, as the CA did in **Clinton**, where the **Act** was interpreted in a way that allowed the excluded matter of sexual infidelity as a trigger to be taken into account as one of the circumstances. The judges looked at the speeches in Parliament, and the **Act** as a whole, and this purposive approach to statutory interpretation is supposed to give effect to what Parliament intended when passing the law. It may have done so, the CA made clear that the decision did not alter the fact that it is still excluded if it is the only trigger.

The nature of law: One role of law is to punish wrongdoing and another is to provide justice, which requires both clarity and fairness in the law. It is arguably fair that as long as there is a sufficient trigger for the loss of control, that there should be a defence to a murder charge. It does not mean D 'gets away with' the killing, only that the conviction will be for manslaughter not murder. D will be punished but the judge can choose the appropriate sentence, depending on the level of fault. It can be said that the law is now clearer because many of the matters are now stated in the **Act** and not left to judicial development. Any of the cases where the defence succeeded can be used to illustrate the importance of fault in criminal liability. The success of the defence indicates that there is a reason for the killing, and thus a lower level of fault. In providing such a defence the law is balancing the interests of the victims of violence and society as a whole (in being kept safe from those who use violence) against those of D (in not being fully liable where there is a lower degree of fault) and hence achieving a degree of justice. Any murder cases (and these would include voluntary manslaughter) have a connection with morality because many people see the taking of a life as both immoral and illegal. The law should therefore enforce morality and punish D for taking a life.

Self-test questions

1. To what charge does the **Coroners and Justice Act 2009** apply?
2. What three things need to be proved for **s 54**?
3. What amounts to a qualifying trigger?
4. State two 'characteristics' which are not attributable to the reasonable person
5. What 'trigger' is excluded by the Act?

Answers to tasks and self-test questions are on my website at www.drsr.org/publications/tasks. For some interactive exercises, click on 'Free Exercises'.

Chapter 10 Voluntary manslaughter under the Homicide Act 1957 – Diminished responsibility

"... a state of mind so different from that of ordinary human beings that the reasonable man would term it abnormal." Lord Parker

By the end of this Chapter, you should be able to:

- Explain the main legal requirements in proving diminished responsibility
- Explain how the law applies in practice by reference to cases
- Identify possible criticisms for an evaluation of the law

Diminished responsibility comes under the **Homicide Act 1957 s 2(1)** as amended by **s 52** of the **Coroners and Justice Act 2009**. This section came into force in October 2010 and states:

"A person who kills or is a party to the killing of another is not to be convicted of murder if he was suffering from an abnormality of mental functioning which:

(a) arose from a recognised medical condition,

(b) substantially impaired D's ability to:

understand the nature of his conduct; or

form a rational judgement; or

exercise self-control.

and

(c) provides an explanation for D's acts and omissions in doing or being a party to the killing"

Examination pointer

The old law will be useful in evaluating the defence for an extended writing question. For problem questions, it is the later cases and the **Act** that are important. Also, as you will have seen, there is an overlap between diminished responsibility and loss of control, so you may well have to apply both. Look carefully at the given facts and watch for words like 'abuse' or 'depression'. Long-term abuse may be relevant to loss of control or result in a recognised medical condition such as 'battered woman's syndrome' or trauma. Look at the following example.

Example

A man's wife is dying and in terrible pain. Over a period of several months, she begs him to end her suffering. He is getting very upset and severely depressed. One night she screams at him "for once in your life act like a man and help me die". He finally snaps and smothers her. This could be 'loss of control' so you would apply the law under **s 54** and **s 55**. There is evidence of loss of self-control, by things 'done or said', a person with normal levels of tolerance and restraint will be someone who had gone through several months of being tormented by such requests and so arguably would act in the same way. What if he had spent a couple of days thinking about it, trying to find the courage? Under the old law, he may fail due to the 'sudden and temporary' rule. This no longer applies – but a loss of control defence may still fail if there was a cooling-off period so you can refer to his 'severe depression' and bring in **s 2** as an alternative. In **Bailey 2002**, a 74-year-old man killed his wife, who had motor neurone disease and wanted to die. The evidence was that he had not lost control but his defence of diminished responsibility succeeded.

In **Zebedee 2011** (unreported), D had killed his father who was suffering from Alzheimer's disease. He admitted killing him but denied murder. He said that he snapped after remembering alleged abuse by his father that he had suffered as a child, but there was no evidence to support this. He argued both diminished responsibility and loss of control, saying that his ability to exercise control had been impaired by an adjustment order resulting from the earlier abuse. As for loss of control, he said this was caused by his father whistling a tune over and over, soiling himself and making a gesture which recalled the abuse. Both defences were put to the jury but rejected.

There are four matters under the amended **s 2**

- **D suffers from 'an abnormality of mental functioning'**
- **The abnormality arises from a 'recognised medical condition'**
- **The abnormality substantially impaired D's ability to do one or more of three specified things**
- **The abnormality of mental functioning provides an explanation for D's acts and omissions**

Let's look at each of these.

An abnormality of mental functioning

As this expression indicates, there is an overlap with the general defence of insanity. It covers more than 'defect of reason' though, which is the test for insanity. In **Byrne 1960**, Lord Parker CJ defined abnormality of mind (the old expression) as "a state of mind so different from that of ordinary human beings that the reasonable man would term it abnormal". D was described as a sexual psychopath. While suffering from powerful urges he strangled and then mutilated a young woman. These urges did not prevent him knowing what he was doing (he would have therefore failed on insanity) but he found it difficult, if not impossible, to control them. His defence of diminished responsibility succeeded and he was acquitted of murder.

Cases on the old law will still be relevant in deciding whether there was an abnormality of mental functioning, as the phrase is very similar. It is a matter for the jury based on medical evidence. It is likely that **Byrne** will be followed so that 'abnormality of mental functioning' will be interpreted as a condition which is so different from that of ordinary people that reasonable people (and the jury) would regard it as abnormal.

Arising from a recognised medical condition

In all cases, medical evidence will be needed because the abnormality of mental functioning must arise from a 'recognised medical condition'.

This is perhaps wider than the old law (and a lot less complex) and covers both physical and psychiatric conditions. Disorders such as post-traumatic stress disorder, Gulf War syndrome, paranoid personality disorder, battered woman's syndrome and pre-menstrual stress are all likely to be recognised medical conditions. We looked at **Thornton** with loss of control. She was suffering from 'battered women's syndrome' and at her retrial the jury accepted the defence of diminished responsibility. In **Martin 2001**, a Norfolk farmer was convicted of murder after killing an intruder. On appeal, he succeeded in arguing diminished responsibility due to a 'paranoid personality disorder'.

In **Freaney 2011**, a woman was cleared of the murder of her severely autistic 11-year-old son. Her son needed 24-hour care and help with dressing, washing, brushing his teeth and eating. He was not toilet trained and still wore nappies. She murdered him using her coat belt and when she was sure he was dead, she lay down on the bed beside him and tried to commit suicide. She denied murder but admitted his manslaughter on the grounds of diminished responsibility. The jury accepted that she was suffering from 'extreme mental stress' at the time she strangled her son and her plea of diminished responsibility succeeded. She was given a supervision order.

Evaluation pointer

Reference to a recognised medical condition is clearer than the old law, which was complex and hard for juries to understand. However, one problem that remains is one that the Law Commission recognised. It had recommended that developmental immaturity in those under 18 should be included within the definition of diminished responsibility as a recognised medical condition. This was because there is evidence to show that parts of the brain which play an important role in the development of self-control do not mature until 14 years of age. The Government did not act on this suggestion. To an extent, it is covered where the lack of maturity is caused by a medical disorder such as autism, but this clearly won't cover all young defendants, so children of 10 or over who kill can be convicted of murder even where there is evidence they had an abnormality of mental functioning due to their immaturity. The level of fault is lower in such cases but if the defence fails the conviction will be for murder.

The **Act** is clear that the abnormality of mental functioning must arise from a 'recognised medical condition'. This means that the recognised medical condition must cause the abnormality of mental functioning.

In **Gibbon 2015**, D had a grudge against a neighbour. He took two knives from his kitchen and attacked her, stabbing her more than 30 times. He was charged with murder and argued that he was suffering from an abnormality of mental functioning caused by depression. Although depression is a medically recognised illness, the jury rejected the defence of diminished responsibility because at the time of the killing the depression did not cause an abnormality of mental functioning. The killing was planned and premeditated. He was convicted of murder.

Evaluation pointer

In **Inglis 2010**, (see murder) a mother was convicted of murder and sentenced to life imprisonment for killing her disabled son. Once murder is established the judge has no discretion, so Mrs Inglis was sentenced to life imprisonment even though it was accepted she acted in what she believed were her son's best interests (although this was reduced to a starting point of 9 years rather than the usual 15, on compassionate grounds). Mrs Freaney succeeded in the defence and was convicted of manslaughter, the judge gave her a supervision order but there was no prison sentence. The vast difference in the sentences in **Freaney 2011** and **Inglis** shows the difficulty in having a mandatory life sentence. As stated earlier, justice requires that the law should apply equally in practice as well as in theory.

Diminished responsibility and intoxication

In **Tandy 1989**, an alcoholic strangled her 11-year-old daughter after learning that she had been sexually abused. She had drunk almost a whole bottle of vodka and was suffering from an abnormality of mind at the time of the killing. The CA upheld the conviction for murder and held that the abnormality had to be caused by the disease of alcoholism rather than by the voluntary taking of alcohol. It could succeed if the first drink was involuntary but on the evidence, this was not the case. The CA established the principle that drink is only capable of giving rise to this defence if it either causes brain damage or produces an irresistible craving so that consumption is involuntary.

So an abnormality caused by taking drugs or drink would not suffice unless there is an associated medical condition such as alcoholism, now usually referred to as alcohol dependency syndrome. However, if D is intoxicated *as well as* suffering from one of the above causes the defence may succeed. This was stated in **Fenton 1975**, confirmed in **Gittens 1984** (where she was drunk but also suffered from chronic depression) and approved by the HL in **Dietschmann 2003**. It is thus a well-established rule which will still apply.

Key case

In **Dietschmann**, D had savagely attacked someone whilst suffering depression following the death of his girlfriend. He was also drunk. The HL made clear that D had to show that even without the drink he had sufficient 'abnormality of mind' (as in **Fenton** and **Gittens**). However, they added that he did not have to show that he would have killed even if not intoxicated, because the 'abnormality' did not have to be the *only* cause of the killing. This means D only needs to satisfy the jury that, as well as (but not *because of*) being drunk, he had an abnormality which substantially impaired his responsibility. He need not show he would still have killed even if he had been sober.

Principle: The members of the jury must ask themselves whether D had satisfied them that, *despite the drink*, his mental abnormality substantially impaired his responsibility. If so the defence may succeed, if not the defence is not available.

Evaluation pointer

These are difficult issues. Not least if you happen to be on the jury! You will have to try to ignore the intoxication and determine whether the other causes were enough substantially to impair D's ability. Not an easy task. The **Dietschmann** case highlights the difficulties. Does it solve any? Would you be able ignore the intoxication in such cases if you were on the jury?

If alcoholism as a disease is argued, you will have to decide if the first drink taken was voluntary or involuntary.

The rules were clarified in the next case.

In **Wood 2008**, the CA confirmed that **Dietschmann** did not alter the principle that voluntary consumption of alcohol does not amount to an abnormality of the mind, but said that it did establish that a defence of diminished responsibility would not fail merely because D had consumed alcohol voluntarily before killing. The CA agreed that **Tandy** should be re-assessed in cases where there was 'alcohol dependency syndrome'. In **Wood**, D had been diagnosed with this syndrome and killed in a frenzied attack whilst drunk, having woken after a party to find a man attempting to have oral sex with him. The CA held that it was not a requirement that the syndrome caused brain damage (as required in **Tandy**). The only question for the jury was whether it constituted an abnormality of mind (now mental functioning). If it did not, diminished responsibility based on the consumption of alcohol would fail. If it did, the jury must consider whether D's responsibility was substantially impaired because of the syndrome. The jury should focus exclusively on the effect of alcohol consumed as a direct result of the illness or disease and ignore the effect of any alcohol consumed voluntarily.

In **Dowds 2012**, in an appeal to the CA after the **2009 Act** came into force, D argued that acute intoxication was a recognised medical condition. He and his partner had a long history of drunkenness and violence, and both had been drinking when he attacked her with a knife and killed her. His appeal failed and the CA held that the new law was not intended to change the rule that voluntary intoxication was not capable of establishing diminished responsibility.

So, if D has a medical condition and is also drunk the jury should ignore the drink and just consider the medical condition (**Dietschmann**).

If the intoxication *results from* a medical condition, such as alcohol dependency syndrome, the jury can consider the drink but must ask whether it amounts to an abnormality (**Wood**).

In **Mitchell 2016**, D had a volatile relationship with a man and they both had issues with drink. After a drunken argument one night she stabbed him and killed him. She was charged with murder. After some appeals and a retrial she was found guilty of manslaughter due to diminished responsibility.

The medical evidence was that she had alcohol dependency syndrome and that her intoxication had impaired her capacity to form a rational judgment and to exercise self-control.

The **Coroners and Justice Act 2009** does not change the rules on this (**Dowds 2012**).

Example

After Tony came back from fighting in the war in Iraq he was diagnosed with post-traumatic stress disorder (PTSD), which causes him to have violent outbursts. One night, after several drinks, he gets into a fight and kills someone. He is charged with murder and pleads the defence of diminished responsibility. The PTSD will be a recognised medical condition, so the jury will then have to decide whether the PTSD itself substantially impaired his ability to exercise self-control, ignoring the effect of the drinks he had consumed.

Substantially impaired D's ability

Under the old law, in **Lloyd 1967**, substantially impaired was said to mean the impairment need not be total but must be more than trivial or minimal. In **Campbell 1987**, the medical evidence was that D had epilepsy which could make him "vulnerable to an impulsive tendency". The defence failed because 'vulnerable to' indicates that it was not substantial.

Key case

In **Golds 2016**, the position was restated under the new law. The SC held that the judge is not normally obliged to direct the jury as to the meaning of 'substantial' unless there is any misunderstanding and the jury asks for clarification. However, if an explanation were needed, the **Act** did not change the old law on the meaning of the word as stated in **Lloyd**. The SC added that **Lloyd** did not suggest it would be enough merely to show that the impairment was more than trivial, only that it fell between the two extremes of trivial and total. The SC made clear that it must *be* more than trivial, but that *any* impairment that is more than trivial will not necessarily suffice.

Principle: 'Substantial' is as established in **Lloyd**, between the two extremes of trivial and total.

Note that the substantial impairment must occur at the time of the killing. In **Fairweather 2016**, D committed two killings over a period of three months. He claimed he was suffering a psychotic episode at the time and had heard voices telling him to kill. He pleaded diminished responsibility. The court heard evidence that he had autism spectrum disorder. That would be an abnormality of mental functioning arising from a recognised medical condition. However, the jury did not accept that he was psychotic at the time of the killings and rejected the defence.

There is some difference with the previous law. Under **s 2** as amended by the **Coroners and Justice Act**, it is not D's mental responsibility that must be substantially impaired, it is D's ability to do one of three things:

- to understand the nature of his conduct, or
- to form a rational judgement or,
- to exercise self-control

Although not specified in the old law, these matters are much as before. Someone with learning difficulties may not understand the nature of the act, nor be able to form a rational judgement, nor exercise self-control. D succeeded in **Byrne 1960** because he was unable to exercise self-control. Severe stress, as in many of the mercy killing cases, would perhaps prevent D being able to form a rational judgement.

Note that only one of the three things is needed, not all.

In **Redfern 2014**, D had been taking prescribed drugs which caused depression. During a period of depression he killed his wife and daughter. The court accepted his plea of diminished responsibility because the depression had caused an abnormality of mental functioning which had substantially impaired his ability to form a rational judgement.

In **Dantes 2015**, D suffered from paranoid schizophrenia and in a frenzied attack he killed his parents by repeatedly stabbing them. He was suffering from a recognised medical condition which caused his abnormality of mental functioning at the time of the killing. The expert witnesses agreed that this abnormality substantially impaired his ability to exercise self-control. The defence of diminished responsibility succeeded.

In **Daley 2016**, again D suffered from paranoid schizophrenia. He had braked suddenly and the driver behind bumped into him and got out of the car to ask why D had stopped. D said he thought he was under attack and stabbed V many times. He was charged with murder. The jury unanimously accepted the evidence that he was suffering from paranoid schizophrenia at the time. This had caused an abnormality of mental functioning which substantially impaired his ability to exercise self-control.

In **King 2016**, D killed his wife while suffering from dementia (an abnormality of mental functioning). The evidence showed that the dementia had affected the part of his brain responsible for forming rational decisions. In accepting the defence, the judge said that the dementia caused an abnormality of mental functioning and that his ability to form a rational judgment was substantially impaired by this at the time of the killing.

Provides an explanation for D's acts and omissions in doing or being a party to the killing

That the abnormality of mental functioning must 'provide an explanation for D's acts and omissions' is clarified in **s 52(1)(C)** of the **Act** as meaning that it 'causes, or is a significant contributory factor in causing, D to carry out that conduct'.

This was introduced to the defence by the amendments made by the **Coroners and Justice Act 2009**. It means that there must now be some causal connection between D's abnormality of mental functioning and the conduct.

In **Mann 2015**, D killed his seriously ill wife while suffering from depression after caring for her round the clock. They had been happily married for nearly 60 years but she had been very ill and was increasingly suffering from dementia and did not want to return to hospital. She said he "had promised to help her go". He had been in the army and killed her with a single stab wound. The judge accepted the expert evidence that the depression caused an abnormality of mental functioning which substantially impaired his ability to exercise self-control and that this abnormality had provided an explanation for the killing because it was a significant contributing factor to it.

So it is clear that the abnormality must cause the killing or make a significant contribution to it.

Example: Applying the 2009 Act to Wood, above.

Alcohol dependency syndrome was confirmed to be a recognised medical condition in this case.

The jury would also need to be convinced that:

Wood was suffering an abnormality of mental functioning which arose from his alcohol dependency syndrome

This abnormality substantially (not trivially, but not necessarily totally, using **Lloyd**) impaired his ability to do **one of** the following:

- understand the nature of his conduct: quite likely, the evidence showed he did not know what he was doing at the time

- form a rational judgement: also likely as it was doubtful he could form any judgement at all
- exercise self-control: not clear on the facts but we only need one of these, not all three

Finally, the abnormality of mental functioning must provide an explanation for his acts. This is an issue of causation, and again is quite likely as he would not have killed if not suffering from the syndrome, so this made a significant contribution to his actions

An example of a case showing the two partial defences overlap is **Morgan 2016**. D strangled his girlfriend after the relationship started to go wrong and she threatened to show videos of them having sex to his ex-wife and daughters. He argued that the killing was the result of a loss of self-control and also that his responsibility for the killing was diminished by the fact that he was suffering from Asperger's syndrome and this was an abnormality of mental functioning which substantially impaired his ability to form a rational judgment and exercise self-control, and which provided an explanation for his actions. The jury rejected both partial defences. In planning the killing and then taking steps to cover it up, D appeared to have understood what he was doing and had been able to form a rational judgment and exercise self-control. The planning also indicated that he had not lost control (this defence would probably not have succeeded anyway, as he seemed to be acting in a considered desire for revenge).

Task 20

Go to the Law Commission website at www.lawcom.gov.uk and look at the 2004 report on 'Partial defences to murder' or the 2006 report on Murder, manslaughter and infanticide' (click on projects and type in murder or manslaughter). You will find lots of information which you can refer to in an essay on voluntary manslaughter or justice. You can see how far the LC's proposals for reform have been addressed. Reference to these (and quotes from the LC) will enhance an answer and show you have done some independent research. It is also useful in a discussion of whether justice is now better served and/or whether more reform is needed.

Burden of proof

Unlike loss of control, where the prosecution has to show that D was *not* provoked, D must prove diminished responsibility. It was confirmed in **Wilcocks 2016** that the **Act** has not changed this. The standard of proof is the balance of probabilities, i.e., the civil standard. Remember D will need to provide medical evidence to support the plea of diminished responsibility.

Evaluation pointer

There may be a sense of injustice where a jury decision is made based on what is justified rather than by using the legal tests. The defence may succeed or fail for moral reasons, rather than legal ones.

Examples can be seen in cases of 'mercy killings', such as **Bailey 2002**. A jury may accept a plea of diminished responsibility even where there is little evidence for it. This may be due to sympathy for the accused, or because the mandatory life sentence means that if the defence fails, the sentence will be life for murder. Accepting the defence means that a discretionary sentence can be given, taking into account the circumstances. Whilst this may 'do justice' in a particular case, it is arguably stretching the law to fit the facts.

It also works both ways. In **Sutcliffe 1981**, the 'Yorkshire ripper' case where D had committed a series of brutal murders, the defence was rejected by the jury (on the direction of the judge) despite strong medical evidence to the contrary and the fact that both the defence and prosecution accepted it. Presumably, the brutality of the murders persuaded the jury that a life sentence was appropriate.

Abolishing the mandatory life sentence for murder could be discussed in an evaluation. It would perhaps avoid the uncertainty of relying on the jury's sympathy or revulsion.

Examination pointer

Remember that there is an overlap between loss of control and diminished responsibility. Look back at cases like **Thornton**. Long-term abuse may be relevant to loss of control or result in a recognised medical condition such as 'battered woman's syndrome' or trauma. You may well have to discuss both defences. Look carefully at the given facts and watch for words like 'abuse' or 'depression'.

Problems and reforms

In its 2004 report 'Partial Defences to Murder' the Law Commission described the current law on murder as "a mess" and recommended a complete review of the law. They said:

> *"Over the centuries the law of homicide, including the law of murder, has developed in a higgledy-piggledy fashion. The present law is a product of judge made law supplemented by Parliament's sporadic intervention. The outcome is a body of law characterised by a lack of clarity and coherence."*

The **Coroners and Justice Act** only addresses a few of the problems seen in their report.

See the summary at the end of the fatal offences for more on the problems and reforms

Summary

Abnormality of mental functioning: will be interpreted as for abnormality of mind ...	... so different from that of ordinary human beings that the reasonable man would term it abnormal **Byrne 1960**
Substantially impaired	Impairment need not be total but must be more than trivial or minimal **Lloyd 1967**
It is D's ability to do one of three things which must be substantially impaired	These are: to understand the nature of his conduct; to form a rational judgement; to exercise self-control.
Alcoholism, or alcohol dependency syndrome, may lead to a successful defence but only if the first drink was involuntary	**Tandy 1989/Wood 2008**
If D is intoxicated *as well as* suffering from a abnormality of mental functioning the defence may succeed, but the jury must ignore the intoxication	**Dietschmann 2003**
The **Coroners and Justice Act 2009** does not change the rules on intoxication	**Dowds 2012**
The abnormality of mental functioning must provide an explanation for D's conduct	A causation issue; did the abnormality of mental functioning cause D to act that way?

Links to the non-substantive law

ELS: For links to the English legal system, look back at the diagram and examples in the introduction to Part 1. As the charge would be murder, which is an indictable offence, the case will be tried in the Crown Court and the maximum sentence is life, as for murder. The difference with the defence succeeding is that this sentence is now discretionary so the judge can choose a sentence appropriate to the facts. A jury will decide on the facts of the case and this could have its advantages. Much will depend on the type of killing. In euthanasia cases juries have been sympathetic as in **Gilderdale 2010**. However, if D has killed a child, or the killing is seen as immoral, a jury is more likely to find D guilty even if the facts suggest a defence was available, as in **Sutcliffe**. Statutory interpretation can be linked to this topic as the judge may need to interpret the **Homicide Act**, as amended by the **Coroners' and Justice Act**. However, you can also note that the law is clearer now so this may be easier, as seen in the many cases since the later **Act** seen in this Chapter. A 'recognised medical condition' is more understandable for juries than the old law and it will be easier for D to get reliable medical evidence. This may involve access to justice as although it may be less expensive than before, it is still costly.

The nature of law: Much of what was said in the last Chapter applies here too. One role of law is to punish wrongdoing and another is to provide justice, which requires clarity and fairness in the law. It can be said to be fair that as long as there is a sufficient abnormality of mental functioning, there should be a defence to a murder charge. It does not mean D 'gets away with' the killing, only that the conviction will be for manslaughter not murder. D will be punished but the judge can choose the appropriate sentence in an attempt to achieve justice on the given facts. Again as with the other partial defence, it can be said that the law is now clearer because many of the matters are now stated in the **Coroners and Justice Act** and not left to judicial development. Any of the cases where the defence succeeded can be used to illustrate the importance of fault in criminal liability. The success of the defence indicates that there is a reason for the killing, and thus a lower degree of fault. An important role of law is to provide justice. The vast difference in the sentences in **Freaney 2011** and **Inglis 2010** shows the difficulty in having a mandatory life sentence, so the availability of both partial defences can be said to achieve greater justice. A final point is that it is unfair and inconsistent, and therefore unjust, that the burden of proof is on D. Unlike other defences, D must prove diminished responsibility. It was confirmed in **Wilcocks 2016** that the **Act** has not changed this, so it is arguable that the law has not played a very admirable role by keeping this rule. The law had a good opportunity to achieve greater equality and fairness by changing the rule when passing the **Act**.

Self-test questions

1. Have you achieved the aims set out at the beginning of the Chapter?
2. From which case did the opening quote come?
3. What type of evidence will be required for this defence?
4. Who has the burden of proving the defence?
5. Which Act amended the **Homicide Act s 2** on the defence of diminished responsibility?

Answers to tasks and self-test questions are on my website at www.drsr.org/publications/tasks. For some interactive exercises, click on 'Free Exercises'.

Chapter 11 Gross negligence manslaughter and constructive or unlawful act manslaughter

"A verdict of manslaughter may, depending on the circumstances, be appropriate both by reason of an unlawful and dangerous act, and by reason of gross negligence". Rose LJ

By the end of this Chapter, you should be able to:

- Explain the four legal requirements in proving gross negligence manslaughter
- Explain the three legal requirements in proving constructive manslaughter
- Explain how the law applies in practice by reference to cases
- Identify possible criticisms for an evaluation of the law

Gross negligence manslaughter

This type of manslaughter occurs when someone owes a duty to another person, but is 'grossly negligent', with the result that the person dies.

Example

Kylie is looking after a 2-month-old baby for the evening. She gets very drunk and falls over whilst carrying the baby. Kylie passes out and the baby is smothered. If the baby dies then Kylie may be guilty of gross negligence manslaughter. She will owe a duty to the baby in her care, and getting so drunk whilst looking after a young child is likely to be sufficiently negligent.

The rules on gross negligence manslaughter were clarified by the HL in **Adomako 1994**.

Key case

In **Adomako**, an anaesthetist had failed to monitor a patient during an operation. The patient later died as a result. The doctor was accused of manslaughter.

The CA held that in order to prove gross negligence manslaughter there must be:

- A risk of death
- A duty of care
- Breach of that duty

Gross negligence as regards that breach, which must be sufficient to justify criminal liability

The CA also gave examples of the type of conduct which might amount to such negligence. When the case went to the HL, the test was confirmed but the HL rejected the idea of setting out particular examples. Lord Mackay said that the jury would have to decide whether *"involving as it must have done a risk of death"* D's conduct fell below the standard expected to the extent *"that it should be judged criminal"*. On the facts, this was the case here, and the conviction was upheld.

It seemed that this replaced reckless manslaughter, which Lord Mackay said in **Adomako** no longer existed. Before looking at the rules on gross negligence manslaughter, we'll take a brief look at this issue. You won't need to apply it, but it could be useful when evaluating the law.

Evaluation pointer

In **Seymour 1983**, D was driving recklessly, and crushed his girlfriend between his lorry and a car, killing her. The HL said that if there was an 'obvious and serious' risk of injuring someone (objective recklessness), D was guilty of manslaughter. However, in **Adomako**, the HL seemed to reject reckless manslaughter and as this was a unanimous decision, it could be taken as a statement of the current law. The judgment was, however, somewhat complex and matters were further complicated by Lord

Mackay who, having said in **Adomako** that reckless manslaughter no longer existed, also said, "*I consider it perfectly appropriate that the word reckless be used in cases of involuntary manslaughter*". This left the matter somewhat uncertain, and it is wrong that the law is not clear.

Many objective reckless manslaughter cases involved driving incidents and there is now a statutory offence of causing death by dangerous driving, so arguably reckless manslaughter is not needed. However, some cases came outside the 'motor manslaughter' category and so are not covered by statute. In **Khan and Khan 1998**, the CA said that there were only **two** types of involuntary manslaughter: unlawful act manslaughter and gross negligence manslaughter. This apparently confirmed **Adomako**, that reckless manslaughter no longer existed. However, doubt was again cast on this in **Lidar 2000**.

In **Lidar**, a group of men had a fight in the car park of a pub. When two of them got in a car and started to drive off, a 3rd leant in the window of the car and the fight continued. They drove off with him half in the window and at some point he fell off and suffered injuries from which he died. The jury was directed in terms of recklessness and the driver was convicted of manslaughter. The CA upheld the conviction, possibly relying on Lord Mackay's reference in **Adomako** to it being "perfectly appropriate" to use the word reckless. As a driver owes a clear duty to other road users there is no doubt a finding of gross negligence manslaughter would have been possible, so there was no need to confuse the matter by reference to recklessness

For application purposes you need to know the rules on gross negligence manslaughter and unlawful act manslaughter, so let's look at the requirements for each.

The requirements for gross negligence manslaughter

The **Adomako** requirements were confirmed in **Misra 2004**.

Key case

In **Misra**, also a medical negligence case, it was argued that the uncertainty in the law of gross negligence manslaughter meant that it infringed the **European Convention on Human Rights**. The CA rejected this argument and held that the offence had been sufficiently clearly set out in **Adomako**. Grossly negligent treatment, which exposed a patient to the risk of death, and caused death, would make the doctor liable for manslaughter.

The CA also said that it had been 'clearly established' that a risk of death was needed; a risk of bodily injury or injury to health was not enough.

As well as a **risk of death**, the death must have occurred as a result of a **breach** of a **duty** owed by D to V. Then the jury must decide whether D's breach of duty was **grossly** negligent and therefore criminal.

Principle: There must be a risk of death, a risk of bodily injury or injury to health is not enough.

Let's look at these four requirements.

Risk of death

In **Misra 2004**, the CA confirmed that a risk of death was needed, not just a risk of harm. This will still be quite wide. Activities which are dangerous in themselves, such as taking people mountaineering or white-water rafting would be included. Ordinary activities which have the potential to be dangerous could also involve a risk of death. This would cover driving a train or piloting a ferry. Such activities are not dangerous in themselves, but if a train or ferry is handled negligently or poorly maintained, there is a risk of death, so the driver or company may be liable.

Duty

It was not made fully clear in **Adomako** whether the ordinary civil test for duty is enough. Later cases suggest that it is. In **Wacker 2003**, the Ds were transporting about 60 illegal immigrants in a lorry. For some time during the journey there was no ventilation. Most of the immigrants died and the Ds were charged with gross negligence manslaughter. The judge referred to **Adomako** and the 'ordinary principles of the law of negligence'. A duty will therefore be owed to anyone foreseeably affected by D's actions. The CA held that they had assumed a duty of care for the victims and rejected their appeal against conviction.

Task 21

Look back at Chapter 2 and reread the following manslaughter cases. What was the duty and how was it breached?

Stone and Dobinson 1977

Pittwood 1902

Key case

Khan and Khan 1998 is a case worth knowing because gross negligence manslaughter, constructive manslaughter and omissions were all discussed. It also seems to confirm that there are only two types of manslaughter, and that reckless manslaughter no longer exists. The Ds had supplied drugs to a young prostitute. She went into a coma but they left her and when they returned the next day, she had died. This would be a failure to act, an *omission* (not getting medical help). The trial judge referred to 'manslaughter by omission' and found them guilty. The CA allowed the appeal and stated that there were only two types of involuntary manslaughter. These were unlawful act manslaughter (which requires an act, not an omission) and gross negligence manslaughter (which requires a pre-existing duty, as in **Stone and Dobinson**). The CA held that there was no such duty between a drug dealer and a client. D could not be guilty of either type of manslaughter.

Principles: There are only two types of involuntary manslaughter. Gross negligence manslaughter requires a duty, which does not arise between a drug dealer and a client.

In **Khan**, the CA refused to find that a duty was owed by a drug dealer to a client. However, they did suggest that such a duty *could* arise. If the facts were capable of giving rise to a duty, then the judge should give the jury *"an appropriate direction which would enable them to answer the question whether on the facts as found by them there was such a duty"*.

The CA restated this in **Evans 2009**. The judge will direct the jury as to whether the facts were *capable* of giving rise to a duty; the jury must then decide whether in fact they did. The CA also held that the duty in cases of gross negligence manslaughter was not confined to family and professional relationships.

In **Evans**, the CA held that if a person created, or contributed to, a situation which was life threatening then a duty to take reasonable steps to save that life would arise. D had supplied heroin to her 16-year-old half-sister, who had injected it herself. When she showed symptoms of having overdosed her sister took no action, fearing she would get into trouble. She and her mother put the girl to bed but she was dead the next morning. The CA noted that cases had not been clear on whether the judge or the jury should decide on whether a duty was owed. The CA held that whether a duty of care *could* exist was a question of law for the judge. However, it was for the jury to look at the facts to decide whether such a duty had been established. That a duty was owed in **Evans** was decided on the basis of owing a duty after creating a dangerous situation as in **Miller**. It could have been decided on the principle that a duty can be owed on the basis of an assumption of responsibility.

Examination tip

You can see from **Evans** and the other cases on duty and omissions, that there is an overlap. Both **Fagan** and **Miller** could have been decided on the basis of a continuing act or of creating a dangerous situation. **Miller** and **Evans** could have been decided on the basis of an assumption of responsibility or of creating a dangerous situation.

Breach of duty / the conduct amounted to gross negligence

In civil law, breach means D has not reached the standard expected of a reasonable person. However only if D is *grossly* negligent will there be criminal liability. This is for the jury to decide. Lord Mackay said in **Adomako** that whether the conduct justified a criminal conviction was "supremely a jury question". Thus the jury must look at the circumstances and decide whether D's conduct was sufficiently grossly negligent to be deemed criminal. This was confirmed in **Misra 2004**. First there must be a breach (has D acted like a reasonable person?), then this breach must be seen by the jury as sufficiently negligent to be deemed criminal.

In **Warner 2014**, a caretaker was convicted of gross negligence manslaughter when he failed to replace a gap in the barrier of a walkway and a child fell to her death. He had breached his duty of care to users of the walkway and the court said his failure to replace the barrier had been "thoroughly irresponsible".

In **Wood and Hodgson 2003**, a 10-year-old girl was visiting the Ds. She found some ecstasy tablets hidden in a cigarette packet and took some. She later died in hospital and they were charged with gross negligence manslaughter. Applying the rules:

Risk of death: It is known that ecstasy can kill so there is a risk of death.

Duty: they owed her a duty of responsibility (**Stone and Dobinson**) as a visitor and/or as a child in their care.

Breach: There was evidence that they had hidden the tablets, and that they had attempted to treat her, but they did not call an ambulance for some time. They had **breached** their duty to her by not taking reasonable care.

Gross negligence: However, the jury found that they had not shown a sufficiently high level of negligence to be deemed criminal.

Result: They were not guilty of gross negligence manslaughter.

Evaluation pointer

In **Adomako**, the CA had set out a list of what type of conduct might be deemed sufficiently negligent. The HL rejected this on the basis that it could confuse juries who might think that only those situations would suffice. They thought it better to leave it to the jury to decide on the facts whether the conduct was sufficiently bad to be deemed criminal. It is therefore not at all clear what exactly does amount to criminal negligence. It is hard for a jury to decide what was sufficiently negligent if the law is not clear. The Ds in **Wood and Hodgson** seemed just as 'thoroughly irresponsible' as the caretaker in **Warner** but they were not found sufficiently negligent, whilst he was, even though the level of fault appears to be very similar.

In **Willoughby 2004**, D was the owner of a disused public house in Canterbury. He had recruited a local taxi driver to help him set fire to the building for financial purposes. The taxi driver was killed when the building collapsed and D was convicted of gross negligence manslaughter. On appeal, the CA said that the judge should have directed the jury on unlawful act manslaughter rather than gross negligence manslaughter. They made it clear that either may be appropriate, depending on the circumstances. The opening quote came from this case. (On the facts, the jury had accepted that D had committed arson which is an unlawful act, and this caused death, so the manslaughter conviction was upheld.)

Examination pointer

For a problem question look for clues in the scenario, you may need to discuss both types. The CA in **Adomako** indicated that it could also be gross negligence manslaughter where, e.g., an electrician caused a death by faulty wiring. This was *obiter dicta* because it was not relevant on the facts of the case. It could be referred to if the given scenario involved such circumstances, or something similar. Although not binding, *obiter dicta* can be used as *persuasive precedent*.

As we saw in **Willoughby**, the two types of manslaughter overlap. If you think it is constructive manslaughter, discuss this first, but if, e.g., there is doubt as to whether there is an act or omission, or whether the act is unlawful, go on to gross negligence manslaughter as an alternative. If, as in **Willoughby**, there is some doubt as to whether a duty is owed, you could start with gross negligence manslaughter and go on to constructive manslaughter as an alternative.

Evaluation pointer

Although on the facts, the conviction in **Willoughby** was upheld, it does highlight the difficulties. The overlap is not always clear. If the judge has trouble identifying whether it is gross negligence or unlawful act manslaughter, then arguably the law is still too uncertain, as argued in **Misra**. It is also unclear whether the civil test for duty is enough. It would seem so, but if it is, then another criticism is that it should not be. The functions of the criminal and civil law are very different.

You could also consider how far the law should impose a duty on a drug dealer to his client. Although the CA declined to find there was a duty in **Khan**, there could arguably have been a common law duty, as in **Stone and Dobinson**. The decision may be one of policy rather than law. Taking on responsibility for an invalid is sufficient to establish a duty of care, responsibility for a prostitute to whom D had supplied drugs is not. This seems more of a moral judgment than a legal one. It is another area that needs clarification.

Task 22

Make up a scenario and apply the rules to decide whether there is liability for manslaughter.

Reforms

The Law Commission published a consultation paper on manslaughter in 1994, followed by a report in 1996: *Legislating the Criminal Code: Involuntary Manslaughter* (Report 237). It suggested that involuntary manslaughter should be abolished and replaced with three new offences:

- reckless (subjective) killing (D sees a risk of death or serious injury)
- killing by gross carelessness (the risk of death or serious injury was obvious (objective) and the conduct fell far below what was expected)
- corporate killing (similar to killing by gross carelessness but death is due to management failure)

This would simplify and clarify the law. The offence of killing by gross carelessness would solve the **Khan**-type problem, as there would be no need to prove a duty. Having such a serious crime relying on the common law for its development is questionable. The courts themselves have indicated it is the role of Parliament to create the law on such a major issue. The government has concentrated on voluntary manslaughter reform and suggested reforms of involuntary manslaughter have not been taken up.

Task 23

Go to the Law Commission website at www.lawcom.gov.uk and look at the 2006 report on Murder, manslaughter and infanticide' (click on projects and type in murder or manslaughter). As with tasks 19 and 20, you will find lots of information which you can refer to in an essay on the manslaughter or justice. Quotes from the LC will enhance an answer and show you have done some independent research. Unlike the proposals for reform of the partial defences, gross negligence manslaughter has not changed, so arguably reform is still needed if justice is to be done.

Evaluation pointer

Having such a serious crime relying on the common law for its development is questionable. The courts themselves have indicated it is the role of Parliament to create the law on such a major issue. The public have long called for change. The Law Commission proposals are no longer new. Another problem in relation to both types of involuntary manslaughter is that they cover such a wide range. The level of fault involved can vary enormously from something just short of intent to kill to the virtually accidental. Justice requires greater clarity in the law.

Summary

The **Adomako 1994** requirements as confirmed in **Misra 2004** are:

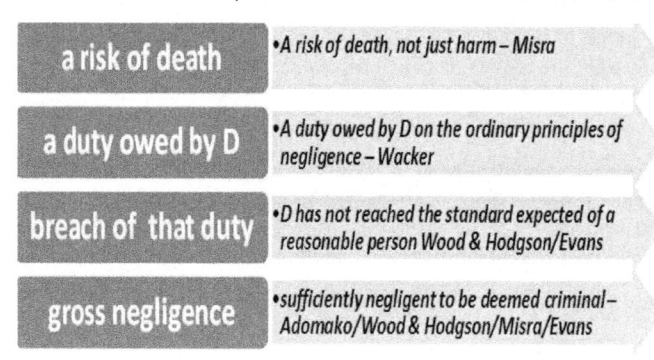

a risk of death	• A risk of death, not just harm – Misra
a duty owed by D	• A duty owed by D on the ordinary principles of negligence – Wacker
breach of that duty	• D has not reached the standard expected of a reasonable person Wood & Hodgson/Evans
gross negligence	• sufficiently negligent to be deemed criminal – Adomako/Wood & Hodgson/Misra/Evans

Unlawful act or constructive manslaughter

This second type of manslaughter is 'constructed' from an act which is both unlawful and dangerous and which causes death, but with a *mens rea* that does not need to match the act (we saw constructive liability with **s 47** and **20** and also with murder). This is why it called both constructive manslaughter (because of constructive liability) and unlawful act manslaughter (because it requires an unlawful act). Either term is acceptable in an examination.

The requirements for unlawful act manslaughter

Actus reus

There are three separate issues to address in the *actus reus*

- an unlawful act

- which is dangerous
- which causes death

Unlawful act

An act is only unlawful for the purposes of constructive manslaughter if it is a crime. Criminal damage is a common example, as in **Hancock and Shankland 1986**. Battery is another.

Examples

In **JF 2015**, the Ds were teenagers who had set fire to an old duvet in a derelict building. The fire spread and a homeless man was killed by the fumes. The unlawful act was criminal damage by fire. They were convicted of manslaughter and this was upheld on appeal.

In **Lamb 1967**, D pointed a loaded gun at V, his friend, as a joke. Because they did not understand how a revolver works, they thought that there was no danger in pulling the trigger. D did so and V died. The court said the unlawful act must be a crime. Although the act could have been a battery, it was not because he did not have *mens rea*, he did not see the risk of harm. As he was not guilty of battery, he was not guilty of manslaughter.

It must be an act not an omission. In **Khan and Khan 1998**, the charge of unlawful act manslaughter failed because there was no act, just an omission to get medical help.

Task 24

Look up these cases and identify the unlawful act. Then make a note of how causation in fact and in law is proved and how these apply.

Hancock and Shankland 1986

Pagett 1983

Nedrick 1986

Which is dangerous

Whether the unlawful act is dangerous is an objective test. It was stated in **Church 1967** that

> "the unlawful act must be such as all sober and reasonable people would inevitably recognise must subject the other person to, at least, the risk of some harm resulting therefrom, albeit not serious harm".

Key case

In **Church**, D had knocked a woman unconscious and then, wrongly believing her to be dead, threw her in the river to dispose of the 'body'. The CA held that it did not matter that D did not see any risk of harm. In this case, D did not see any such risk as he thought she was dead! So, the principle is that if reasonable people would see the risk of harm, this will be enough. D was guilty of manslaughter because reasonable people would see that throwing someone into a river carries a risk of harm.

Principle: A dangerous act is one which sober and reasonable people would recognise as risking some harm occurring.

In **R v M (J); R v M (S) 2012**, two Ds were involved in a violent incident at a nightclub after being asked to leave. One of the doormen collapsed from shock shortly afterwards and died. The CA rejected their appeal against a manslaughter conviction and confirmed that it was not necessary for D to have foreseen any specific harm to the victim. What mattered was whether '*reasonable and sober people*' would have recognised that the unlawful activities subjected the victim to the risk of some harm. On the facts, it was clear that sober and reasonable people observing the events would have recognised that the doormen involved in the effort to control the Ds were at the risk of some harm.

Note that if there is a high risk of death then a murder charge may be more appropriate. In **Stephen-Port 2016**, D had lured gay men to his house at different times and given them high doses of GHB (a date-rape drug) in order to have sex with them. In four of the cases the men died. The court decided that due to the number of incidents and the fact that D had administered the drugs on several occasions, there was a high enough risk of death, which D knew about, to provide evidence of intent and to make the offences murder rather than manslaughter.

Physical assaults will usually be deemed dangerous, unlawful acts like robbery and burglary will depend on the circumstances.

In **Dawson 1985**, during an attempted robbery of a garage, the Ds had frightened V with an imitation pistol. He suffered from a heart condition and subsequently died. They were found not guilty of manslaughter because a reasonable person would not have been aware of the heart condition, and so would not see the act as dangerous. The court recognised that fear could be foreseen, but as physical harm could not be, the act was not dangerous in the true sense.

Evaluation pointer

Both **Church** and **Dawson** show that for an act to be deemed dangerous there must be a risk of physical harm. It appears that this does not include psychiatric harm. In many other areas of law, physical harm has been extended to include psychiatric. It can be argued that 'dangerous' should include an act which could cause psychiatric harm. **Dawson** can be criticised on the basis that a robbery with imitation firearms could be construed as dangerous. The reaction of a victim to such a robbery could be unpredictable. Someone might decide to 'have a go' and this would certainly be dangerous, whether the guns were real or not. **Dawson** was *distinguished* in the next case.

In **Watson 1989**, burglars entered a house and saw an elderly man, but continued with their act of burglary. They were charged with manslaughter when he died of a heart attack. The man's frailty was obvious and the Ds saw this. Their knowledge could be attributed to the reasonable person who could therefore see the danger of the act, thus **Dawson** could be distinguished. (Note that on the facts their conviction was quashed on the causation issue, because there was not enough evidence that the shock of seeing burglars caused death.)

In **Bristow 2013**, a man died after intervening in a burglary at an off-road vehicle repair shop. The Ds argued that the burglary was not dangerous until after V arrived and the escape car was driven dangerously, i.e., the risk of harm became apparent. At this point there was no evidence as to who was driving so no-one was guilty. The CA held that this was not like **Dawson** or **Watson,** and although burglary was not dangerous in itself, the particular circumstances could make it so. Here the risk was obvious from the outset of the burglary because of the nature of the premises and their geography. There was a limited escape route with nearby residential accommodation. The reasonable person would see a risk of harm being caused to anyone trying to intervene or prevent escape.

In Dawson, the robbery was not dangerous because V's heart condition was not obvious – reasonable people would not see any risk of harm.

In Watson, the burglary became dangerous once the man's frailty was obvious – reasonable people would now see the risk of harm.

In Bristow, the burglary was dangerous from the start because the risk was obvious to reasonable people at that stage.

In **JF 2015**, the CA restated the law on unlawful act manslaughter and made clear that the test for dangerous comes from **Church** and is 'purely objective'. The fact one of the Ds had a low IQ and both were young was not relevant, it was enough that a reasonable person would see the act as dangerous.

Evaluation pointer

Whether the unlawful act is dangerous is an objective test, based on what a reasonable person would see as dangerous. It is not relevant that D didn't see it as dangerous. For such a serious offence it can be argued that a subjective test should be used. This is particularly the case where there seems to be a lower level of fault because D is young or has a low IQ, as in **JF**. Objective recklessness was abolished a long time ago as regards the *mens rea* for criminal damage, yet it is still used for the 'dangerous' requirement for a manslaughter charge.

Examination pointer

Take care when applying the rules in a problem scenario. Students often misunderstand the point of **Dawson** and confuse it with the thin skull rule. This rule may well be relevant but it will only apply once the act is found to be unlawful and dangerous. It is a causation issue. In **Dawson**, the question was whether the act was dangerous. The answer was 'no' because a reasonable person would not know of the heart condition. If the act *had* been dangerous then D would 'take the victim as he finds him'. Thus, D would be liable for the death even though a person without a heart condition would not have died.

Example

Consider the following imaginary cases:

1. *You are angry and wave your fist at Cathy. She is of a very nervous disposition and dies of fright.*

2. *You are angry and throw a brick at Kate, which misses. She is of a very nervous disposition and dies of fright.*

In the first case, your action may be unlawful (causing fear is an assault), but is unlikely to be seen as dangerous. Much may depend on whether you know she is of a nervous disposition, if not, you are not guilty of Cathy's manslaughter. It ends there.

In the second, your act is both unlawful and dangerous. The next question is whether you caused Kate's death. You cannot argue that most people would not have died, and that Kate's nervous disposition caused her death. Under the thin skull rule you must 'take your victim as you find her'. You are guilty of manslaughter.

Causes death

The usual rules of causation apply, i.e., D must make a significant contribution to the death and the chain of causation must not be broken. Let's look at the cases in your task.

Examples

Hancock and Shankland – throwing concrete blocks onto a taxi would be criminal damage, thus unlawful. Throwing concrete blocks off a bridge is dangerous. The damage caused the driver's death.

Nedrick – setting fire to something belonging to someone else is a type of criminal damage (arson) and so again unlawful. It is also clearly dangerous and the fire caused death.

Pagett – shooting at the police is both unlawful and dangerous. D made a significant contribution to the girl's death and the police didn't break the chain of causation by firing back because it was a natural reaction (foreseeable). The shooting caused death.

In all the above cases the Ds were guilty of manslaughter. As were the Ds in **JF**, where the CA held that the unlawful act was criminal damage by fire, and the fire caused the man's death.

Causation is not always easy to prove and problems have arisen in several cases. Compare the following two decisions.

In **Cato 1976**, D supplied, and assisted V to take, heroin which resulted in death. It was held that he had unlawfully administered a drug which caused death and so was guilty of manslaughter.

In **Dalby 1982**, the CA quashed the conviction because although D had supplied drugs (an unlawful act) this had not caused death. V had injected himself and this broke the chain of causation.

In **Cato**, D actually injected V so there was no break in the chain of causation. In **Dalby**, V's own act broke the chain.

In **Kennedy 1999**, D mixed the drug and handed the syringe to V and this sufficed even though, as in **Dalby**, V injected himself. In **Dias 2002**, V injected himself, as in **Dalby**. The CA quashed D's conviction on the issue of causation and criticised the decision in **Kennedy**. The conflicting case law led to the CCRC referring **Kennedy** back to the CA on the issue of causation. In **Kennedy 2005**, the CA said causing your own death was not unlawful, so nor was encouraging another to. However, participating in the administration of a 'poison' or 'noxious thing' is a crime, and so forms the basis for a manslaughter charge. The case then went to the HL.

Key case

In **Kennedy 2007**, the HL quashed the conviction and held that in the case of a fully informed adult self-administering the drug it would never be appropriate to find the supplier guilty of manslaughter. D had not administered the drug so this was not an unlawful act. He had committed an unlawful act in supplying the heroin, but this did not cause the victim's death.

Principle: If an adult self-administers a drug the supplier will not be guilty of manslaughter.

Application of the three essentials can be seen in **Carey and Others 2006**. A teenage girl died from a heart attack following an attack on her and three other girls. The group who carried out the attack were charged with manslaughter. The CA confirmed the three elements, (i) that there was an unlawful act, (ii) which was dangerous in the sense that the unlawful act subjected V to the risk of physical harm, and (iii) that the unlawful act caused her death. As regards the unlawful act, the prosecution relied on the public order offence of 'affray'. This is using or threatening unlawful violence towards another, which would cause a person of reasonable firmness present at the scene to fear for his/her personal safety. The CA confirmed, following **Church**, that 'dangerous' was an objective test. Affray was not dangerous in the required sense because it would not have been recognised by a 'sober and reasonable bystander' that an apparently healthy 15-year-old was at risk of suffering harm as a result. On causation, both **Dawson** and **Watson** were discussed. It was agreed that it was not foreseeable that an apparently healthy 60-year old man would suffer shock and a heart attack as a result of an attempted robbery (**Dawson**), but it was foreseeable that an obviously frail and very old man was at risk of suffering shock leading to a heart attack as a result of a burglary committed at his home late at night (**Watson**). The current case involved a healthy young girl, so was nearer to **Dawson** than **Watson**. It had been argued that V was running from the attack so, as in

Roberts 1971, this did not break the chain of causation. However, the CA felt that she was not running away, merely running home, because there was no longer any threat by then. Although V had suffered a punch to her face, an unlawful act, this minor injury did not cause her death. The act of affray was unlawful but not dangerous, so the manslaughter charge failed.

This can be compared to **R v M (J); R v M (S) 2012**, above. A similar violent incident was held to be a substantial cause of the doorman's shock and had significantly contributed to his death. The shock and the increase in blood pressure led to his collapse and an internal rupture, from which he died. Shock was foreseeable, and there was found to be no break in the chain of causation between the violence and the death.

Before going on to *mens rea*, let's recap with an imaginary scenario.

Example

Vic decides to kill himself and jumps off a tall building, checking before he does so that no one is underneath. Dave is a resident of the building who is having a violent row with his wife. He fires a gun at her and misses, hitting Vic as he passes the window. Vic is thrown off course by the blow and lands on a pedestrian, Sue, killing her. Vic survives. Can anyone be charged with manslaughter?

Look at the three requirements. Vic's act is *dangerous* and *caused her death*, but is not *unlawful*. Vic is unlikely to be found guilty of manslaughter. Dave's act is both *dangerous* and *unlawful*. However, did it *cause death*? Unlikely, Vic's jumping would be the cause. Dave is also unlikely to be found guilty of manslaughter.

Mens rea

There is no special *mens rea* for this type of manslaughter. It is the *mens rea* for the unlawful act. There is therefore no need to prove *mens rea* as regards the death, only the unlawful act. Let's take one of the earlier examples a step further.

Example

Going back to **Nedrick 1986**, the unlawful act was arson, a form of criminal damage. The *mens rea* for this is intent or recklessness. There is no need for D to intend, or to recognise a risk of, death, only to intend or see a risk of the damage. Arson was clearly intended, so *mens rea* is easy to prove for a manslaughter charge to succeed.

In **JF 2015**, above, the CA made clear that the state of mind of D and the dangerousness of the act were to be differentiated. The first is a matter of *mens rea* and requires that D intended the unlawful act, here criminal damage, or was reckless in the subjective sense, i.e., recognised the risk of damage and carried on anyway. The second is a matter of *actus reus* and is an objective question – would reasonable people see the act as dangerous? The prosecution has no need to prove *mens rea* as regards the death, or even harm, only the damage. They intended to start a fire (and recklessness would be enough) so had *mens rea*. Their act was dangerous in the objective sense, as setting a fire is seen as dangerous by most people. The convictions were upheld.

Task 25

Explain the term constructive liability as it applies to manslaughter and write a few sentences regarding whether you believe that this type of liability achieves justice.

The only other point on *mens rea* is to remember that it must coincide with the *actus reus*. As we saw this is widely interpreted. Thus in both **Thabo Meli 1954** and in **Church 1967**, the Ds were guilty of unlawful and dangerous act manslaughter on the basis of a 'series of acts'.

Evaluation pointer

The Law Commission has criticised the fact that the *mens rea* for this type of manslaughter may be for some quite different offence (constructive liability, where the *actus reus* and *mens rea* don't match). Manslaughter is a very serious offence but the *mens rea* may be for a minor crime, such as criminal damage. Arguably, manslaughter should have a *mens rea* of its own and D should at least be subjectively reckless about causing death or serious injury. The convictions in **JF** can support this view.

Summary

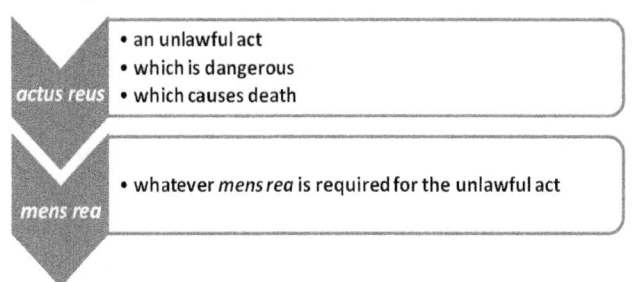

actus reus
- an unlawful act
- which is dangerous
- which causes death

mens rea
- whatever *mens rea* is required for the unlawful act

Task 26

Make up a scenario and apply the rules to decide whether there is liability for manslaughter. Use the recap, but be sure to add cases.

Links to the non-substantive law

ELS: For links to the English legal system, look back at the diagram and examples in the introduction to Part 1. Manslaughter is an indictable offence, so the case will be tried in the Crown Court and the maximum sentence is life, as for murder. The difference with manslaughter is that the sentence is discretionary so the judge can choose a sentence appropriate to the facts. A jury will decide on the facts of the case and this could have its advantages. However, there are difficulties for a jury in gross negligence manslaughter. The jury must look at the circumstances and decide whether D's conduct was sufficiently grossly negligent to be deemed criminal. It is hard for a jury to decide what was sufficiently negligent if the law is not clear. For unlawful act manslaughter the jury has the important role of deciding whether the act was dangerous.

The nature of law:

Gross negligence manslaughter: One role of the law is to achieve justice and part of this is to ensure fairness. As said above, the Ds in **Wood and Hodgson** seemed just as 'thoroughly irresponsible' as the caretaker in **Warner** but they were not found sufficiently negligent, whilst he was. Deciding what amounts to gross negligence (the fault element) is insufficiently clear and justice also requires clarity. Any inconsistency in the law is going to be unfair to someone, and arguably the law cannot achieve justice if it is not both fair and clear.

As seen in **Willoughby**, the judge had trouble identifying whether it was gross negligence or unlawful act manslaughter. Again, this suggests the law is still too uncertain, as argued in **Misra**.

If the role of law is to punish those who are blameworthy then it is arguable that there should have been a conviction in **Khan**. The Ds showed a high level of fault because it would have been easy to get help, even anonymously, but they did nothing. The law should not consider the morals of D or the victim when deciding on fault. Why should a prostitute not be owed a duty by the supplier of drugs?

Constructive manslaughter: The main point here is that made earlier with **s 47**, **s 20** and murder. The role of law is to achieve justice and to punish those found blameworthy. Constructive liability goes against justice. D should only be liable where fully blameworthy for the crime, i.e., with the *mens rea* for the offence actually committed, especially in such a serious crime as manslaughter. It seems particularly unjust where the unlawful act is only a minor offence such as a battery or criminal damage, as the *mens rea* for that offence will suffice to go with the *actus reus* of causing a death and result in the full offence of manslaughter.

Another point is that having an objective test for whether an act was dangerous is unjust. If D did not see the act as dangerous, as in **JF**, there is a lower level of fault and it is arguable there should not be criminal liability for such a serious offence.

Self-test questions

1. What are the elements required to prove gross negligence manslaughter?
2. Can you commit either type of manslaughter by omission?
3. From which case did the opening quote come?
4. What were the facts and principle in **Church**?
5. What is the difference between **Cato** and **Dalby**?
6. What did the HL decide in **Kennedy 2007**?

Answers to tasks and self-test questions are on my website at www.drsr.org/publications/tasks. For some interactive exercises, click on 'Free Exercises'.

Summary and evaluation of the fatal offences

Murder

Actus reus: The unlawful killing of a human being under the Queen's peace

Mens rea: Malice aforethought, i.e., intention to kill or seriously injure

Task 27

Note the principle and brief facts of the following cases

- Fagan
- Stone and Dobinson
- Roberts
- Cheshire
- DPP v Smith
- Blaue

Key criticisms of **actus reus, mens rea** *and murder*

A point that relates to any of the key criticism sections is that a question could just focus on a very small part of the law, especially if it is mixed with one of the concepts. An example is in the specimen paper for 2017 where there is a question on the rules on loss of control in relation to sexual infidelity and whether they achieve justice. The focus in such a question is more on justice than the rules themselves. The rules would clearly need to be explained (with reference to **Clinton**) and then an explanation of justice with reference to different theories of justice, followed by a discussion on whether the specific rules on sexual infidelity achieve justice (and in whose opinion).

All these criticisms can be used in a discussion of whether justice is achieved and many also relate to fault.

- D is not usually liable for an omission but can be in certain circumstances; there is a degree of uncertainty in such cases e.g., Bland, Gibbins & Proctor
- Sometimes questions arise about whether someone who is 'brain dead' or a foetus in the womb is a human being. In AGs Reference (No 3 of 1994) 1997, the HL held that a foetus was not a human being for the purpose of a murder conviction. However, if the foetus is injured, and dies from that injury after being born, that could amount to murder. Arguably, there should be greater clarity on this.
- The rules on what will break the chain of causation may be difficult for a jury to understand
- The law on intent has developed but is arguably still unclear
- The mandatory life sentence for murder means the judge has no discretion and cannot take into account the very different circumstances between some killings, in euthanasia cases. A discretionary sentence could remove the need for the special defences (voluntary manslaughter) as the circumstances could be taken into account by the judge
- Murder is a common law offence. Should there be a statutory definition? If so, should it contain more than one degree of murder as in the USA (and as recommended by the Law Commission – see below)? This could again remove the need for the special defences.

- The *mens rea* for murder is intent to kill or seriously injure, for such a serious crime should it only be intent to kill?

Note that where the *actus reus* and *mens rea* do not match this lack of correspondence is known as 'constructive liability'. It is called constructive liability because liability is constructed from the *actus reus* of one offence and the *mens rea* of another e.g., for murder, liability is constructed from the *actus reus* of murder and the *mens rea* of causing serious harm. This applies to unlawful act (also known as constructive) manslaughter and to **s 47** and **s 20** of the **Offences against the Person Act**.

In general, the LC is against constructive liability and prefers to uphold the correspondence principle. Constructive liability relates to both fault and justice, because D is liable for a crime where there is a lower level of fault than the crime suggests, which is not just.

Reforms

In its 2006 report 'Murder, manslaughter and Infanticide' the Law Commission noted four particular problems with the law on homicide and said:

If excessive force is used in self-defence this should come within the partial defences.

It is not right that duress cannot be a defence to murder in any circumstances.

The serious harm rule is wrong and there should be intent to kill, or at least intent to cause serious harm knowing there is a risk of death.

The two-category structure of murder or manslaughter is out-dated. The LC recommended a three-tier structure for homicide, which would cover

- 1st-degree murder
- 2nd-degree murder
- Manslaughter

These are explained further under 'involuntary manslaughter' below because they relate to all three types of homicide. Only the first of these would have a mandatory life sentence, the other two would have discretionary life i.e., up to a maximum of life at the judge's discretion.

The LC also wanted a new **Homicide Act** not only to deal with the partial defences but also to clarify the law. They said that a new Act should provide clear and comprehensive definitions of the homicide offences and the partial defences.

These recommendations have not been taken up, although the self-defence issue is now covered by the 'fear of serious violence' trigger for loss of control in the **Coroners and Justice Act**.

Voluntary manslaughter

Loss of control under the Coroners and Justice Act 2009

Diminished responsibility under s 2 Homicide Act 1957 (as amended by the Coroners and Justice Act 2009)

Loss of control s 54
- did D lose self-control?
- was the loss of self-control triggered by something specified in **s 55**?
- would a person of D's sex and age have reacted in the same way in D's circumstances?

Loss of control s 55(1) : triggers
- D's fear of serious violence from V against D or another identified person
- a thing or things done or said (or both) which:
  (a) constituted circumstances of an extremely grave character, and
  (b) caused D to have a justifiable sense of being seriously wronged
- **Excluded matters:**
  S 54(4) revenge
  S 55(6) sexual infidelity
  Inciting the violence or the things done or said for the purpose of using violence.

Diminished responsibility
- an abnormality of mental functioning
- which arises from a 'recognised medical condition'
- and substantially impaired D's ability to do one or more of
  (a) understand the nature of his conduct, or
  (b) form a rational judgement or
  (c) to exercise self-control
- and provides an explanation for D's acts and omissions:

Task 28

From which cases did the following principles come?

- That sexual infidelity may be relevant to the circumstances of D, even though excluded by s 55
- That an 'abnormality of mind' (now mental functioning) for diminished responsibility is one that reasonable people would term abnormal
- An abnormality caused by alcoholism may be accepted as diminished responsibility
- Impairment of responsibility need not be total but must be more than trivial
- Where there is evidence of intoxication as well as another cause of 'abnormality' the jury should ignore the intoxication

In its 2004 report 'Partial Defences to Murder' the Law Commission said

> "Over the centuries the law of homicide, including the law of murder, has developed in a higgledy-piggledy fashion. The present law is a product of judge made law supplemented by Parliament's sporadic intervention. The outcome is a body of law characterised by a lack of clarity and coherence."

The **Coroners and Justice Act** only addresses some of the problems seen in the report

Key criticisms of murder and the special defences

All these can be used in a discussion of whether justice is achieved. Although most suggest the law is not achieving justice, the first three suggest it has improved. Many also relate to fault as the defences indicate there is a lower level of fault, so D should not be guilty of murder but of manslaughter.

- The defence of provocation, now loss of control, has been improved by the Coroners and Justice Act, although some argue that it is still unclear. One improvement is that reacting in fear of serious violence is a stated to be qualifying trigger, thus clarifying this somewhat
- The removal of the need for a 'sudden and temporary' loss of control is an improvement. However, the fact that any loss of control must be shown goes against the Law Commission's proposals and prevents the defence clearly extending to cases of abuse against women, who may be physically weaker and liable to even greater abuse if they lose control and fight back
- The 'fear of serious violence' trigger addresses the 'all-or-nothing' nature of self-defence. If excessive force is used, there may now be a defence of loss of control
- Diminished responsibility is not a satisfactory alternative for abused women as it indicates they are mentally unbalanced
- Where there is evidence of intoxication as well as another cause of 'abnormality' the jury has to perform an almost impossible task of separating the one from the other – Dietschmann
- 'Abnormality of mental functioning' is difficult for the jury to understand and medical evidence is often complex and contradictory
- Diminished responsibility is sometimes dependent on whether the killing was morally wrong – Bailey/Sutcliffe
- Success may depend on which defence is raised in the first place. What was then provocation failed in the case of Cocker 1989, but diminished responsibility succeeded in Bailey 2002 in similar circumstances
- For diminished responsibility the burden of proof is on D
- There is an overlap between diminished responsibility and loss of control where the killing has been due to a mental state such as depression or long-term abuse – (Aluwahlia and Thornton)
- The difficulties of these defences for the jury could lead to inconsistency. Juries may differ in their decisions
- Should the mandatory life sentence for murder be abolished? If it was, then it could be argued that these defences would not be necessary. On the other hand, abolishing them and leaving the issue as one of sentencing would remove the role of the jury. It is arguably better for a jury to decide, for example, how a 'reasonable man' would act
- Should the LC's recommendations of a three-tiered system have been taken up? If it was, then again it could be argued that these defences would not be necessary

Task 29

Pick out a few of the criticisms which make sense to you. Add a few sentences to expand on each of the points you choose. Where possible, refer to cases to support your comments. You'll soon find you have a good base for an evaluation question.

Examination pointer

Remember what I said earlier: if a crime can be committed recklessly, there is no need to discuss intent. Also, don't start an answer with "D will be guilty (or not) of ….." You need to identify and apply the law in a logical manner to reach a conclusion as to whether D is guilty. Finally, always read the question carefully to see if a particular offence is mentioned, you should only discuss those offences which you are asked to discuss as you cannot get marks for irrelevant material.

Involuntary manslaughter

Gross negligence manslaughter

The **Adomako 1994** requirements as confirmed in **Misra 2004** are:

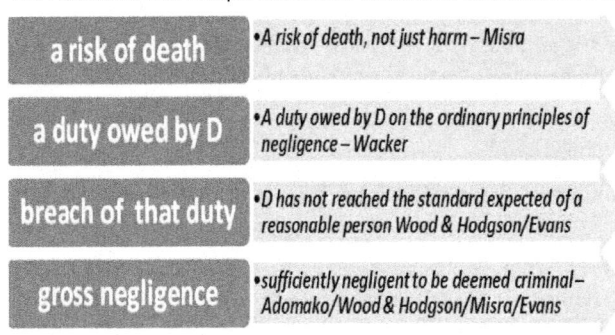

a risk of death	• A risk of death, not just harm – Misra
a duty owed by D	• A duty owed by D on the ordinary principles of negligence – Wacker
breach of that duty	• D has not reached the standard expected of a reasonable person Wood & Hodgson/Evans
gross negligence	• sufficiently negligent to be deemed criminal – Adomako/Wood & Hodgson/Misra/Evans

Constructive or unlawful act manslaughter

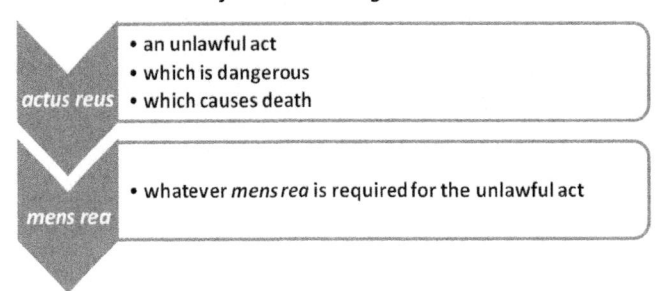

actus reus
- an unlawful act
- which is dangerous
- which causes death

mens rea
- whatever *mens rea* is required for the unlawful act

Key criticisms of unlawful act and gross negligence manslaughter

All these can be used in a discussion of whether justice is achieved and the problem with the *mens rea* for both these offences can be related to fault.

- unlawful act manslaughter covers a wide range of behaviour
- it is hard to find an unlawful act and/or causation in some of the decisions on unlawful act manslaughter
- the *mens rea* for unlawful act manslaughter may be for a quite different offence (see below*)

- whether the unlawful act is dangerous is an objective test, it can be argued that a subjective test should be used for such a serious offence
- identifying whether it is gross negligence or unlawful act manslaughter can be difficult, even for a judge – Willoughby 2004
- it is not fully clear what gross negligence amounts to

*As with murder, where the *actus reus* and *mens rea* do not match. This lack of correspondence is known as 'constructive liability'. Liability is constructed from the *actus reus* of one offence and the *mens rea* of another e.g., for unlawful act manslaughter also known as 'constructive' manslaughter liability is constructed from the *actus reus* of manslaughter and the *mens rea* of the unlawful act, which may be completely different and sometimes quite minor.

In general, the LC is against constructive liability and prefers to uphold the correspondence principle. As I said earlier, constructive liability relates to both fault and justice because D is liable for a crime where there is a lower level of fault than the crime suggests, which is not just. This is particularly true with unlawful act manslaughter as the *mens rea* may be for a minor offence like criminal damage, where the level of fault is low.

Proposals for reform

In its 2006 report 'Murder, manslaughter and Infanticide' the Law Commission proposed the three-tier system mentioned above. It is here in full as it applies to all three types of homicide.

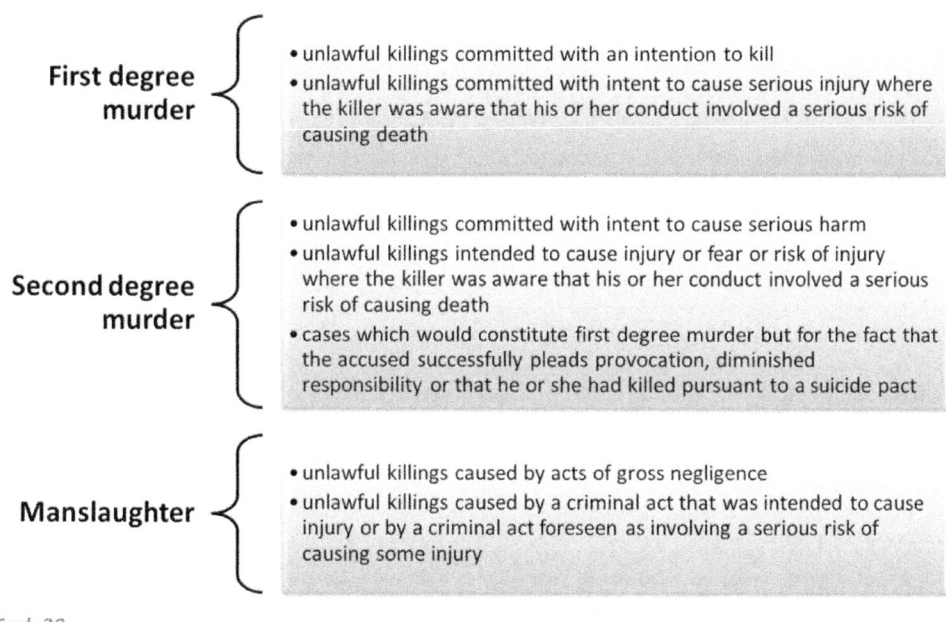

First degree murder
- unlawful killings committed with an intention to kill
- unlawful killings committed with intent to cause serious injury where the killer was aware that his or her conduct involved a serious risk of causing death

Second degree murder
- unlawful killings committed with intent to cause serious harm
- unlawful killings intended to cause injury or fear or risk of injury where the killer was aware that his or her conduct involved a serious risk of causing death
- cases which would constitute first degree murder but for the fact that the accused successfully pleads provocation, diminished responsibility or that he or she had killed pursuant to a suicide pact

Manslaughter
- unlawful killings caused by acts of gross negligence
- unlawful killings caused by a criminal act that was intended to cause injury or by a criminal act foreseen as involving a serious risk of causing some injury

Task 30

Pick out a few of the criticisms which make sense to you. Add a few sentences to expand on each of the points you choose. Where possible refer to cases to support your comments. Look also at what proposals for reform are currently being pursued by the Law Commission (www.lawcom.gov.uk). You'll soon find you have a good base for an evaluation question.

Examination pointer

If the scenario involves a death the charge will be murder or manslaughter. Which you need to discuss will depend on the facts. Murder rarely comes alone into a scenario so you often have to discuss both murder and some type of manslaughter or attempt. Look for clues so you can identify the appropriate charge. If there are no clues to a specific charge, just a death, consider whether a charge of murder may not lead to a conviction for murder for some reason (for example because intent or causation is hard to prove).

If there is intent to kill and D's act caused a death **the charge is murder**.

If there is intent to kill and D's act caused a death but there is evidence of loss of control or diminished responsibility **the charge is still murder**. If the defence succeeds the conviction is for manslaughter.

If there is intent to kill but D's act did not cause a death **the charge is attempted murder**, as in **White**.

If there is no intent to kill but D's act was unlawful and did cause a death **the charge is manslaughter** (constructive/ unlawful act).

If there is no intent to kill and no unlawful act consider whether a duty is owed. If so **the charge is manslaughter** (gross negligence).

Chapter 12 Theft

"... in a prosecution for theft it is unnecessary to prove that the taking is without the owner's consent ..." *Lord Steyn*

By the end of this Chapter, you should be able to:

- Explain both the *actus reus* and *mens rea* of theft
- Explain how the law applies in practice by reference to cases
- Identify possible criticisms for an evaluation of the law

As you can see from the quote, theft is wider than just taking something without permission. It is defined in the **Theft Act 1968 s 1(1)** which says a person is guilty of theft:

'*if he dishonestly appropriates property belonging to another with the intention of permanently depriving the other of it*'

The offence of theft comes under **s 1**. The following sections then explain each part of the *actus reus* and the *mens rea* in the definition. You will need to learn these too.

Task 31

There are 3 parts to the *actus reus* and 2 to the *mens rea*. Read the definition again and try to identify each of them before going on.

Examination pointer

Giving sections of **Acts** will enhance your answer. One way to remember them is to note that they are in order. **S 1** is the offence itself and then: 'dishonestly' **s 2**, 'appropriates' **s 3**, 'property' **s 4**, 'belonging to another' **s 5**, 'with the intention of permanently depriving the other of it' **s 6**. Subsection 1 of each of the sections explains each term.

So you could say "D may be charged with theft under s 1(1) of the Theft Act 1968. The actus reus is the appropriation of property belonging to another. It could be argued here that the items are not property. This is further defined under s 4(1) which states ...":

Section 1:
a person is guilty of theft if

he dishonestly appropriates property belonging to another with the intention of permanently depriving the other of it

Section 2	Section 3	Section 4	Section 5	Section 6
dishonestly	appropriates	property	belonging to another	with the intention of permanently depriving the other of it

Further subsections may then add to this.

We'll look at each part of the *actus reus* and then the *mens rea*. Did you spot which was which?

The actus reus is

- appropriates s 3 (conduct)
- property s 4 (circumstance)
- belonging to another s 5 (circumstance)

The mens rea is

- dishonesty – s 2
- with the intention of permanently depriving the other of it – s 6

Actus reus

Appropriation s 3(1)

This term covers many more types of conduct than 'take'. It is defined in **s 3** as

'any assumption by a person of the rights of an owner'

Assumption here means take over e.g., you 'assume' someone's identity if you pretend to be them. For theft, you assume someone's rights in property.

The best way to approach this is to consider what rights an owner has in the first place. If you own something, you have a right to do what you like with it. So you can use it, alter it, damage it, destroy it, lend it, sell it, give it away etc. If someone else does any of these things with it then they may well have *appropriated* it because they have 'assumed' your rights.

At one time, it was thought that you could not appropriate something if you had authorisation from the owner, i.e., consent. This caused problems – and much case law.

In **Lawrence 1971,** the HL held there could still be an appropriation even if the owner consented. They found a taxi driver guilty of theft after he took more money than the correct fare (about £7 instead of 55p) from a foreign student. The student had offered him his wallet after he said £1 wasn't enough. He argued it could not be theft because the student gave him the wallet. The House disagreed. The decision was not without its critics. There is an offence under **s 15** of the **Act** of 'obtaining property by deception' which would have covered this type of conduct. Why then, it has been argued, did the House need to interpret **s 3** so widely? The next case appeared to complicate matters further.

In **Morris 1984,** Ds switched labels on goods in a supermarket with intent to pay the lower price. The question was, had an appropriation taken place? The CA held that appropriation took place when D assumed *any* of the rights of the owner, so it occurred as soon as the goods were removed from the shelf with intent to pay the lower price. It could therefore be appropriation even before they switched labels. The HL's interpretation was narrower. Although Lord Roskill said that **s 3** meant interference with *any* of the rights of the owner, he later made clear that there must be 'an *adverse* interference' with those rights'. Thus appropriation only took place when D did something unauthorised, in this case, switching labels. In the case of someone swapping labels for a joke, Lord Roskill said that they would not, without more, have 'appropriated'.

Evaluation pointer

This seems to contradict **Lawrence**, which allowed for an appropriation even with the owner's consent or authorisation. In **Morris,** Lord Roskill said appropriation *wouldn't* occur if the owner had expressly or impliedly consented – and goods are removed from a supermarket shelf with the owner's consent. The House did not need to decide on the issue because both D's had done something 'adverse' by switching labels, the owner did not authorise label switching. The student consented in **Lawrence,** so which case do you think is to be preferred? Another matter for discussion is the difficulty for juries; the practical joker example shows how far appropriation (*actus reus*) and dishonesty (*mens rea*) are linked.

So, according to **Morris**, it can be theft even if you don't take anything. *Mens rea* may be harder to prove before D gets to the check out, but if, as in **Morris**, you intend to pay less than you should, then you intend permanently to deprive the owner of the difference in price. This is also likely to be seen as dishonest. The HL considered the matter again in the next case.

Key case

In **Gomez 1993**, D was the assistant manager of a shop. He was asked by an acquaintance to obtain some goods in exchange for two stolen cheques. Knowing that the cheques were stolen, D got the shop manager to authorise the sale of the goods to the acquaintance. The CA allowed his appeal against a conviction for theft because the manager had consented. Based on **Morris**, there was no appropriation and so no theft. The prosecution appealed to the HL. The appeal raised the question of whether – and how – the earlier two cases could be reconciled. The House decided to revert to **Lawrence.** They held that it was a clear decision that an act could be an appropriation even if done with consent. They declared **Morris** to be incorrect on this point. Lord Keith said that although a customer putting items into a shopping basket is not a thief, the customer has appropriated those items.

Principle: An appropriation can occur even if done with consent.

So has **Gomez** made the issue certain? Maybe not. In **Galasso 1993,** the same year, the CA seemed to view **Gomez** as not going as far as Lord Keith suggested. Later cases were not always consistent. A narrow interpretation of **Gomez** was seen in **Mazo 1996**. The CA accepted that an appropriation could take place with the owner's consent, but only if that consent had been induced by deception or fraud. In this case, although there was evidence that V did not have full mental capacity, it was held that a gift of a number of cheques she had made to D, her maid, was valid, there was insufficient evidence of any deception. There was therefore no appropriation and D's appeal against her conviction for theft succeeded. However, the next case shows a wider interpretation.

Key case

In **Hinks 1998**, the CA again held that appropriation did not depend on whether there was consent, and said that consent was only relevant to the issue of dishonesty. Here, a man of limited intelligence had been persuaded to give Mrs Hinks, who claimed to be his 'carer', £60,000 over a period of a few months. The CA upheld the conviction for theft. Her appeal was rejected by the HL. Lord Steyn made the point in the opening quote, confirming the *ratio decidendi* of **Lawrence**, and continuing that it went 'to the heart of' the present case. Thus, even a gift could amount to an appropriation. It should be noted that the HL decision was only a 3-2 majority and Lords Hutton and Hobhouse argued strongly that there was no appropriation.

Principle: In a prosecution for theft it is unnecessary to prove that the taking is without the owner's consent.

In **Briggs 2004**, the CA considered another case where V had been deceived into parting with money. The D was dealing with the purchase of a house on behalf of elderly relatives. The relatives gave authority for money for the purchase to be transferred to the seller's solicitor. They believed they were getting title to the property but in fact, title was transferred to D. Their consent to the transfer was therefore induced by fraud. D argued that property was not appropriated where, by fraud, an owner was induced into parting with it. The CA agreed. They noted that if there could be an appropriation in such cases there would be little need for many of the deception offences (these have since been repealed and replaced by the fraud offences, but they were very similar to theft in cases like this where someone has been deceived into parting with property or money).

Evaluation pointer

It can be argued that the interpretation of appropriation in **Gomez** and **Hinks** was too wide. As the CA pointed out in **Briggs**, it means that many of the deception offences would be redundant. It is unlikely that Parliament would have legislated on these if they had intended appropriation to include situations where V is deceived into parting with something. Maybe the minority argument in **Hinks** was correct. However, a case like **Mazo**, where there was not enough evidence of deception and no appropriation, would come under neither offence. A prosecution against **Briggs** would probably have succeeded had D been charged with one of the deception offences.

Hinks makes clear that consent is not relevant to appropriation, but is to dishonesty. Thus, the fact that V has consented may be relevant to whether D was dishonest. Otherwise, you could be guilty of theft of a genuine gift. Lord Keith intimated this in **Gomez** when he referred to Lord Roskill's joker in **Morris**. There may be appropriation in such cases, but if it isn't done dishonestly and with intent permanently to deprive then *mens rea* won't be proved.

Examination pointer

It follows from **Gomez** that where consent is obtained by deception the charge may be theft under s 1. As the matter is not fully clear, you may need to refer to, e.g., **Briggs** to support the alternative argument that there is no appropriation. Then go on to look at *mens rea*. Even if there is an appropriation, a prosecution may fail on this issue.

If you come by something innocently but then deal with it dishonestly this can be theft. As we saw, **s 3(1)** defines appropriation as being *'any assumption by a person of the rights of an owner'* it continues *'and this includes, where he has come by the property (innocently or not) without stealing it, any later assumption of a right to it by keeping or dealing with it as owner.'* This would apply if you picked up a mobile phone by mistake, but after getting home decided to keep it.

S 1(2) provides *"it is immaterial whether the appropriation is made with a view to gain or is made for the thief's own benefit"*. This means taking and destroying something is still appropriation. Taking something and giving it away would also come within this section.

Examination pointer

A problem question will usually involve one or two particular issue e.g., it may be arguable whether there is an 'appropriation' or whether the property 'belongs to another'. As I pointed out earlier, **s 1** defines theft. The other sections merely expand on each part of the definition. They aren't offences in themselves. So you should avoid statements like "D will be guilty of appropriation under **s 3**". All 5 elements have to be proved. If they are then D will be guilty of theft under **s 1**. If any one of them can't be proved, D is not guilty of theft. Take each part of the definition and apply these logically to the given facts and you should get your marks.

Task 32

You pick up a watch in a jeweller's intending to steal it. You see a shop assistant looking over at you and put it back. Are you guilty of theft? Think about this as you read this Chapter. We'll come back to it.

Property s 4(1)

Property includes,

> *"money and all other property, real or personal, including things in action and other intangible property"*

Real property relates to land; personal would be anything else. Tangible property is something you can touch like a book or a car. Intangible means things you can't touch such as the right to the balance in a bank account or the copyright on a song. These are called 'things in action' because they are rights which can only be enforced by a court action, e.g., by suing someone for stealing the lyrics of a song and making a record. The section goes on to say that (with a few exceptions) land can't normally be stolen. Just about everything else can be though.

In **Kelly 1998**, an artist was given access to the Royal College of Surgeons to draw specimens. He took some body parts and when accused of theft argued it was not 'property'. You can't own someone's body. The CA held it was theft and that parts of a body could come within **s 4** if they had been treated in some way e.g., by preserving them for medical purposes.

In **Marshall 1998,** Ds acquired underground tickets from travellers and then sold them. On appeal, they argued the tickets were not property belonging to another. The CA held that there was appropriation of property (the tickets themselves) belonging to London Underground (who 'owned' them).

In **Oxford v Moss 1978,** an examination paper was taken by a university student prior to the exam. This was not theft of the paper, as he intended to return it. Knowledge of what was on the paper was appropriated, but this was held not to be property.

So, you can steal most things including money and rights. However **s 4(3)** excludes wild plants (unless taken for "reward or sale or other commercial purpose") and **s 4(4)** excludes wild creatures (unless they have been tamed or kept in captivity).

Example

Whilst exercising his rights of access to open land under the **Countryside and Rights of Way Act 2000**, Chris picks some wild mushrooms and then sells them to the local restaurant. He also takes home a rabbit to show his kids. The first is theft because he has taken them for "reward or sale or other commercial purpose". The second isn't unless the rabbit had been someone's pet. In that case, it would also be theft.

Examination pointer

Watch for references to the subsections in a problem question. In my example above you would need to pick up on the fact that although **s 4(1)** includes most things, according to **s 4(3)** you can't normally steal wild plants. Then go on to say it may be 'property' in this case because selling them would be for "reward or sale or other commercial purpose" under **s 4(3)**. As regards the rabbit, this would not be theft if it is wild, but if 'tamed' it can be, **s 4(4)**. Don't worry too much if you can't remember the numbers of all the subsections though – no-one's perfect!

Belonging to another s 5(1)

This is also wide and is not confined to property actually owned by another, having possession or control of it can suffice. **S 5(1)** states,

> 'Property shall be regarded as belonging to any person having possession or control of it, or having in it any proprietary right or interest ...'

Example

You lend a coat to a friend, Sue, for the evening. Whilst she is dancing, someone takes it. They have appropriated property belonging to you, as you owned it. They have also appropriated property 'belonging to' Sue as she had possession at the time.

You can have control of property without knowing of its existence. Thus such property can be stolen. In **Woodman 1974**, the owner of a disused business premises sold a load of scrap metal. He didn't know the buyers had left some behind. D went onto the property and took some of the remaining scrap. He was convicted of theft. The owners of the premises no longer owned the metal, as they had sold it, but they did have 'control' of it.

There is a difference between something which is lost and something which is abandoned. The first belongs to someone so keeping it could be theft, the second does not so can't be.

Example

You have some old books which you don't want anymore. You leave them at college hoping someone may find them useful. You have abandoned them so they cannot then be stolen.

In **Hibbert & McKiernan 1948**, it was held that taking lost golf balls on a golf course was theft. They had been lost, not abandoned.

In **Rickets 2010**, the court considered whether goods left in bags outside a charity shop were 'property belonging to another'. D had argued that they had been abandoned and therefore did not constitute 'property belonging to another'. The court held that if goods were left outside a charity shop then it could be assumed that it was the owner's intention to donate them as a gift to the shop. Therefore, they were not abandoned, but remained the property of the person who had left them until taken in by the charity. Removing the goods before this time could therefore amount to theft. A second point arose as regards control. Some property was also taken from a bin outside another charity shop and the question again was whether it 'belonged to another' The court held that it did: the bin was in close proximity to the charity shop, it could therefore be inferred that the bin was under the control of the charity shop.

It is even possible to steal your own property if someone else has a right to it. **S 5** says *'having in it any proprietary right or interest ...'*. This is illustrated by **Turner 1971**, where a garage had a right to hold D's car until their bill was paid. Turner was thus guilty of theft when he took it back without paying the repair bill.

Examination pointer

Look out for situations where someone else has possession or control of the property, or where it is debateable whether something has been abandoned and be prepared to discuss these points. Note also that the definition is 'belonging to *another'*. It doesn't say you have to appropriate it from a *particular* person.

Obligation to deal with the property in a certain way

> **S 5(3)** provides, *'Where a person receives property from or on account of another, and is under an obligation to the other to retain and deal with that property or its proceeds in a particular way, the property or proceeds shall be regarded (as against him) as belonging to the other'.*

Example

Your mother gives you £20 and asks you to do the shopping tomorrow. You *received* property, the £20. You are *obliged* to *retain* it until tomorrow, and to *deal with* it by doing the shopping. You may have been given the £20, but under **s 5(3)** it *belongs* to your mother.

In **Davidge and Burnett 1984**, D was given money by her flatmates to pay bills. She spent it on Christmas presents. She was found guilty of theft as she had an obligation to deal with it in a certain way (pay the bills) and had not done so.

In **Hallam & Blackburn 1995**, investment advisers were convicted of theft when they did not invest sums entrusted to them. However, there must be an obligation to deal with it in a particular way and thus there was no conviction in **Hall 1973**. A travel agent paid deposits for flights into his firm's account and was later unable to repay the money. He was not guilty of theft as there had been no special arrangements for the deposits to be used in a particular way.

Property received by mistake

S 5(4) provides,

> *'Where a person gets property by another's mistake, and is under an obligation to make restoration (in whole or in part) of the property or its proceeds or of the value thereof, then to the extent of that obligation the property or proceeds shall be regarded (as against him) as belonging to the person entitled to restoration, and an intention not to make restoration shall be regarded accordingly as an intention to deprive that person of the property or proceeds'*

Put simply – and it needs to be – this means that if you are given something by mistake (and so have an obligation to give it back), keeping it can be theft. It would cover overpayments of wages as in **AG's Reference No 1 of 1983**, where D knew she'd been overpaid and simply left the money in her account. The same applies if you buy goods from a shop and are given too much change by mistake. Essentially the excess belongs to the shop so you are obliged to give it back. Keeping it is theft of that amount.

Task 33

Look at the following situations. Decide if the *actus reus* of theft has occurred and explain the significance of any particular sections in each case.

Sam gets home from college to find she has picked up the wrong coat by mistake. She decides to keep it.

Peter buys a book to read on his journey home and thinks it is such rubbish he leaves it on the train in disgust. Susan picks it up and takes it home.

Simon pays a local builder £100 to buy sand to build a patio. The builder buys himself a second-hand dishwasher instead.

Mary buys a CD and gives a £20 note. She is given change from a £50 note and keeps it.

Mens rea

The **Theft Act 1968 s 1(1)** says that a person is guilty of theft if,

'*he **dishonestly** appropriates property belonging to another with the **intention of permanently depriving the other** of it*'

You saw that 'appropriates' 'property' and 'belonging to another' relate to the *actus reus*. 'Dishonesty' and 'intention permanently to deprive' relate to *mens rea*. Every one of these elements must be proved, or the prosecution will fail.

In **Gomez 1993**, the distinction was made between an honest shopper and a thief. A person who takes an item off a supermarket shelf appropriates it. Only the fact that a shopper means to pay the right price stops them being a thief. This is because they are not being dishonest. They have no *mens rea*. In **Madely 1990**, Richard Madely was found not guilty of theft when he absentmindedly forgot to pay for some goods. The prosecution could not prove theft because he lacked *mens rea*.

Going back to the situation in Task 32, you may be found guilty of theft of the watch. The *actus reus* is the appropriation (by picking it up – **Gomez**) of property (the watch) belonging to another (the shop). You also have *mens rea*, you intended permanently to deprive the shop and your actions were dishonest. Let's look at these two issues now.

Dishonesty

The **Theft Act** does not define dishonesty but it does provide three specific situations where the person is *not* deemed dishonest:

S 2(1)(a) provides that a person's appropriation of property belonging to another is not to be regarded as dishonest if 'he appropriates the property **in the belief that he has in law the right to deprive the other of it**, on behalf of himself or a third person.'

S 2(1)(b) provides that it is not dishonest if a person 'appropriates the property **in the belief that he would have the other's consent** if the other knew of the appropriation and the circumstances of it'.

S 2(1)(c) provides that a person is not dishonest if 'he appropriates the property **in the belief that the person to whom the property belongs cannot be discovered** by taking reasonable steps'.

In each case it is D's belief that matters. The belief does not have to be reasonable, just *honestly held*. It is subjective, so it is *D's* belief that is important. However, D will need to persuade a jury that it was honestly held. The less reasonable it is, the harder it will be to convince a jury of this.

Example

You're having coffee with a friend. She goes to the loo leaving her coffee and her handbag on the table. You wait for a while, but need to leave to catch your bus. You drink her coffee and take £50 from her bag (some friend). Can you rely on **s 2(b)**? You'll need to convince a jury that you believe she would have consented in the circumstances. This may not be hard in relation to the coffee; after all, it was going cold. It will be a lot harder to convince the jury that you believed your friend would consent to taking the £50 though.

In **Small 1987**, D had taken a car which had been left for over a week with the keys in the ignition. Two issues arose. He argued it had been abandoned and so he believed he had a right to take it – **s**

2(1)(a). The CA quashed his conviction and made clear that the issue under **s 2** is whether a belief is *honestly* held, not whether it is reasonable. The second issue was not pursued, but if the car *was* abandoned then it did not 'belong to another'. Thus, there would be no *actus reus* and no need to look at dishonesty at all.

Example

You take a bicycle which belongs to a friend. You could argue under **s 2(1)(a)** that the friend owed you money so you believed you had a legal right to it. Alternatively you could argue under **s 2(1)(b)** that you believed the friend would have consented in the circumstances. Under **s 2(1)(c)** you could argue that you thought the friend had left the country and so couldn't be traced by taking reasonable steps.

In a case such as **Small s 2(1)(c)** it could also have been argued that the owner couldn't be traced by taking reasonable steps, though with a car it would be harder to convince a jury he honestly believed he couldn't trace the owner as cars must be registered.

Note that **s 2** relates to *mens rea* not *actus reus*. So a *belief* that you had a legal right to something is enough, even if you are wrong. Similarly if the other person doesn't consent but you believed they would this will suffice. Lastly, a *belief* you could not trace the owner by taking reasonable steps would be sufficient. You do not actually have to *take* reasonable steps to find the owner.

Examination pointer

Watch for the above points, especially for **(c)**. The issue is one of *mens rea* not *actus reus*. It is a common mistake in examinations for candidates to say that as no steps were taken D was dishonest, but it is D's belief that is important, not D's actions. Also note that if one of these three beliefs applies then that may show D is not dishonest. In all other cases the **Ghosh** test is needed (see next).

The Ghosh test

In addition to **s 2**, which merely shows when D is *not* dishonest, (and despite the opening quote) the courts have developed a test for dishonesty. It comes from the case of **Ghosh 1982**.

Key case

In **Ghosh**, a surgeon claimed fees for operations he had not performed. The question was whether the prosecution had proved that he had acted dishonestly. The CA laid down what is now known as the 'Ghosh test'.

Lord Lane said that the jury must determine whether "*according to the ordinary standards of reasonable and honest people what was done was dishonest. If it was not dishonest by those standards, that is the end of the matter and the prosecution fails. If it was dishonest by those standards then the jury must consider whether the defendant himself must have realised that what he was doing was by those standards dishonest*".

This means that there are two questions for the jury

- Was D's act dishonest by the ordinary standards of reasonable and honest people? If not, stop here, if so, ask the second question:
- Did D realise the act would be regarded as dishonest by such people?

If the jury can answer 'yes' to both parts D is dishonest.

As is often the case, it is a two-fold test with both a subjective and objective element. The first, 'objective' test, is what reasonable and honest people would have thought about D's actions. The jury will look at what D did and ask themselves whether they think that action was dishonest. The second, 'subjective' test, is what D believed reasonable and honest people would think. Here the jury will have to decide what *D* was thinking in relation to that action. This is harder.

Evaluation pointer

Does the **Ghosh** test make things clear for a jury? Is it too wide? In this sort of case, where D claims fees for operations he has not performed, the question is probably not a difficult one for the jury to answer. It may be harder where D's actions have some 'do-good' element. Might a jury decide on moral rather than legal grounds? Writers often refer to the 'Robin Hood' type scenario. If D (Robin) takes from the rich and gives to the poor the jury may not consider this conduct dishonest. The problem is that members of the jury will probably differ on what they regard as dishonest. This could result in different verdicts, depending on the composition of the jury. A jury with several people on it who believe in animal rights may not regard removing animals from a laboratory as dishonest, for example. The answer to the first question would therefore be 'no'. Whatever D thinks is then irrelevant because once the first is answered in the negative there is no need to consider the second question. Motive is not normally relevant in criminal law (except in sentencing) but it may matter to a jury.

Let's reverse the facts in the Robin Hood case. This time Robin steals from the poor and gives to the rich. Now would the jury think it dishonest? Quite likely. Morally this may be OK, but legally it means that the same facts can lead to a conviction or acquittal depending not only on motive, but also on who the victim is. Arguably, taking from one person should not be any different to taking from any other.

The CA noted the lack of clarity in the law and attempted to put it right in **Ghosh**. It is by no means certain that they have done so. The second part of the test is only partly subjective. It is what D (subjective) thinks ordinary people (objective) would regard as dishonest. It is hard for the jury to know what D thought reasonable people *would* regard as dishonest. D's own circumstances and upbringing would be reflected in the subjective part of the test. D may have some very odd ideas about what is regarded as dishonest. So, it isn't only a hard question for the jury to answer, the test is complicated in itself. However, for the moment we are stuck with it.

We saw earlier that **s 1(2)** provides *"it is immaterial whether the appropriation is made with a view to gain or is made for the thief's own benefit"*. This touches on dishonesty as well as appropriation. It means that the Robin Hood argument should fail even though Robin isn't gaining a benefit.

Added 2018: The **Ghosh** test was criticised by the SC in **Ivey v Genting Casinos 2017**. The court held that what D thought ordinary people would regard as dishonest was irrelevant. There were still two questions. The first question was to ascertain what D believed to be the facts. This belief must be genuinely held but need not be reasonable. The second question was whether D's conduct was dishonest by the standards of ordinary decent people, a purely objective question without the subjective element of the **Ghosh** test. The case involved a fairly complex trick by which D won a substantial sum at cards. He did not think what he had done was cheating, but the casino thought otherwise. Using the **Ghosh** test he would not be guilty as if he didn't think he was cheating he presumably did not think ordinary people would see his actions as dishonest. The SC noted that *"the capacity of all of us to persuade ourselves that what we do is excusable knows few bounds"*. The HC and CA had decided the issue under the civil law (breach of contract) so the ruling is not necessarily binding precedent, but as it was a SC case it is likely to be followed. The test suggested in **Ivey** is the test used in civil law and if followed it puts civil and criminal law on a par, which seems sensible.

Examination pointer

When discussing the *mens rea* of theft you may need to look at both **s 2** and **Ghosh**. Look for clues in the scenario set, e.g., any reference to being owed money should point you to **s 2(1)(a)**, taking from a friend or colleague to **s 2 (1)(b)**, something found to **s 2(1)(c)**. Reference to D's age or mental capacity requires you to discuss that it is what *D believes* that is important, not what is *reasonable*. If these don't apply, or may not succeed, then explain and apply the **Ghosh** test (but note **Ivey**).

Task 34

Look at the following situations. State which belief under **s 2(1)** you can argue and whether you think you'll convince the jury you honestly held that belief.

- You find a football in your garden and keep it
- You take some money from a friend's bag in an emergency
- You find a £2 coin in the street and keep it
- You find a handbag containing a wallet and credit cards in the street and keep it

Note that under **s 2(2)** the fact that you are willing to pay for the property does not mean you are acting honestly. At first glance, you may think it unfair to find D guilty of theft in such a case but compare the following two situations.

- D takes a bottle of milk from a neighbour's doorstep and leaves more than enough money to replace it
- D is a very rich employer and really likes a vintage car belonging to an employee. One day D takes the car and leaves double what it is worth

In the first situation, you may think it is unfair to find D guilty, but if it weren't for **s 2(2)** the employer wouldn't be guilty either. Anyone could take anything they wanted as long as they could pay for it. Also in the first case D could use the **s 2(1)(b)** defence.

Summary of Dishonesty

- Does s 2(1)(a) apply? Belief in a right to the property
- Does s 2(1)(b) apply? Belief in consent
- Does s 2(1)(c) apply? Belief that the owner can't be found
- If the answer is 'Yes', D is not dishonest
- If the answer is 'No', apply the Ghosh test

Intention permanently to deprive

S 6(1) provides that this will exist where D's *'intention is to treat the property as his own to dispose of regardless of the other's rights'*.

In **Raphael and another 2008**, D had taken the victim's car by force (robbery) and had then demanded payment for it to be returned. The CA noted that **s 6(1)** included an intention to 'treat the thing as his own to dispose of regardless of the other's rights' and said *"it is hard to find a better example of such an intention"* than an offer to return the property to the owner in return for a sum of money. The return of the property was subject to a condition that was inconsistent with the rights of the owner, i.e., the demand for payment.

It will also exist where property is borrowed *'for a period and in circumstances making it equivalent to an outright taking or disposal'*. This means it is not usually theft if you mean to return the item. This would apply to borrowing but could be different if you have used it and so reduced its value.

Example

You borrow a month's season ticket intending to return it later. You use it for three weeks and are charged with theft. You can argue that you had no intention permanently to deprive the owner of it. This argument is likely to fail. The use of it for this period will make it 'equivalent to an outright taking' and so come within **s 6**.

In **Lloyd 1985,** D borrowed some films from the cinema where he worked and copied them. The CA held **s 6** would apply if D used something so that "all the goodness or virtue is gone". On the facts this was not the case so there was no liability. This narrow interpretation of **s 6** has been seen as rather too generous to D and later cases have shown a significant widening of it.

In **Velumyl 1989,** D took money from his employer's safe intending to return it. The CA held that this was sufficient, as he had treated the money as his own. It was also made clear that as he would be unable to replace the exact notes taken he had intended to deprive the owner of those notes. D's best hope in a case like this is to convince the jury that the intention to put them back showed the conduct was not dishonest.

The broader approach is seen again in **Lavender 1994** and **Marshall 1998.**

In **Lavender**, D took some doors from his flat which belonged to the council. He hung them in his girlfriend's flat which belonged to the same council. Arguably, he hadn't intended permanently to deprive the council of the doors as he merely moved them around. The court held D had treated the doors as his own to dispose of regardless of the other's rights.

In **Marshall**, the CA held that acquiring underground tickets from travellers and then selling them was within the scope of **s 6**. The Ds had treated the tickets as their own to dispose of regardless of London Underground's rights.

Evaluation pointer

It can be argued that the **Lloyd** approach is too narrow but the wider approach in these later cases can also be criticised. It means that D is liable even where there does not appear to be any intent permanently to deprive.

Another case which illustrates **s 6** is **Cahill 1993**. Very early one morning D took a pile of newspapers from a newsagent's doorstep on his way home. He was very drunk at the time and couldn't fully explain what he intended to do with them. His conviction was quashed because the judge's direction to the jury only went as far as *'to treat the property as his own'* and did not add *'to dispose of regardless of the other's rights'*. Had the direction been given correctly he may have been found to have *mens rea*. Much would depend on where he dumped them, close by or not. The newspapers would be worthless after the end of the day. If they didn't find their way back to the shop then 'all the goodness or virtue' would be gone.

Examination pointer

If given a scenario like **Velumyl**, you could argue that D may not be dishonest under **s 2**. Suggest D may have believed that the owner would have consented (perhaps borrowing from the employer had been allowed before). Or D believed they had a right to it (perhaps they were owed wages). Alternatively rely on the **Ghosh** test. The jury may consider that by intending to return the money, D was not dishonest by ordinary standards.

A final point:

In **Small 1987**, D had taken a car. It may be hard to prove intention permanently to deprive in such a case because a car is easily traceable. (It was for this reason that a separate offence of taking without consent was later added to the **Theft Act.**) You should look for clues in the scenario as to the type of property that has been taken.

Task 35

Consider the following situations and decide if **s 6** is satisfied:

- Dave takes Steve's tickets for that night's pop concert and returns them the next day.
- Frank takes £10 from his mother's purse and puts it in his pocket. His sister sees him and says she will tell if he doesn't return it. He puts it back.

- Ellie borrows a book from a friend and reads it. She then throws it away.

Recap

Let's look back at the Task where you took a watch and put it back.

You appropriated (by picking it up) property (the watch) belonging to another (the shop). You have the *actus reus* for theft. Do you have *mens rea*? It may be difficult to find evidence but you know you acted dishonestly. You know 'ordinary reasonable people' would regard the fact that you only put it back because someone was watching as dishonest. You can argue that you didn't keep it so haven't permanently deprived anyone. This actually doesn't matter. It is *intent* to do so that makes it theft. Intent relates to *mens rea* (what you think) not *actus reus* (your actual conduct). Again, it will be hard to prove, but yes, technically you have committed theft. As has Frank in the above task, although he may be able to argue under **s 2(1)(b)**, that he believed his mother would have consented in the circumstances.

Summary

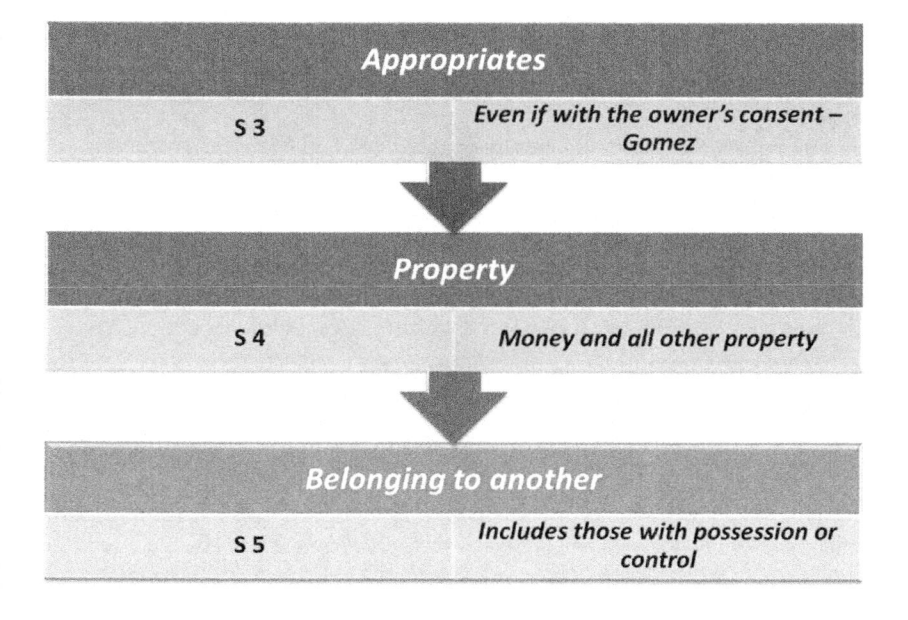

	Appropriates
S 3	Even if with the owner's consent – Gomez

	Property
S 4	Money and all other property

	Belonging to another
S 5	Includes those with possession or control

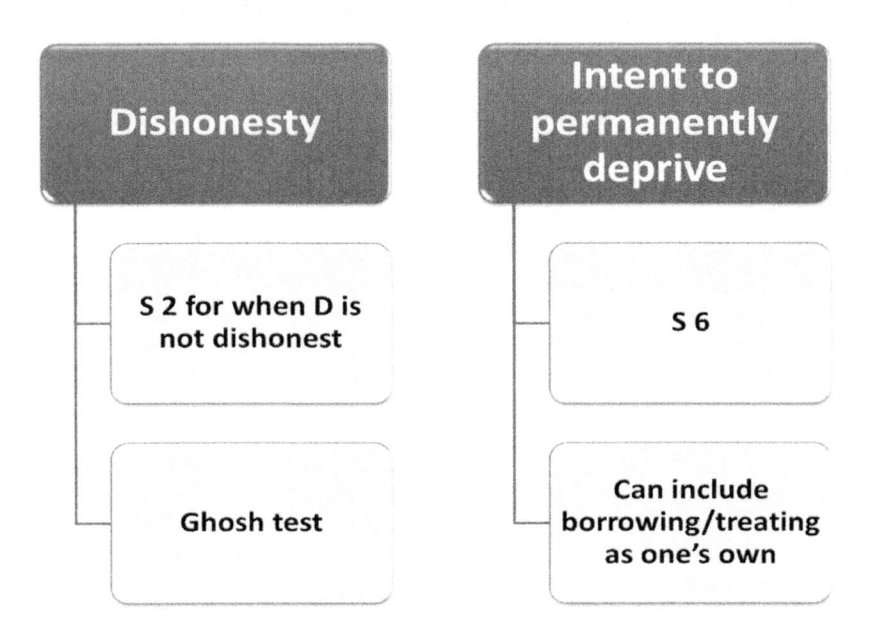

```
┌─────────────────┐           ┌─────────────────┐
│                 │           │   Intent to     │
│   Dishonesty    │           │  permanently    │
│                 │           │    deprive      │
└────────┬────────┘           └────────┬────────┘
         │                             │
         ├──┬──────────────────┐       ├──┬──────────┐
         │  │ S 2 for when D is│       │  │   S 6    │
         │  │  not dishonest   │       │  │          │
         │  └──────────────────┘       │  └──────────┘
         │                             │
         │  ┌──────────────────┐       │  ┌──────────────────┐
         │  │                  │       │  │   Can include    │
         └──│   Ghosh test     │       └──│ borrowing/treating│
            │                  │          │   as one's own   │
            └──────────────────┘          └──────────────────┘
```

Links to the non-substantive law

ELS: For links to the English legal system, look back at the diagram and examples in the introduction to Part 1. Theft is an either-way offence so can be heard in either the magistrates' court or the Crown Court. The jury plays an important role in theft as it must decide whether D's act was dishonest by the ordinary standards of reasonable and honest people. There may be an advantage to having a jury hear the case, especially if there was a good reason for the theft (as in the Robin Hood example). However, one disadvantage is that as discussed above, the **Ghosh** test has proved problematic for juries to understand.

The nature of law: The role of law is to protect property as well as people, so a person who has taken something from another should be punished. However, a balance may need to be considered where there is a reason for the theft. **S 2** of the **Theft Act** addresses this by providing for three situations where D will not be found dishonest and so will not be guilty of theft even though appropriating another's property. This tips the balance in D's favour where there is an honest belief that the property could be taken for one of the three reasons (and thus a lower level of fault). In most cases this is fair, but the owner of the property may not think that it achieves justice. Another role of the law is to protect those who may be vulnerable, so it is important that the law has decided that there must be real consent before D can argue an appropriation was by consent. The decision in **Hinks**, following **Lawrence**, achieved justice and protected a man of limited intelligence in the first and a person with limited language skills in the other, and of course the law provided protection for the future for other vulnerable people that may be persuaded to consent to the appropriation. The only problem with this is the slight inconsistency in the case law. This lack of clarity means justice is hard to achieve. Another point on the role of law in protecting people is that it is fair that a person cannot avoid a conviction for theft by making a payment for the property. This is explained above in my example of the employer taking the vintage car. If the case goes to the Crown Court and is heard by a jury morality may come into the decision. If D had good reason for the theft, for example, stealing food for the starving, members of the jury may see it as morally justified and be reluctant to convict.

Self-test questions

1. When can wild plants or animals be classed as property?
2. Did **Gomez** follow **Morris or Lawrence** on the issue of consent?
3. What was appropriated in **Hinks**?
4. What are the 3 statutory beliefs in **s 2**?
5. Do these beliefs have to be reasonable?
6. When can borrowing amount to intent permanently to deprive?
7. Can you state all the section numbers dealing with each part of the actus reus and mens rea?

Answers to tasks and self-test questions are on my website at www.drsr.org/publications/tasks. For some interactive exercises, click on 'Free Exercises'.

Chapter 13 Robbery

"What is a robbery, ladies and gentlemen? Well, in very crude terms, it is a theft that has been carried out through violence." **R v West 1999**

By the end of this Chapter, you should be able to:

- **Explain the *actus reus* and *mens rea* of theft and what turns it into robbery**
- **Explain how the law applies in practice by reference to cases**
- **Identify possible criticisms for an evaluation of the law**

Robbery is essentially a type of aggravated theft. **S 8** of the **Theft Act 1968** makes it a more serious offence if D uses force (or the threat of force) in order to steal. **S (8)(1)** provides:

"A person is guilty of robbery if he steals, and immediately before or at the time of doing so, and in order to do so, he uses force on any person or puts or seeks to put any person in fear of being then and there subjected to force".

It is an indictable offence and carries a maximum life sentence.

Let's look at each part of this offence to clarify what is needed. It's easier than it might look.

Actus reus

There are several parts to this.

- steals
- immediately before or at the time of doing so
- in order to do so
- uses force on any person or puts or seeks to put any person in fear

Steals

Robbery involves a theft PLUS the force element. It is therefore necessary to prove all the *actus reus* and *mens rea* elements for theft before considering whether there may be a robbery. An example we looked at with theft is **Raphael and another 2008**. D had appropriated property (the car) which belonged to another (the owner). He had acted dishonestly and intended permanently to deprive the owner of it (by treating it as his own regardless of the other's rights). He had therefore committed theft. When he took the car, he had hit the man with an iron bar. This turned the theft into robbery.

As you have to prove theft, it follows that you can also use the defences to theft. This means that the **s 2(1)** defences will apply here too. Thus in **Robinson 1977** D threatened V with a knife in order to get money he was owed. He believed he had a legal right to the money (even though he knew he had no right to use a knife to get it) so had a defence under **s 2(1)**. If there is no theft then there can be no robbery.

Task 36

Look back at the *actus reus* and *mens rea* of theft. Be sure you can explain:

Appropriation – property – belonging to another

Dishonesty – intention permanently to deprive

If all these can be proved *and* there is the additional element of force, it may be a robbery.

Immediately before or at the time of doing so

The use (or threat) of force must be before or during the theft. This seems to suggest that the use of force once the appropriation has taken place would not be enough to make it robbery. This is not interpreted too strictly by the courts.

Key case

In **Hale 1979,** the Ds entered the victim's house and one went upstairs and stole some items from a jewellery box. The other was downstairs tying up V. The CA declined to quash their convictions for robbery even though the appropriation may have already taken place. The appropriation was seen as a continuing act. Therefore, it was open to the jury to conclude that it continued whilst the victim was tied up.

Principle: An appropriation may be a continuing act.

In **Lockley 1995**, the court confirmed the point in **Hale 1979** that appropriation was a continuing act. Force on a shopkeeper *after* the D's took some beer could amount to robbery. Remember **Fagan** and continuing acts? No? Then have a look at Chapter 1 again.

Examination pointer

A common mistake is for candidates to go straight on to the robbery issues, but you need a theft to have occurred, so if you see a potential case of robbery in an exam question take it step by step. Firstly, consider whether there is appropriation of property belonging to another. Then consider whether it was dishonestly appropriated with the intention of permanently depriving someone of it. If so, you have theft. Go on to consider if there are any additional elements which may turn the theft into an offence of robbery, as in **Raphael**.

In order to do so

So we can see that the appropriation may continue whilst D is removing the goods from the premises. If force is used, or threatened, this may amount to robbery. However, the force or the threat of force must be 'in order to' steal. This means it must be applied with the purpose of facilitating the theft. If the jury is satisfied that D stole something, yet the force or threat of it was not applied in order to steal, they cannot convict under **s 8(1)**. Using force to get away is not 'in order to steal'. It may be theft, but not robbery.

Uses force on any person or puts or seeks to put any person in fear

The word force is not separately defined in the Act. In **Dawson and James 1978**, the CA said that since it was an ordinary word it was for the jury to determine its meaning. In **West 1999**, the judge made the comment in the opening quote. He then continued, "*What does that mean? What it means, ladies and gentlemen, is; if you are in the supermarket and someone puts their hand into your basket and takes your purse out, a pickpocket, that is theft. It has been stolen from you. If you are outside in the street, and you are approached by someone who held a knife at your throat and then took your purse out of your bag, you will have been robbed, because immediately before or during the course of the theft, you were subject to violence or a threat of violence.*" The indication here is that violence is needed, as was the case in **Raphael and another 2008**. However, it is clear from several cases that the use of force can be small. Snatching a bag from someone's grasp was held to be robbery in **Corcoran v Anderton 1980**. Similarly, in **Clouden 1987**, wrenching a shopping basket from someone's grasp amounted to robbery. It will be a matter for the jury and there may be quite a fine line between what amounts to sufficient force and what does not. Snatching a bag (**Corcoran**) or a shopping basket (**Clouden**) from someone's grasp sufficed, but snatching a cigarette from someone's grasp did not qualify as enough force (see below).

Snatching a cigarette from someone's grasp did not qualify as enough force in **P v DPP 2012** because there was no physical contact. Although this does not seem so different from snatching a handbag or shopping basket it can be said that less force would be needed to snatch a cigarette than a bag.

A second point arose in **Corcoran**. The two D's had tried to take the handbag by force. It fell from one D's hands and they ran off without it. The court held that the theft was complete when D snatched the handbag from her grasp. This means that a robbery can occur without anything being taken. This isn't as daft as it seems. You can commit theft without taking something. In **Gomez 1993**, it was said that taking something from a supermarket shelf was appropriation. If done dishonestly it could be theft even though you haven't left the shop, if done with force it can be robbery.

Example

You are in a shop. You put an item in your pocket intending to avoid paying for it. You have appropriated property belonging to the shopkeeper. This would be seen as dishonest in the eyes of 'ordinary' people. You would also be intending permanently to deprive the owner of it. This is theft. If you threaten another shopper to "keep quiet or else" when you take it, then you have used the threat of force in order to steal. This is robbery. In both cases, the crime has been committed even if you drop the item in your hurry to get away

Note that the force or threat can be on 'any person'. As in my example, it need not be on the victim of the theft. If you wanted to gain entrance to a casino at night to steal the profits, then knocking out a security guard would suffice. So might tying up and blindfolding someone whose house overlooks the casino. This would depend on why you did it. If it was to prevent them seeing you and raising the alarm it would be robbery. If it was just to prevent them seeing you and pointing you out at a later date it would not. The difference is that in the first case it is *in order to* steal (without being stopped because the alarm has been raised). In the second it is just to avoid being recognised and doesn't help with the theft.

Task 37

Look back at theft to remind yourself of all the parts to the *actus reus* and *mens rea*. Apply these to **Clouden**. You should end up by establishing theft. Keep your workings; we'll come back to this.

Evaluation pointer

The use of force can be really minor yet the maximum sentence for robbery is life imprisonment. Consider whether this is just. Prior to the Act, the Criminal Law Revision Committee had said that snatching a bag from an unresisting owner would not suffice. **Corcoran** and **Clouden** show that the courts have interpreted the requirement for force very widely. If a person tries to prevent D from taking a bag and there is a struggle then robbery appears an appropriate charge. If, however, there is no resistance then theft would seem to cover it.

Being then and there subjected to force

This means that it must be a threat of immediate force. As with the 'immediately before or at the time' element there is no set time limit. It will be a matter for the jury to decide based on all the circumstances. If the force is used just before or just after (**Hale**) then it may be robbery. However, if D threatens force in a week's time if the security guard doesn't look the other way tonight, it is unlikely to be robbery.

In **R v DPP; B v DPP 2007**, some boys pushed another boy around and took his mobile phone and other items. They were charged with robbery under **s 8**. V said he had not felt particularly scared and the D's argued that as he was not frightened there was no robbery. The court interpreted the Act and held that it was the intention of D rather than the fortitude of V that was important. If this were not the case, guilt would be dependent on how brave, or not, the victim was. This was not what Parliament would have intended and not what the **Act** implied. They had intended to scare him and some force had been used so their convictions were upheld.

Mens rea

Firstly, because robbery requires that a theft took place, the prosecution will need to prove the *mens rea* for the theft. This is dishonesty and intention permanently to deprive. We also saw above that this means D can use the **s 2** arguments to show lack of *mens rea* in relation to dishonesty. In **Robinson 1977**, D had a defence under **s 2(1)** because he believed he had a legal right to the money.

As regards the *mens rea* for the robbery itself, the **Act** is not clear and there is no case authority. It is most likely to be intention as to the use or threat of force. Robbery requires force 'in order to' steal and recklessly using force would probably not meet this requirement. Thus, in an examination scenario, it is best to say that the force or threat of it must be intentional.

Task 38

Find the notes you made in the last task on **Clouden**. Now add the additional *actus reus* and *mens rea* for robbery. OK? Now you should be able to tackle an exam question on robbery.

Examination pointer

You may have a scenario which appears to be a robbery because there is evidence of force. Go through all the elements of theft and then **s 8**. If you then fail to prove robbery on one of the above issues say that although D is unlikely to be convicted of robbery a theft conviction would be possible. The overlap between theft and robbery means you often need to discuss both, so read the question carefully and look for clues as to *how* the theft happens; if force is used then it may make it robbery.

Summary

actus reus
- steals
- uses force
- or puts someone in fear
- immediately before or at the time

mens rea
- as for theft
- dishonesty
- intent to permanently deprive
- s 2 defences may apply

The final part of the *mens rea*, applicable to robbery but not theft, is intention as to the use of force.

Links to the non-substantive law

ELS: For links to the English legal system, look back at the diagram and examples in the introduction to Part 1. Also look at the last Chapter as robbery requires a theft to have occurred so the same issues apply. The difference is that robbery is seen as much more serious, so even though it could just involve the snatching of a bag, it is an indictable offence, so triable only in the Crown Court, with a maximum sentence of life imprisonment. The **s 8** of the **Theft Act** has been interpreted quite widely in respect of the force being 'immediate' and 'in order to steal'. Had the literal rule been used in **Hale** or **Lockley** they would not have been guilty as the theft had already been committed.

The nature of law: The matters mentioned in the theft Chapters will also apply to robbery, as a theft is needed first. In addition, the role of law is to punish those at fault and for robbery there is a higher degree of fault seen in the intentional use or threat of force. The maximum sentence for robbery is therefore higher than for theft, up to a possible life sentence. On this point, it is arguable that the use of force should be greater than that seen in **Corcoran** and **Clouden** because of the possibility of a life sentence. It seems unjust to have that possibility when the force is really minor. Finally, we saw in relation to theft that D's interest is protected by **s 2** but that the victim may not feel justice is achieved. This is even more the case with robbery, as V will have been subjected to force, or at least the threat of it, but **s 2** still applies, as in **Robinson**.

Self-test questions

1. *What turns theft into robbery?*
2. *What are the five elements to theft?*
3. *How was appropriation treated in **Hale**?*
4. *What amounted to force in **Corcoran**?*
5. *What is the mens rea for robbery?*

Answers to tasks and self-test questions are on my website at www.drsr.org/publications/tasks. For some interactive exercises, click on 'Free Exercises'.

Chapter 14 Attempts

"... a person may be guilty of attempting to commit an offence to which this section applies even though the facts are such that the commission of the offence is impossible" **Criminal Attempts Act 1981 s 1(2)**

By the end of this Chapter, you should be able to:

- Explain the actus reus of attempt
- Explain the mens rea of attempt
- Explain how the law applies in practice by reference to cases
- Identify possible criticisms for an evaluation of the law

What is an attempt?

It is defined in the **Criminal Attempts Act 1981 (CAA) s 1(1)** which provides:

> *"If with intent to commit an offence to which this section applies, a person does an act which is more than merely preparatory to the commission of the offence, he is guilty of attempting to commit the offence"*

The *actus reus* is that D 'does an act which is more than merely preparatory'. The *mens rea* is 'intent to commit an offence'.

Example

In **Holt and Lee 1981**, two people in a restaurant made a plan to avoid paying for their meal by telling the waiter they had already paid another member of staff. They were overheard discussing this plan by an off duty policeman. They were charged with attempt (at inducing the restaurant to forgo payment). They had gone far enough with their plan to be seen as doing *an act which is more than merely preparatory* and they *intended* to induce the restaurant to forgo payment.

Actus reus: *more than merely preparatory*

Cases based on the common law before the Act was passed had produced various tests for attempt. Most of these required a very close proximity to the actual crime: D must have reached the point of no return, i.e., had done all but the last act of committing the main offence. Another test was based on a series of acts, where D did several things which taken together created liability. Many convictions failed because D was not sufficiently close to committing the crime. The Law Commission felt that there was no 'magic formula' and the test in **s 1** is based on its proposals. The **CAA** requires that an act is 'more than merely preparatory'. This is a matter for the jury. Although the requirement under the **CAA** seems wider (more than merely preparatory can come a lot sooner than a last act) it is still not always easy to know where to draw the line. If D shoots someone and leaves them for dead, but they survive, then D can be charged with attempted murder without any problem. In **White 1910** (see Chapter 2), D gave his mother poison but she died before it took effect. He had not caused her death so the murder charge failed. He was found guilty of attempted murder. Difficulties arise where it is not so clear cut. In **Gullefer 1987**, D had put a bet on a dog race and, seeing that his dog was clearly going to lose, jumped on to the track to try and stop the race. He would then have got his stake back. A charge of attempted theft failed because D had done no more than prepare to get his money back. He had not started on the act of stealing, which would have entailed going to the bookmaker and obtaining a refund. In **Campbell 1991**, a conviction of attempted robbery was overturned on appeal on the basis that D's act was no more than preparatory. He was arrested within a yard of a post office carrying a fake gun. He said he had intended to rob it but had changed his mind and was walking away.

A controversial case on this issue is **Geddes 1996**. D was found in a boys' toilet in a school. He then ran off when challenged by a teacher. He left behind a bag containing a large knife, a roll of tape and rope. He was convicted of attempted false imprisonment but this was again overturned on appeal. He had *mens rea* but insufficient *actus reus* because he had not at the time approached any victim.

A case more in line with the later test of 'more than merely preparatory' is **AG's Reference (No 1 of 1992) 1993**. D had dragged a girl into a shed and tried to rape her but could not get an erection. He was found guilty of attempted rape. In **Boyle and Boyle 1987**, the D's were found by a door with a broken lock and hinge and were found guilty of attempted burglary.

Evaluation pointer

It can be said that this offence causes problems for the police. If they arrest D too early the charge will fail. However, if they wait until the act is clearly 'more than merely preparatory', they could be putting people in danger, which was one of the problems with the old law. Take **Campbell**, for example. Should the police have waited until he entered the post office? If the gun had been real, they would have been risking people's lives. This will often be a difficult operational decision to make. The same can be said with **Geddes**. There was held to be no attempt because he had not approached any victim but there was clear evidence of his intentions and if he had not been challenged by the teacher, someone might have been abducted.

Other examples

Some cases since **Geddes** have found the act more than 'merely preparatory' even though D was still in the early stages of committing the crime (arguably more so than in **Geddes**). In **Tosti 1997**, D was examining a padlock on a barn door while deciding whether he could break in and this was enough for attempted burglary. In **Toothill 1998**, D knocked on a woman's door intending to commit rape and this was enough for attempted burglary (at that time rape was one of the ways to commit burglary, though this is no longer the case).

Task 39

What effect does the issue of causation have as regards whether there is a crime or an attempted crime? Give a case example.

Attempts to do the impossible

The Act states in **s 1(2)** that a person may be guilty of attempting to commit an offence: *"even though the facts are such that the commission of the offence is impossible"*.

The Act seems clear, but in **Anderton v Ryan 1985**, the HL seemed to prefer to follow the earlier common law which was that there was no liability if a crime was physically or legally impossible. D had bought what she *believed* to be a stolen video recorder. It wasn't, in fact, stolen but she was charged with the attempted handling of stolen goods. The CA reversed the decision of the magistrates to acquit, and allowed the prosecution's appeal. The HL reversed that decision and the conviction was quashed. This meant that, despite the wording of the Act, impossibility could be a defence. This state of affairs did not last long. The HL accepted that it had made a wrong decision and in **Shivpuri 1987**, it used the *1966 Practice Statement* to overrule its own earlier decision. In **Shivpuri**, D had brought a substance into the UK believing it to be heroin. It turned out to be a harmless vegetable matter. He was convicted of attempting to deal in prohibited drugs and the HL upheld the conviction. Also in **Jones 2007**, D was convicted of attempting to incite an underage girl to have sex with him, even though the 'girl' was actually an adult policewoman who had responded to his advertisement for young girls to have sex with him in return for payment. Several texts were exchanged and eventually a meeting was arranged and he was arrested. He had argued that the offence was impossible as the girl did not exist; it was an adult he had incited. The CA followed **Shivpuri** and rejected his appeal against conviction.

Impossibility therefore no longer seemed to be a defence to an attempt to commit a crime. However, in **Pace and Rogers 2014**, the CA held that the *mens rea* for attempt was intent to commit the main offence. This meant 'all the elements' of the offence. In this case, the police had mounted an operation with the idea of clamping down on the sale and disposal of stolen scrap metal. They offered some goods to scrap metal dealers indicating the goods were 'a bit naughty'. The appellants purchased the goods and were subsequently charged and convicted of attempting to convert criminal (stolen) property. In allowing their appeal the CA said that the principal offence was only committed where the property really was criminal property. Here it was actually the property of the police and not stolen. This meant they could not be guilty of attempt because there was no intent to convert criminal property, so no *mens rea*.

Evaluation pointer

The CA recognised in **Pace and Rogers** that the decision could have significant effects on later cases and that the courts "do not always reveal a consistency in approach". This shows that the **Criminal Attempts Act** has not sufficiently clarified the law on this area, which goes against the idea of justice, which demands clarity.

Examination pointer

Look for clues in a problem scenario, particularly as to whether the main crime takes place. If D tries to commit an offence but fails, there may be an attempt. D can be convicted of the preliminary crime even if the main offence never occurs. Note that attempt can come into a question with one of the other crimes. Thus, you should discuss attempted murder if D tries to kill someone but fails, or attempted theft if the *actus reus* of theft cannot be proved. In these cases, you should use the **Criminal Attempts Act** once you have established that the main crime has not been proved.

Mens rea

The Act says "with intent to commit an offence" so the *mens rea* is intent and nothing less. Intent was defined in **Mohan 1975** as a decision to bring about the prohibited consequence no matter whether the accused desired that consequence or not.

Intention is required for attempt even if recklessness would be enough for the principal offence. This was confirmed in **Millard & Vernon 1987**, where some football fans had been convicted of attempted criminal damage. The CA allowed their appeal on the basis that even though recklessness was enough for criminal damage, it was not enough for an attempt to commit this offence. *Mens rea* is therefore more limited in an attempt than in the main offence. In **Whybrow 1951**, it was held that for attempted murder intent to kill is required, even though intent seriously to injure is sufficient *mens rea* for murder itself.

In **Pace and Rogers**, the CA again made clear that the *mens rea* was intent and that a suspicion (that the goods were stolen) was not enough. It also made clear that it must be intent to commit *all* the elements of the main offence.

One other point on *mens rea* and impossibility is that it will not be attempt if D intends to carry out an offence only in certain conditions, which then do not exist. An example of a 'conditional attempt' is where D intends to steal something but it is not there. D will not be guilty of attempted theft even though there was intent to steal.

Finally, note the overlap between offences, e.g., between **s 18** and attempted murder. It is sometimes a matter of chance that V did not die, for example, due to prompt medical treatment. In **R v Z 2017** (unreported), a Year 10 schoolgirl thought a school friend had been involved in some online bullying she had suffered. Telling her that she had a present for her she arranged a meeting, and while the girl shut her eyes and waited for the present Z stabbed her. Fortunately, the girl sensed something was wrong and opened her eyes, therefore managing to avoid a fatal wound. The knife went through her school blazer and shirt but only a short way into her body. Although not a deep cut there was a wound and Z intended at least serious harm, so it could certainly be **s 18**. The girl had only survived because she jumped back. The jury found that Z had intended to kill the girl, so she was convicted of attempted murder.

Examination pointer

R v Z is an example of the overlap between **s 18** and attempted murder. However, for attempt you need the *mens rea* of intent to kill. Although intent seriously to injure is enough for both murder and **s 18**, it is not enough for attempted murder. In **R v Z** the jury found there was intent to kill but if there had only been intent seriously to injure the conviction would have been for **s 18**, wounding with intent.

Summary

- *Actus reus* is an act which is more than merely preparatory
- Impossibility is no longer a defence to an attempt – Shivpuri/Jones
- Although there must be intent to complete all the elements of the main offence – Pace and Rogers
- *Mens rea* is intent to commit the main offence
- This means intent to complete all the elements of the main offence – Pace and Rogers
- The main offence need not occur

Links to the non-substantive law

ELS: For links to the English legal system, look back at the diagram and examples in the introduction to Part 1. The HL accepted that it had made a wrong decision in **Anderton** and in **Shivpuri** it used the *1966 Practice Statement* to overrule its own earlier decision and create a new precedent. Note that as regards the courts and sentencing, this will depend on what was attempted. Attempted assault would be a summary offence, for example, and attempted robbery would be indictable.

The nature of law: As a major role of law is to achieve justice, which requires the law to be clear and accessible, any inconsistency or lack of clarity in how the law deals with attempts can be discussed in a question on justice. The CA recognised in **Pace and Rogers** that the courts "do not always reveal a consistency in approach". This shows that the **Criminal Attempts Act** has not sufficiently clarified the law on this area.

Another role of law is to protect the public and this is also an issue with attempts. If the police wait until the act is clearly 'more than merely preparatory' before arresting D, they could be putting people in danger. In **Campbell**, the conviction was overturned but if the police had waited until he entered the post office, they could have been risking people's lives. Also in **Geddes**, there was no attempt because he had not approached any victim, but there was clear evidence of his intentions (a high level of fault) and if he had not been challenged by the teacher, someone might have been abducted.

Also as regards fault, unlike cases of constructive liability discussed earlier, with attempt the fault element is often *higher* than the relevant conduct suggests. This means D is not criminally liable for an attempted crime unless there is specific intent to commit it, even if the offence itself can be committed recklessly, as with criminal damage (**Millard & Vernon**). For attempted murder there must be intent to kill, but murder itself only requires intent seriously to injure, so the full offence requires a lower level of fault than the attempted one. As noted above, if the jury had not found intent to kill in **R v Z 2017**, the conviction would have been for wounding with intent and not attempted murder.

Self-test questions

1. On what issue did **Shivpuri** overrule **Anderton v Ryan?**
2. How is attempt defined?
3. In which Act is attempt defined
4. Why did the CA allow the appeal in **Pace and Rogers**?
5. What was confirmed in **Millard & Vernon** on the issue of mens rea?

Answers to tasks and self-test questions are on my website at www.drsr.org/publications/tasks. For some interactive exercises, click on 'Free Exercises'.

Summary and evaluation of the property offences and attempt

Theft s 1 Theft Act 1968		
s 3	*actus reus*	appropriation
s 4		property
s 5		belonging to another
s 2	*mens rea*	dishonestly
s 6		intent to permanently deprive
Robbery s 8 Theft Act 1968	*actus reus*	theft PLUS force or threat of it in order to steal
	mens rea	as for theft plus intent to use or threaten force
Attempt s 1 Criminal Attempts Act 1981	*actus reus*	an act which is more than merely preparatory
	mens rea	intent to commit the main offence

Key criticisms of theft and robbery

All these can be used in a discussion of whether justice is achieved and many also relate to fault.

- Conflicting cases on appropriation have left the law on theft uncertain
- D can be guilty of theft without actually taking anything
- The Ghosh test is difficult for juries
- D can be guilty of theft of wild plants and animals e.g., if they are used commercially
- The distinction between something lost and something abandoned may not be clear
- The force for robbery can be minor yet the maximum sentence is life imprisonment

Key criticisms of attempt

- The line between what is and is not 'more than preparatory' is still unclear
- The difficulty this poses for juries leads to inconsistency
- Geddes shows the problem of waiting for a final act

- Had the teacher not challenged the man people would have been put at risk, but the court held he had not passed the 'more than preparatory' test
- Similarly, in Campbell, lives could have been put at risk by waiting for D to do more
- The Law Commission suggested adding a new offence of 'criminal preparation' in 2007 but the proposals were not accepted
- Having an offence of criminal preparation would have meant a conviction in cases like Campbell and Geddes
- The Law Commission in its 2009 report said that the 'more than merely preparatory' definition of attempt should stay but still maintained the offence needed amending as regards attempted murder and conditional attempts
- The level of *mens rea* is high, making it more difficult to convict someone of attempt than of the main offence
- This is especially illogical in murder cases where attempted murder is harder to prove than murder itself, as in Whybrow 1951, where it was held that for attempted murder intent to kill is required, even though intent seriously to injure is sufficient *mens rea* for murder itself
- It remains to be seen how far the law on *mens rea* has been clarified by Pace and Rogers 2014
- The sentence is the same as for the full offence even though that offence has not occurred

Chapter 15 Insanity and Automatism

"... and it would be an unfortunate thing if it were left to juries to consider whether some particular act was morally right or wrong. The test must be whether it is contrary to law ..." Lord Goddard

By the end of this Chapter, you should be able to:

- **Explain the different parts of these defences**
- **Explain how the rules on both insanity and automatism apply in practice**
- **Compare the two defences and explain their differences by reference to cases**
- **Identify possible criticisms for an evaluation of the law**

There is an overlap between these two defences so we will look at them in the same Chapter.

Insanity

Insanity can be relevant at three points in time. Whilst awaiting trial, at the time of trial or at the time of the offence. The first two are not strictly defences as they mean D does not stand trial at all. It is the last one that concerns us here.

The burden of proving insanity to the jury is on D, on the balance of probabilities. The prosecution may however, raise insanity, in which case it must be proved beyond reasonable doubt.

Under the **Criminal Procedure (Insanity) Act 1964**, the result of a successful plea of insanity was committal to a secure hospital for an indefinite period. For this reason, it was not often raised in defence. The **Criminal Procedure (Insanity and Unfitness to Plead) Act 1991** amended the 1964 Act and increased the judge's powers to make four orders. The orders were then reduced to three by the **Domestic Violence, Crime and Victims Act 2004**. The judge may now give:

- a hospital order (which can also be accompanied by a restriction order)
- a supervision order
- an absolute discharge

Until 2004 if the charge was murder a hospital order was the only option, but this is no longer automatic.

Examination pointer

If the defence is successful then there is a special verdict. This is "not guilty by reason of insanity". When discussing the effect of a plea of insanity you should refer to the judge's powers under the **1991** and **2004 Acts** as 'orders'. Avoid calling them sentences. Technically, D has been found not guilty.

The defence is based on **M'Naghten's case 1843**.

Key case

M'Naghten fired his gun at the Tory Prime Minister, Robert Peel, but killed his secretary. Medical opinion showed that M'Naghten was suffering from 'morbid delusions'. He was found not guilty. Due to the public reaction to both the crime and the outcome, the House of Lords formulated a set of rules. The **M'Naghten rules** are still used today. There are two main propositions of law.

Firstly, everyone is to be presumed to be sane until proved otherwise.

Secondly, insanity may be proved if, at the time of committing the act, D was *"labouring under such a defect of reason, from disease of the mind, as not to know the nature and quality of the act he was doing, or if he did know it, that he did not know he was doing what was wrong."*

Let's break this defence down into the different parts.

Defect of reason

There has to be a complete deprivation of the powers of reason rather than simply a failure to exercise them. In **Clarke 1972**, D claimed that, due to depression, she had absent-mindedly put some items in her bag and so was not guilty of theft. The judge ruled that this argument amounted to insanity. She promptly changed her plea to guilty, (because this was before the **1991 Act** and it would have meant being sent to a mental hospital). On appeal, the CA held that temporary absentmindedness was not a defect of reason, but it did negate *mens rea*. As she had no *mens rea*, her conviction was quashed.

Task 40

Look back at Chapter 3 on *mens rea* and the case of **Madeley** where the host of a TV show had a similar argument. The court decided he was not guilty. What was the reason in that case?

Disease of the mind

The defect of reason must be caused by a disease of the mind. The meaning of 'disease of the mind' is a legal question for the judge. However, D will need medical evidence from two experts. This is a requirement of **s 1 Criminal Procedure (Insanity and Unfitness to Plead) Act 1991.**

So what constitutes a disease of the mind? In **Bratty v Attorney General for Northern Ireland 1963**, D had killed a girl with her stocking during an epileptic fit. Lord Denning said a disease of the mind was *"any mental disorder which has manifested itself in violence and is prone to recur"*.

In **Kemp 1957**, Devlin J said

> *"the condition of the brain is irrelevant and so is the question of whether the condition of the mind is curable or incurable, transitory or permanent"*.

This indicates a temporary state can still be insanity. In **Smith (Mark) 2012**, D was violent and abusive while travelling on an aircraft and had to be restrained by cabin staff. Evidence from psychiatrists was that he had a brief reactive psychosis characterised by delusions and hallucinations. He was charged with criminal damage and interfering with the performance of the aircraft crew in flight, and was found not guilty by reason of insanity, even though it was a temporary state.

It would appear, though, that it is more often accepted as insanity where the disease is of a permanent nature, or in Lord Denning's words "prone to recur".

A lot of case law turns on this issue of 'disease'. This has led to a distinction between *internal* factors and *external* factors. If the 'defect of reason' is caused by an internal factor (a disease), the defence is likely to be insanity. If it is caused by an external factor (like a blow to the head and concussion), then it is likely to be automatism (discussed below). The distinction is most easily explained by looking at some cases.

Kemp 1957: D had arteriosclerosis (this is a narrowing of the arteries, which reduces the flow of blood to the brain). This caused occasional lapses of consciousness. During one such period, he killed his wife by striking her with a hammer. His defence was treated as insanity.

Quick 1973: A diabetic nurse at a psychiatric hospital attacked one of the patients. He argued that this was because at the time he was suffering from hypoglycaemia as result of failing to eat after taking his insulin. The CA held the 'defect' was caused by an external factor, i.e., the insulin itself. This would be automatism not insanity.

Sullivan 1984: D hit out at someone trying to help him during an epileptic fit, and was convicted of actual bodily harm. The HL confirmed that the appropriate defence would be insanity and that epilepsy was a 'disease of the mind' which had caused a 'defect of reason'.

Hennessey 1989: D was a diabetic. He had taken a car and driven whilst disqualified. He argued automatism caused by failure to take his insulin. The CA upheld the judge's finding of insanity on the basis that the cause was the disease itself, an internal factor.

Burgess 1991: D claimed he was sleepwalking when he attacked his girlfriend. He was charged with wounding with intent and raised the defence of automatism. The judge held that the cause of his 'defect of reason' was an internal factor, a disease of the mind. He was found not guilty by reason of insanity and detained in a mental hospital. However, in **Bilton 2005 (unreported)**, the defence of automatism was successfully used when D raped a girl whilst sleepwalking. A similar illness, rapid eye movement sleeping disorder, was accepted as automatism in **Thomas 2008**, where D had strangled his wife during such an episode.

Task 41

Look at the sequence of events in the diagram. If you take out any 'non-events' it is easier to see what caused the defect of reason. On the left, it is the insulin (external) on the right, the diabetes (internal). Do the same for **Quick** and **Hennessey** and then write a summary of each highlighting the differences.

Diabetes example

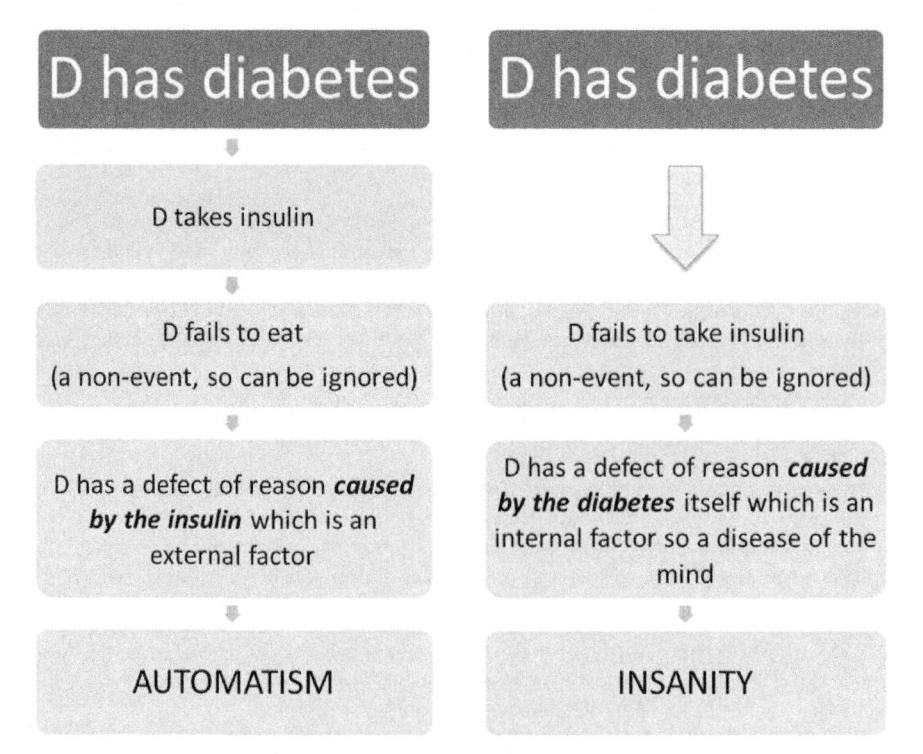

D has diabetes	D has diabetes
↓	↓
D takes insulin	
↓	
D fails to eat (a non-event, so can be ignored)	D fails to take insulin (a non-event, so can be ignored)
↓	↓
D has a defect of reason **caused by the insulin** which is an external factor	D has a defect of reason **caused by the diabetes** itself which is an internal factor so a disease of the mind
↓	↓
AUTOMATISM	**INSANITY**

A 'defect of reason' caused by external factors (automatism) would usually be temporary whereas if caused by internal factors (insanity) it may be more permanent. This would need treating in order to protect the public, so a hospital order may be appropriate. In **Bratty v Attorney General for Northern Ireland 1963**, Lord Denning said a disorder which led to violence and was prone to recur was "the sort of disease for which a person should be retained in hospital rather than be given an unqualified acquittal". Both **Smith (Mark) 2012** and **Burgess 1991** show that a temporary state can amount to insanity, so there is a fine line between the two defences.

Evaluation pointer

In its 'scoping paper' (a paper setting out what is within the scope of the project) on insanity in 2012, the Law Commission said

> "... the law has not adopted a distinction between mental disorders and physical disorders, so that the latter are outside of the scope of the notion of "disease of the mind" in M'Naghten. Instead, it has adopted a distinction between internal and external factors which as we have seen leads to highly illogical results"

In cases like **Bratty** and **Kemp**, the defence of insanity may be appropriate. D's acts were to some extent purposeful and there is a danger to the public. The case of an epileptic thrashing out and hitting someone during a fit would be less easy to justify. There is a problem with finding insanity in respect of people whose conditions are not normally associated with mental disorder. Use the 'diabetes' cases to support a discussion of these problems. **Burgess** is also arguably too wide a definition, and can be contrasted to **Bilton** and **Thomas 2008**. Should a sleepwalker be classed as insane? It leads to a second issue. Once insanity is raised – and remember this can be by the prosecution or the judge as well as D – D will often change the plea to guilty to avoid the insanity verdict. This is what happened in **Sullivan**. He pleaded guilty after the judge ruled the defence was insanity and was convicted of actual bodily harm. In **Quick**, on the other hand, the defect was held to be caused by the insulin itself. D's appeal succeeded because the defence of automatism should have been left to the jury. The lack of consistency goes against the idea of justice as in order to achieve justice the law should be clear and apply equally.

A final point is that the stigma of an insanity verdict may also mean people who genuinely do have a mental problem do not plead the defence.

Not knowing the nature and quality of the act

In **Codere 1916**, this was held to mean the physical nature of the act, not its moral nature.

In **Bratty v Attorney General for Northern Ireland 1963**, a man who killed a girl with her stocking was found not guilty by reason of insanity because it was held that his epilepsy may have prevented him knowing the 'nature and quality' of the act.

In **Burgess 1991**, the fact that he was sleepwalking meant he did not know the nature of his actions. Similarly, in **Sullivan** and **Hennessy**, they were not aware of what they were doing at the time.

If D is suffering from insane delusions the defence of insanity may succeed, however it will not succeed where D knows the nature of the act.

Example

Derek is deluded and throws a baby onto the fire believing it to be a log. The defence may succeed, as Derek did not realise the nature of what he was doing.

Ahmed hears imaginary voices telling him to kill someone. He does this. The defence will fail, as he knew that he was killing someone.

Not knowing the act was wrong

Even if D understands the nature of the act, the defence may succeed if this second part is satisfied. It is a question of whether D realises the act was *legally* wrong, not whether D believes it was morally right or wrong. In **Windle 1952**, D killed his wife with an overdose of aspirin. There was evidence of mental illness but on giving himself up he said 'I suppose they will hang me for this' thereby indicating he knew that what he had done was legally wrong. The conviction was upheld by the CA, where Lord Goddard gave the quote at the beginning of this Chapter. This made it clear that the question was a legal one; the jury were not to consider whether he believed the act was morally right or wrong. If D knows that the act is legally wrong, the defence fails.

In **Dantes 2015** (see diminished responsibility), D suffered from paranoid schizophrenia and he killed his parents by repeatedly stabbing them. The court rejected the insanity defence because although he had a defect of reason caused by a disease of the mind the evidence showed that he knew the nature and quality of his act, and that it was legally wrong. He had said to the police that he had made a "big mistake", which is similar to **Windle**.

Example

Jack goes on a killing spree and murders several young prostitutes. He believes clearing the streets of prostitutes is morally justified. He could not plead insanity, as he knows killing is legally wrong.

The point was reiterated in the following case, where it was also made clear that there was no need for the judge to put the defence to the jury if it was clear D knew the act was legally wrong.

Key case

In **Johnson 2007**, D forced his way into a neighbour's flat, while he was watching television. He shouted at him and became very aggressive. For no apparent reason he stabbed him with a large kitchen knife and was charged with wounding with intent. At his trial, he said that he did not know what he was doing. The medical experts agreed that, at the material time, he had been suffering from a disease of the mind, paranoid schizophrenia. However, the judge held that there was no question of insanity for the jury to consider because he knew what he did was legally wrong. The jury found him guilty and he appealed. He argued that the judge had been wrong to prevent the jury considering the M'Naghten rules. The appeal was dismissed. Following **Windle**, the CA held that even if there was evidence of a disease of the mind, if he knew that what he did was legally wrong there was no issue of insanity to be left to the jury. The judge had therefore been entitled to prevent the jury considering the M'Naghten rules.

Principle: There is no need for the judge to put the defence of insanity to the jury if it was clear D knew the act was legally wrong.

In **Elmi 2016**, D had seriously injured several worshippers in a mosque believing them to be mocking Allah. He had paranoid schizophrenia and suffered from insane delusions, including that he was the Emir of the Islam Republic. The defence of insanity succeeded as the evidence showed that he did not believe what he was doing was either morally or legally wrong. The judge ordered him to be detained indefinitely at a secure mental hospital.

Examination pointer

There is an overlap with diminished responsibility so in a murder case you may need to discuss both. Until the 1991 Act, the only possible order following a successful insanity defence was detention in a mental hospital. It was therefore mainly used in murder cases. Since 2004, there are three possible orders, so the defence may be used for other crimes more often. The defence of diminished responsibility under the **Homicide Act 1957** is wider though (but only applies to murder cases).

Evaluation pointer and proposed reforms

The defence originates from an 1843 case and it is argued that because of medical advances it should be updated. Judges themselves have called for Parliament to look at the insanity defence.

There are arguments that the law could breach **Article 5 of the European Convention on Human Rights** which states that a person of unsound mind can only be detained where proper objective medical expertise has been sought.

The **1953 Royal Commission on Capital Punishment** recommended the abolition of the M'Naghten rules. The **Homicide Act 1957** introduced diminished responsibility shortly after this which addressed some of the criticisms made. In 1975, the **Butler Committee** favoured replacing the rules with a new verdict of 'mental disorder'. This would arise where D was suffering from 'severe mental illness' or 'severe mental handicap'. The burden of proof would also move to the prosecution, which is the norm in criminal law so would better achieve justice and equality.

The **Law Commission's Draft Code** adopted many of Butler's recommendations and specifically accepted that sleepwalking and spasms should come within automatism rather than insanity. The Commission made some further recommendations in 1995 but these were not acted upon, and it identified insanity as an area in need of reform again in 2008. In its 2012 scoping paper, it was noted that the law lagged behind psychiatric understanding. The LC also said *"English law has adopted an unusually, and arguably unjustifiably, narrow interpretation of the 'wrongfulness' limb"* as interpreted in **Windle**. Another point made in the 2012 paper was that the defence was very rarely used, but it was accepted that this did not necessarily mean it did not need attention; on the contrary, it was noted that the complexity of the law and the out-of-date tests were part of the reason for the lack of use. A project has been set up to consider the responses to the scoping paper in 2013 in order to identify *"better and more up-to-date legal tests"*.

Insanity and intoxication

If the defect of reason comes about through intoxication, the insanity defence fails. If it comes from alcoholism, it could succeed as this can be classed as a 'disease'. In **Lipman 1970**, D had taken LSD and had a hallucination where he thought he was fighting snakes. He killed his girlfriend by stuffing a sheet down her throat. He did not know the quality of his act but, as the LSD was voluntarily taken, the defence failed. He was convicted of manslaughter. That voluntarily taken drugs or alcohol will exclude the defence was confirmed in **Coley 2013**, where D had attacked his neighbour and claimed he had blacked out. This 'brief psychotic episode' was caused by taking cannabis. The CA noted that even if there was a disease of the mind, it had been caused by an external factor and so ruled out insanity.

Automatism

We saw in Chapter 2 that the *actus reus* must be voluntary. The defence of automatism arises where D's act was 'automatic' and so was not voluntary. Thus, it is negating *actus reus* rather than *mens rea*. It is also referred to as 'non-insane automatism' to distinguish it from insanity which can be called 'insane automatism'. Automatism is a very limited defence but if successful, it leads to a complete acquittal so it would be preferred to pleading insanity.

D has to show:

- the act was involuntary
- this was due to an external factor

The act was involuntary

Automatism was defined by Lord Denning in **Bratty v Attorney General for Northern Ireland 1963**

> "... automatism means an act which is done by the muscles without any control by the mind such as a spasm, a reflex action or a convulsion or an act done by a person who is not conscious of what he is doing ..."

The difference with insanity lies in what caused the lack of control. If it was a disease of the mind, the defence is insanity. If an external factor, like a blow to the head, the defence is automatism. The LC said in its 2012 paper

> "English case law has drawn a distinction between "insane automatism" (which it classifies as "insanity") and "sane automatism". It has done this by distinguishing between whether the cause of the accused's lack of control was due to an "internal factor" (i.e. some malfunctioning of the person's body) or an "external factor" (such as a blow to the head)".

The LC recognised that this led to 'illogical results'. It also noted the defence had no clearly accepted definition, although the one in **Bratty** was the most often used.

The lack of control must be total.

Key case

In **A-G's Reference (No2 of 1992) 1994**, D killed two people when his lorry crashed into a car on the hard shoulder of the motorway. He pleaded automatism on the grounds that driving for so long on a motorway had resulted in a 'trance like' state and he was suffering from what is called 'driving without awareness'. On referral to the CA, it was held that this did not amount to automatism because his lack of awareness was not total. Thus if D's behaviour is only partly automatic, there is no defence. This confirmed **Broome v Perkins 1987**, where a diabetic, suffering from hypoglycaemia, hit another car.

Principle: If D is able to exercise *some* control, automatism is not available as a defence.

This was due to an external factor

The essence of automatism is that the crime was the result of an external factor causing an involuntary act on the part of the defendant. If it was an internal factor then the defence is insanity. As we saw with insanity, this distinction has produced some fairly bizarre cases. The LC said in its 2012 paper that the *"line drawn between sane and insane automatism can never make medical sense"*.

External factors would include prescribed drugs, such as the insulin in **Quick 1973**. In **Hill v Baxter 1958**, a hypothetical example was given of D being attacked by a swarm of bees whilst driving a car. If this caused a total loss of control, the automatism defence would succeed.

Examination pointer

The defences of insanity and automatism are closely linked so you may need to discuss both. However, note that the automatism defence would be better as it results in an acquittal.

Automatism and intoxication

As D must be acting involuntarily the defence cannot be relied upon if the automatism was self-induced, e.g., by drinking or taking drugs, as in **Lipman 1970** and **Coley 2013**.

In **Quick**, Lawton LJ said

> "A self-induced incapacity will not excuse ... nor will one which could have been reasonably foreseen as a result of either doing, or omitting to do something, as, for example, taking alcohol against medical advice after using certain prescribed drugs, or failing to have regular meals while taking insulin ..."

It would appear from this that if you knew you had a heart condition and then drove you could not argue automatism if you had a heart attack and crashed into someone. However, the rule has not been applied very consistently.

In **Hardie 1985**, D set fire to a bedroom after taking Valium. The court held that he could successfully plead automatism even though the pills were not prescribed by a doctor. A distinction was made between drugs which are meant to calm you and ones which are likely to lead to aggressive or unpredictable behaviour. In the latter case, the defence would fail.

In **Bailey 1983**, D was suffering from hypoglycaemia due to a failure to eat properly after taking insulin. He hit his ex-girlfriend's new boyfriend over the head with an iron bar and was convicted of GBH. The CA rejected his automatism defence, as there was clearly not a complete loss of control over his bodily movements (he went to the man's house armed with an iron bar). They restated that self-induced automatism by voluntarily consuming drink or drugs would not be acceptable. However, even though his state was arguably self-induced, because he could have eaten something, the CA made clear that the defence *could* succeed in such a case because it is not commonly known that failing to eat can cause such results.

Evaluation pointer

The CA in **Quick 1973** implied that failing to eat makes automatism self-induced. It was not fully clear as they merely held that the defence of automatism should have been left to the jury. In **Bailey**, the same court suggested that whilst drink or drugs would mean the defect is self-induced, failing to eat would not. This leaves the law insufficiently clear, as noted by the LC in its 2012 scoping paper.

The rules on insanity and automatism have led to sleepwalkers and diabetics being labelled insane – sometimes. The difference between not taking insulin, and taking it but not eating properly, is small but has a major consequence. The result is either that D is found insane or goes free.

Do you agree with Lawton LJ? In **Quick** he said the defence was a *"quagmire of law seldom entered nowadays save by those in desperate need of some kind of defence"*. Not very reassuring!

Summary

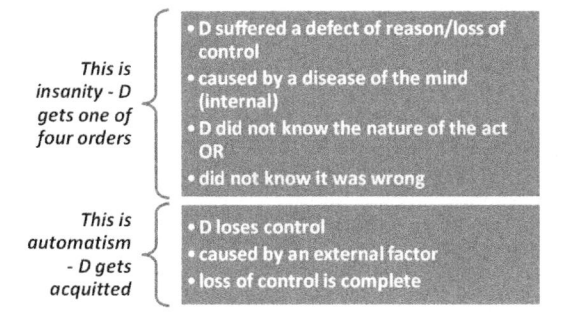

This is insanity - D gets one of four orders	• D suffered a defect of reason/loss of control • caused by a disease of the mind (internal) • D did not know the nature of the act OR • did not know it was wrong
This is automatism - D gets acquitted	• D loses control • caused by an external factor • loss of control is complete

Links to the non-substantive law

ELS: For links to the English legal system, look back at the diagram and examples in the introduction to Part 1.

The nature of law: One role of law is to protect both individuals and society as a whole and another is to do this based on the level of fault involved. Most defences are examples of this. The law makes an act of violence wrong so protects individuals and society, the defences then reflect that D may not be fully blameworthy, or at fault. If D has a defect of reason, and so really does not realise that an act is legally wrong, then there is a low degree of fault. In such cases, the role of law should not be to punish but to protect, and this is done by allowing the judge discretion in which orders to make so that any punishment can reflect the level of fault.

A successful plea of automatism shows D is not at fault, so results in an acquittal not punishment. However, the law is not always consistent and it can hardly be said that a person is at fault when sleepwalking (**Burgess**) or during an epileptic fit (**Sullivan**). This means the law is not fulfilling its role in achieving justice.

Some, such as Hart, would say it is not the role of law to enforce morality and that justice should be based purely on legal rules. An illustration of this is the defence of insanity. In **Windle**, Lord Goddard said *"...it would be an unfortunate thing if it were left to juries to consider whether some particular act was morally right or wrong. The test must be whether it is contrary to law."* However, in its 2012 scoping paper the LC said *"English law has adopted an unusually, and arguably unjustifiably, narrow interpretation of the 'wrongfulness' limb"* as interpreted in **Windle**. There is disagreement on this issue, but the LC is an important legal institution and if it does not believe the rules achieve justice then there is sound reason for arguing that they do not.

Self-test questions

1. From which case do the insanity rules come?
2. From which case does the opening quote come?
3. Which defence applies when the cause is external?
4. Which defence applies when the cause is internal?
5. Give a case example for each of these defences to show this difference

Answers to tasks and self-test questions are on my website at www.drsr.org/publications/tasks. For some interactive exercises, click on 'Free Exercises'.

Chapter 16 Intoxication

"If a man, whilst sane and sober, forms an intention to kill ... he cannot rely on this self-induced drunkenness as a defence to murder." Lord Denning

By the end of this Chapter, you should be able to:

- **Distinguish between voluntary and involuntary intoxication**
- **Explain how the courts treat different types of drug**
- **Explain the difference between specific intent and basic intent**
- **Show how the defence applies by reference to cases**
- **Identify possible criticisms for an evaluation of the law**

Although traditionally this defence only applied to drink, it is now clear that the rules on intoxication apply to both drink and drugs. In cases involving drugs a distinction has been made between those which are commonly known to cause aggressive or dangerous behaviour and those which are not.

Key case

In **Hardie 1985**, D was trying to get his ex-girlfriend to get back together with him. She gave him a sedative (Valium) to calm him down and then left him in her flat. Whilst she was out, he set fire to it. He claimed that he could not remember anything after he had taken the drug. The CA allowed his appeal against conviction and held Valium was *"wholly different from drugs which are liable to cause unpredictability and aggressiveness"*.

Principle: A distinction must be made between drugs which are commonly known to cause aggressive or dangerous behaviour and those which are not. In the latter case, the defence of automatism can succeed.

Thus, 'unpredictable' drugs are treated in the same way as alcohol. With sedatives, the courts will apply a test of subjective recklessness.

Example

D is given anti-depressant drugs by his doctor. They make him feel sick and he doesn't eat for several days. Together with the pills, lack of food has the effect of making him prone to outbursts of violence. During one such period, he lashes out at someone and is charged with assault. He argues intoxication as a defence.

The question will be whether he was reckless, i.e., appreciated the risk that taking the drug would lead to such aggressive and unpredictable behaviour. If he was not told about any possible side effects then it is unlikely he will be seen as reckless. However, if the doctor had warned him to eat regularly to avoid any side effects then his defence will probably fail.

Intoxication is only a defence if it can be shown that due to the intoxication D was incapable of forming the necessary intent. This was established many years ago in **Beard 1920**. The rules for the defence differ depending on whether D was drunk voluntarily or not.

Involuntary intoxication

This would occur where D did not knowingly take alcohol or drugs. An example would be drinking orange juice which someone had 'spiked', e.g., added vodka to. The intoxication must do more than make D lose their inhibitions, though, it must remove *mens rea*.

Key case

In **Kingston 1994**, D was given drinks which had been laced with drugs. He was then photographed indecently assaulting a 15-year old boy. He admitted that at the time of committing the offence that he had the necessary intent, but said that he would not have acted in that way had he been sober. The HL overturned the decision of the CA and held that intoxicated intent was still intent.

Principle: Intoxication is no defence if D had the necessary *mens rea*, even if it is formed whilst involuntarily intoxicated.

In **Allen 1988**, the CA made it clear that the intoxication had to be totally involuntary; not knowing the strength of what you are drinking would not be enough. D had drunk homemade wine not realising it was very strong. He then pleaded involuntary intoxication when charged with indecent assault. The CA held that he had freely been drinking wine, knowing it to be wine. It was therefore voluntary intoxication.

Task 42

Refer to the Chapter on insanity and automatism. Read the facts of **Lipman 1970** again. Make a note of which defence was argued and which succeeded. Why was this? We will come back to this case later to see the overlap between the defences.

Voluntary intoxication

The basic rule on intoxication is that it can provide a defence to crimes of specific intent but not those of basic intent. In simple terms, the distinction is this: if a crime can only be committed intentionally then it is crime of specific intent; if it can be committed with some other form of *mens rea*, e.g., recklessness, it is a crime of basic intent.

Key case

This distinction was made in **Majewski 1977** where the HL held that intoxication could not negate the *mens rea* where the required *mens rea* was recklessness. Essentially getting drunk was seen as reckless in itself. D had been charged with an assault after a pub fight. He argued that he was too drunk to know what he was doing. The HL upheld his conviction and stated that evidence of self-induced intoxication which negated *mens rea* was a defence to a crime requiring specific intent but not to any other crime.

Principle: Intoxication can provide a defence to crimes of specific intent, but cannot negate *mens rea* where the required *mens rea* is recklessness.

Example

Whilst drunk, Sue takes someone's bag and is charged with theft. This is a specific intent crime. Sue's intoxication defence can succeed if she can show that she lacked *mens rea*. The *mens rea* for theft is 'intent permanently to deprive' another. She might show that because she was drunk she thought it was hers and so she had no intent to deprive anyone else of it.

If she destroyed the bag, she could not use the defence to a charge of criminal damage. This offence can be committed by 'intending ... or being reckless as to whether property is destroyed'. The fact that this can be done by 'being reckless' makes it a basic intent crime.

The distinction seemed straightforward but some doubt was cast on it in **Heard 2007**. D had sexually assaulted a police officer whilst drunk and argued intoxication as a defence. He was convicted and appealed on the basis that the crime was 'intentionally' touching another person sexually and thus a specific intent crime. The CA held that basic intent could include intention where the *mens rea* was only for the act itself and nothing further, as here. Specific intent could include recklessness where the offence required *mens rea* for more than the illegal act itself, e.g., a consequence. The CA also noted that not all offences could be categorised as basic or specific offences as some had elements of both.

In **Press & another 2013**, two soldiers were convicted of GBH under **s 18 OAPA** after attacking another two men at a burger stall. The CA confirmed that *"The conventional direction in a case where the prosecution is required to prove a specific intent and the evidence is that the defendant has taken alcohol (or drugs) is that the jury should consider whether the act was accompanied by the required intent even in drink. The fact that the defendant was intoxicated does not constitute a defence"*. If intent had not been proved they would still have been guilty under **s 20** as that is a basic intent crime.

Evaluation pointer and examination pointer

The Law Commission (in its 2012 paper on insanity) said

> *"We define specific intent offences as those for which the predominant* mens rea *is one of knowledge, intention or dishonesty, and basic intent offences as all those for which the predominant* mens rea *is not intention, knowledge or dishonesty (this includes offences of recklessness, belief, negligence and strict liability)"*.

This is what many judges and academics had interpreted **Majewski 1977** as meaning, but **Heard** has introduced some doubt. This provides useful material for a critical evaluation of the defence, but for a problem question I would use the earlier interpretation and just mention briefly that **Heard** has cast some doubt on this.

In **Dowds 2012** (see diminished responsibility), the CA held that voluntary, or self-induced, intoxication was not capable of establishing a defence. Although the case involved the special defence of diminished responsibility, the CA made clear that the rules on intoxication apply to all defences, and to intoxication caused by drugs or other substances as well as alcohol.

Note that if you plead intoxication to a specific intent crime then you will still be guilty of any related basic intent crime. If charged with murder, this would be manslaughter. If charged with **s 18 Offences against the Person Act 1861**, the result would be a conviction under **s 20**. This is because you are using intoxication to negate the *mens rea* of intention. **Majewski** shows, however, that you will still be deemed 'reckless'. If there is no related basic intent crime then D may be acquitted. An example would be theft.

Examination pointer

Look carefully at the facts and at *how* D became intoxicated. First decide if it is voluntary or not. If it is then use **Majewski**, if not then use **Kingston**. You may need both if the matter isn't clear. Look at the type of intoxicant; if it is a drug, you will need to look at the distinction made in **Hardie**, between drugs likely to cause aggression and sedatives. Taking unpredictable drugs is likely to be seen as voluntary intoxication.

Did you do the task on **Lipman 1970**? It can help identify the overlap between defences. Let's look at how:

A possible defence is insanity. He clearly had a 'defect of reason' and he did not know 'the nature and quality' of his act. He thought he was fighting snakes not strangling his girlfriend. However, the defect was not caused by a 'disease of the mind' but by the LSD. This is an external factor so consider automatism. The defence of automatism fails because the loss of control was self-induced (taking LSD). It was voluntary. The defence of intoxication can be argued. The effect of the drug meant he did not have the required *mens rea*. He had no intent to kill or seriously injure so was not guilty of the specific intent crime (murder), but as the intoxication was voluntary, he was guilty of the related basic intent crime (manslaughter).

Evaluation pointer

As we saw when looking at *mens rea* in Chapter 3, the **Criminal Justice Act 1967** requires the jury to decide whether D did 'intend or foresee' the result by reference to 'all the evidence'. **Majewski** seems to dispense with this requirement. If D is drunk that is enough to prove recklessness. No other evidence is required. This favours the prosecution who will not have the usual job of proving *mens rea*. It is also wider than the usual test for recklessness. Usually the prosecution must prove that 'D recognised a risk and went ahead anyway'. Getting drunk hardly has the same level of fault.

The 'Dutch courage' rule

What if D forms the required *mens rea* and *then* gets drunk and commits an offence? This may occur where D becomes intoxicated in order to summon up the courage to commit the offence. This is called the 'Dutch Courage' rule.

In **Attorney-General (AG) for Northern Ireland v Gallagher 1963**, D decided to kill his wife. He bought a knife and a bottle of whisky. He drank the whisky and then stabbed her. The HL held that once a person formed an intention to kill then the defence would fail. Lord Denning made the main speech including the quote at the beginning of this Chapter. He also gave two examples of when intoxication might succeed. Firstly, where a nurse at a christening got so drunk that she put the baby on the fire in the mistaken belief it was a log. Secondly, where a drunken man thought his friend, lying in bed, was a theatrical dummy and stabbed him to death. Lord Denning said that in both cases D would have a defence to a murder charge. This latter is not dissimilar to **Lipman 1970**, where D thought he was fighting snakes and ended up strangling his girlfriend.

Evaluation pointer

In **Gallagher**, the HL held that once a person formed an intention to kill, then the defence would fail. At first glance, this seems fine. After all, D did have *mens rea* because he planned to kill her and went and bought a knife. That he was too intoxicated to possess intent when the act was carried out is arguably irrelevant. It can be seen as inconsistent with the normal rules of law though. The usual requirement is that *mens rea* and *actus reus* occur together.

Lord Denning's examples show that intoxication and mistake are closely linked. We will deal with mistake separately but for the moment let's just look at the overlap.

Intoxication and public policy

Public policy is one reason why the courts will not allow intoxication as a defence. It is not in the public interest to allow people who get drunk and then commit an offence to be able to rely on intoxication as a defence. In **O'Grady 1987**, D hit his friend over the head in the mistaken belief that the friend was trying to kill him. Both of them were drunk at the time. He was convicted of manslaughter and appealed. The CA refused to allow the defence and said:

> "There are two competing interests. On the one hand the interest of the defendant who has only acted according to what he believed to be necessary to protect himself, and on the other hand that of the public in general, and the victim in particular who, probably through no fault of his own, has been injured or perhaps killed because of the defendant's drunken mistake. Reason recoils from the conclusion that in such circumstances a defendant is entitled to leave the court without a stain on his character".

In **Dowds 2012**, Hughes LJ said

> "... public policy proceeds on the basis that a defendant who voluntarily takes alcohol and behaves in a way in which he might not have behaved when sober is not normally entitled to be excused from the consequences of his actions".

Evaluation pointer

The law is complex and juries are confused by the different rules. The **Majewski** 'rules' are less than exact. It is not fully clear which crimes are specific intent, and which are basic. The jury will have to decide whether D was knowingly taking an 'unpredictable' drug or a sedative. This distinction is also unclear. Justice demands greater clarity.

Task 43

Draw up a flow chart or diagram using the following cases. Note for each whether insanity, automatism or intoxication applied and why.

Lipman 1970

Bailey 1983

Hardie 1985

Hennessy 1989

Summary

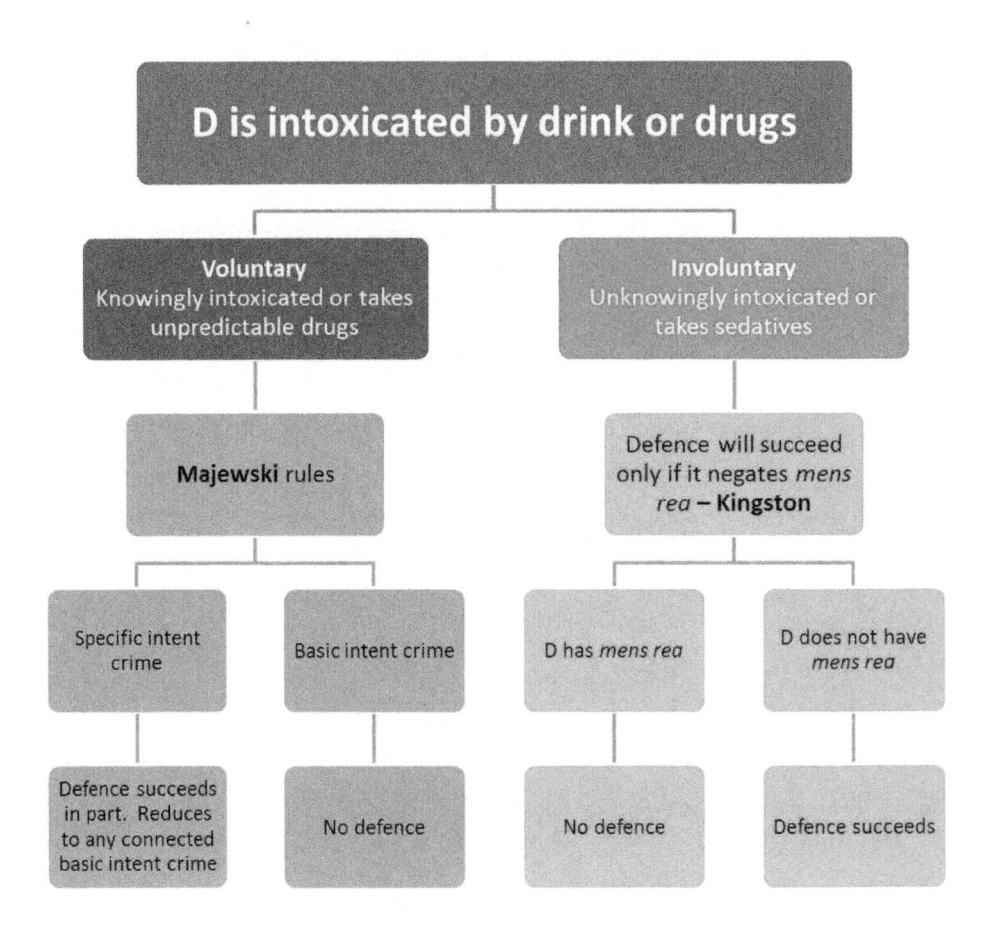

```
                    D is intoxicated by drink or drugs
                    ┌──────────────────┴──────────────────┐
              Voluntary                              Involuntary
   Knowingly intoxicated or takes         Unknowingly intoxicated or
        unpredictable drugs                       takes sedatives
              │                                        │
                                            Defence will succeed
         Majewski rules                   only if it negates mens
                                              rea – Kingston
         ┌────┴────┐                        ┌────────┴────────┐
   Specific intent  Basic intent      D has mens rea    D does not have
       crime          crime                                 mens rea
         │              │                    │                 │
   Defence succeeds
   in part. Reduces   No defence        No defence       Defence succeeds
   to any connected
   basic intent crime
```

Links to the non-substantive law

ELS: For links to the English legal system, look back at the diagram and examples in the introduction to Part 1. Note in relation to juries, that a jury has an almost impossible task in some cases where intoxication is only one factor among others, as seen in **Dietschmann**.

The nature of law: As stated in the last Chapter, most defences are examples of the role of law in punishing those at fault. If a defence applies D may be acquitted, or convicted of a lesser crime where the judge can take into account the level of fault involved when sentencing.

The law attempts to achieve justice by protecting both individuals and society as a whole. The defence of intoxication rarely succeeds unless it completely removes the required fault element. Thus D was found guilty in **Kingston**. If the defence does succeed the law does not accept there is no fault at all, but for crimes where the *mens rea* is intent the conviction can be reduced, e.g., from murder to manslaughter.

To achieve justice the law must balance the interests of the public against those of D. In **O'Grady 1987**, when D had acted due to a drunken mistake, the CA said:

"There are two competing interests. On the one hand the interest of the defendant who has only acted according to what he believed to be necessary to protect himself, and on the other hand that of the public in general, and the victim in particular who, probably through no fault of his own, has been injured or perhaps killed because of the defendant's drunken mistake. Reason recoils from the conclusion that in such circumstances a defendant is entitled to leave the court without a stain on his character".

The rules on intoxication are therefore very strict. As seen in **O'Grady**, people need to be protected from those who get violent when drunk, and justice would not be achieved if the law allowed D a defence when violence was committed due to voluntarily taking drink or drugs. It is right that the law should punish those at fault, and there is an element of fault in getting drunk, but it is arguable whether the decision in **Majewski** achieves justice for D. The test for recklessness is that D recognised a risk and went ahead anyway. This is not quite the same as D got drunk.

Self-test questions

1. What is the difference between specific and basic intent?
2. Name a crime for each type
3. What is 'Dutch courage' and will it provide a defence?
4. If D successfully pleads intoxication to a specific intent crime such as murder what is the result?
5. From which case did the opening quote come?

Answers to tasks and self-test questions are on my website at www.drsr.org/publications/tasks. For some interactive exercises, click on 'Free Exercises'.

Chapter 17 Self-defence and the prevention of crime

"... a person defending himself cannot weigh to a nicety the exact measure of his necessary defensive action." The Privy Council in **Palmer 1971**

By the end of this Chapter, you should be able to:

- Explain the defences of self-defence and prevention of crime
- Identify the principles on which these defences rely and how they overlap
- Refer to appropriate case examples
- Identify possible criticisms for an evaluation of the law

The law allows a defence where D is doing something that would otherwise be an offence, but is acting to protect certain public and/or private interests. The term 'public and private defence' covers prevention of crime (public defence), self-defence, defence of another and defence of property (private defences).

Prevention of crime

This is public defence. It is a statutory defence found in **s 3(1)** of the **Criminal Law Act 1967**, which provides that a person:

> "... may use **such force as is reasonable in the circumstances** in the prevention of crime, or in effecting or assisting in the lawful arrest of offenders or suspected offenders or of persons unlawfully at large".

The main point is that the defence is only available if the force used is *reasonable in the circumstances*.

Example

I see a man grab a woman and try to snatch her handbag. I pull him away and cause bruising. I can use **s 3** as a defence if charged with battery. I was using 'reasonable' force to prevent a crime.

Self-defence

This is private defence. It is a common law defence developed by the courts. However many of the matters which have arisen are now covered by **s 76** of the **Criminal Justice and Immigration Act 2008**. Although usually referred to as self-defence, it covers force used in defence of another. In my example, I am also defending the woman, so could use self-defence as well as prevention of crime.

As seen in my example, the defences overlap, so the principles developed by the courts are essentially the same. In **Hitchins 2011**, the CA held that there was no difference between self-defence under the common law and **s 3**. **S 76** applies to both and is "intended to clarify the operation of the existing defences" in particular, as to whether the degree of force used was reasonable in the circumstances.

There are two main questions to consider:

Did D honestly believe the action was justified? (What D thought; a subjective question)

Was the degree of force reasonable in the circumstances? (What a reasonable person would do; an objective question)

The burden is on the prosecution to satisfy the jury that D was *not* acting in self-defence. They will have to convince the jury that in the circumstances, the action was *not* justified, or that *unreasonable* force was used.

Examination pointer

As with consent, self-defence is usually seen with the non-fatal offences against the person. For example, battery is the *unlawful* application of force. If D acted in self-defence and did not use excessive force, then the 'unlawful' part of the *actus reus* is missing. However, self-defence can apply to murder. The main issue would be whether killing someone was using excessive force. This will be a question for the jury based on the circumstances, or the circumstances as D believed them to be. If the person was armed and dangerous, that circumstance may justify extreme force. Note that if the defence succeeds D is acquitted.

Did D honestly believe the action was justified?

This subjective question is whether the particular D believed that the action which made up the offence was justified.

S 76(7) confirms the opening quote from **Palmer 1971**, stating that D *"may not be able to weigh to a nicety the exact measure of any necessary action"* and that if D only did what was *"honestly and instinctively"* thought to be necessary this would be strong evidence that only reasonable action was taken.

This means excessive force may be acceptable if D 'honestly and instinctively' thought it necessary in the circumstances. However, **s 76(6)** provides that the degree of force is not to be regarded as reasonable if it was disproportionate in the circumstances as D believed them to be. The force should not be disproportionate, but this is considered in the circumstances as D believes them to be; it is a subjective test. If D mistakenly believes someone is being attacked or threatened, then self-defence may be relied on, even if there was no actual threat. This was seen in **Williams (Gladstone) 1987**. A man saw a woman being robbed by a youth and struggled with him. D came on the scene and believed the youth to be under attack. He punched the man and was charged with actual bodily harm. His defence succeeded. The court held that he was to be judged on the facts *as he saw them*.

Was the degree of force reasonable in the circumstances?

This second question is objective and a matter for the jury to decide based on the circumstances of the case, and the nature of the threat. Early cases indicated that in order for the defence to succeed, D should show there was no possibility of retreat. However, in **McInnes 1971**, the CA said that a person is not obliged to retreat from a threat in order to rely on the defence, but that this may be evidence for the jury when considering whether force was necessary, and if so whether it was reasonable. As we saw above, **s 76(6)** provides that the degree of force is not to be regarded as reasonable if it was disproportionate. So D does not have to retreat, but if leaving the scene is an easy option then it may mean any force used isn't seen as reasonable.

There must however, be a perceived threat. In **Malnik v DPP 1989**, D had armed himself with a martial arts weapon and gone to visit a man whom he believed had stolen some cars. He was arrested when approaching the house. He argued that the man was known to be violent, so having the weapon with him for protection was justified. The court held that the defence was not available because there had been no imminent threat; he had put himself in danger by going to the house. Again, in **Burns 2010**, there was an easy alternative. A prostitute agreed to go with D in his car but later changed her mind and wanted to return to where he had picked her up. He tried to remove her forcibly from the car and she suffered cuts and bruises. The court held that he had used unreasonable force, which was therefore unlawful and a battery. It resulted in harm, so was ABH. The CA upheld his conviction and held the use of force was unjustified; he could have regained possession of the car simply by driving her back.

Example

I disturb a burglar in my house and, feeling rather brave, hit him over the head with a china vase. While he lies unconscious at my feet, I kick him in the ribs a few times to punish him for daring to enter my house. The first action may be self-defence. The second is not. There is no threat and I am merely exacting revenge.

In **Martin 2001**, the court confirmed that the reasonable force test is objective and up to the jury to decide.

Key case

In **Martin**, the jury rejected a plea of self-defence by a farmer who shot and killed a 16-year old burglar and seriously injured another. According to evidence, they were retreating and posing no threat, and the jury felt that using a pump-action shotgun was excessive force in the circumstances. In the CA, Woolf LCJ confirmed that the farmer was entitled to use reasonable force to protect himself and his home, but that the members of the jury were *"surely correct in coming to their judgment that Mr Martin was not acting reasonably"*.

Referring to the subjective and objective questions, he went on to say,

"As to the first issue, what Mr Martin believed, the jury heard his evidence and they could only reject that evidence, if they were satisfied it was untrue. As to the second issue, as to what is a reasonable amount of force, obviously opinions can differ ... it was for the jury, as the representative of the public, to decide the amount of force which it would be reasonable and the amount of force which it would be unreasonable to use in the circumstances".

Principle: Whether the degree of force was reasonable is an objective question for the jury to decide.

In **Dawes 2013** (see loss of control), D argued that he acted in self-defence when he stabbed the man he found with his wife. The jury rejected the defence because he had acted unreasonably in the circumstances.

S 76 states that the degree of force used by D was not 'reasonable in the circumstances' if it was disproportionate.

Otherwise, **s 76** provides that what is reasonable is decided by reference *"to the circumstances as D believed them to be"*, so there is a subjective element. If D is mistaken the jury must consider the circumstances that D believed, not the actual circumstances.

Example

A man approaches me to ask directions. I mistakenly believe I am about to be attacked and hit him over the head with my umbrella. If I am charged with battery or actual bodily harm, the jury must decide if hitting him with an umbrella was justified in the circumstances that I believed, i.e., that I was being attacked.

The **Act** merely restates the law; it neither changes it nor arguably clarifies it. Cases since may have clarified matters somewhat.

In **Oye 2013** the CA held that D can be mistaken about the circumstances, even if suffering from delusions, but not the reasonableness of force, because that is purely an objective test. D had believed he was being confronted by evil spirits and punched two police officers, in one case causing a fracture. He said he acted in self-defence. The CA accepted that he genuinely believed he was being confronted by evil spirits, but that his response was disproportionate and not reasonable in the circumstances, so the defence failed. In **Press & another 2013**, the CA further clarified the subjective and objective elements of the defence. Whether D believed in the circumstances and that force was necessary are both subjective, so any mental disorder is relevant at this point. Whether the force was reasonable is purely objective so 'a test solely for the jury and not for D'. This explains the decision in **Martin** and is a useful case as it covers all the main features of the defence.

Key case

In **Press**, two soldiers were convicted of GBH after attacking another two men at a burger stall. One said he thought he was being threatened by the two men and so acted in self-defence. The men said they did nothing to provoke the violence. The soldier was suffering from post-traumatic stress disorder (PTSD).

The CA noted that **s 76(7)** required the jury to consider whether D 'honestly and instinctively' thought that the force used was necessary and also whether the force used was proportionate in those circumstances. In dealing with D's PTSD, the CA clarified the subjective and objective elements of self-defence.

The three main points for the jury to consider are

- whether D genuinely believed in the circumstances (subjective)
- whether D 'honestly and instinctively' thought that the force used was necessary (subjective)
- whether the force was reasonable (or proportionate) in all the circumstances (objective)

The CA held the PTSD was relevant to the first question of whether D held an honest belief that he was being threatened, because he would have been hypersensitive to threatening situations.

It was also relevant to the second question, which was not whether a reasonable person would have thought the degree of force used was necessary but whether D did. A person suffering from a PTSD may hold such a belief when a reasonable person would not.

However, unlike the earlier stages where D's belief may be the governing factor, the reasonableness of the response is a test solely for the jury and not for D. The jury may take into account the 'agony of the moment' factors, and recognise that D may not have time to weigh things up in a considered manner, and if D does no more than seems honestly and instinctively to be necessary, that is itself strong evidence that it was reasonable. However, it is only evidence and the jury must decide objectively whether D has gone beyond what was reasonable in the circumstances.

Finally the CA confirmed that D cannot rely on a mistaken belief 'which was the result of voluntarily taken drink or drugs'. The conviction stood.

Although arguably the **Act** does little to clarify the law, as the CA pointed out in **Oye** it is perhaps better that judges can base their decisions on an Act of Parliament rather than the common law.

In **Williams (Gladstone) 1987**, above, D successfully argued self-defence based on his mistaken belief that his actions were justified because he believed he was defending the youth. In **Martin 2001**, Woolf LCJ confirmed that

> "In judging whether the defendant had only used reasonable force, the jury has to take into account all the circumstances, including the situation as the defendant honestly believes it to be at the time, when he was defending himself. It does not matter if the defendant was mistaken in his belief as long as his belief was genuine".

In **Hargreaves 2010** (see GBH), D said that she had kicked out at her boyfriend as she believed he was going to attack her. This amounted to self-defence, because a mistaken belief can be relied on as long as genuinely held; she was not guilty of grievous bodily harm.

Even though a mistaken belief can be relied on if genuinely held, the force used must be reasonable in the circumstances. In **Daley 2016** (see diminished responsibility), D had braked suddenly and the driver behind bumped into him and got out of the car to ask why D had stopped. D stabbed him many times. He was suffering from paranoid schizophrenia and said he thought he was under attack. He was charged with murder. The jury rejected the defence of self-defence because even though he might have believed he was under attack, the amount of force used was unreasonable (though the jury accepted the defence of diminished responsibility).

Examination pointer

There are two ways to approach self-defence. Reasonable force can, for example, make a battery lawful, eliminating part of the *actus reus*, so there is no offence. Alternatively, reasonable force means self-defence can be used as a defence to a battery charge. Either approach is acceptable.

If a mistake is used to justify self-defence, you will need to discuss **Williams** as confirmed by **Martin** and by **s 76**, i.e., that the mistake must be genuine but does not have to be reasonable.

Self-defence and intoxication

In **O'Grady 1987**, D hit his friend over the head in the mistaken belief that the friend was trying to kill him. Both of them were drunk at the time. He was convicted of manslaughter and appealed. The CA rejected his appeal and said he could not rely on a drunken mistake to justify his actions. It was not fully clear whether this would apply to specific intent crimes such as murder, but in **Hatton 2005**, the CA said the rule applied whether the charge was murder or manslaughter. **S 76(5)** confirms that D cannot rely on a mistaken belief caused by voluntary intoxication. Therefore, D can use the defence based on an unreasonable mistake, but not a drunken one.

Evaluation pointer

The courts are reluctant to allow intoxicated mistake to support the defence for public policy reasons. It is not in the interests of society. In **O'Grady**, the CA said, "*Reason recoils from the conclusion that in such circumstances a defendant is entitled to leave the court without a stain on his character*".

It is arguable that policy issues are a matter for an elected government and Parliament, not the courts. A related problem is that, if successful, the defence leads to an acquittal, "without a stain on his character". On the plus side, it can be said that **s 76** has clarified some of the uncertainties.

Task 44

Discuss what defence(s) Amy should use in the following situations, using a case to support this and explaining whether it is likely to be successful and, if so, the effect it will have.

1. Amy is walking down the street one dark and rainy night when a young man steps out of a doorway right in front of her. Being a paranoid sort of person, she thinks she is being attacked and strikes out in alarm, cutting his cheek. In fact, he was just coming from his own house.

2. Walking home from the pub in a drunken haze Amy sees what she thinks is a man with a weapon coming towards her. She picks up a brick and hits him over the head, causing severe concussion and a nasty cut. It turns out he is from the local radio and is interviewing people on the streets for their views on violence at closing time.

3. Amy is walking down the street when she sees someone whom she believes is assaulting a young man. She intervenes and attacks him but he promptly arrests her. It turns out he is a policeman in plain clothes.

Summary of key issues

- Did D honestly believe that self-defence was justified? Williams (Gladstone)
- Was the force reasonable in the circumstances? Martin
- D is judged on the facts as they are believed to be, even if that belief is mistaken. Williams (Gladstone)/s 76
- D cannot rely on a drunken mistake. O' Grady/Hatton/s 76

Links to the non-substantive law

ELS: For links to the English legal system, look back at the diagram and examples in the introduction to Part 1. A jury is particularly involved with this defence as it includes consideration of what a reasonable person would have done, always a matter for a jury to decide.

The nature of law: The role of law is to protect both individuals and society as a whole. It seems fair that if D acted reasonably in self-defence the law should not mete out a punishment. However, if successful, the defence leads to an acquittal so the victim may well feel that justice was not achieved, as there is no punishment at all. This is particularly the case when the self-defence is mistaken, i.e., there was no danger. This 'all or nothing' nature of the law on self-defence has been criticised by the Law Commission. If D acted mistakenly in self-defence there is at least some fault shown in this, but as long as the belief was genuine the result is an acquittal. It may be better for self-defence to be a partial defence, like loss of control, at least in a murder case.

Self-test questions

1. What are the two main questions for the jury?
2. Why was self-defence rejected by the jury in **Martin**?
3. Can you rely on a mistaken belief to justify using force?
4. What was decided in Hatton and confirmed by **s 76**?
5. What is the result of a successful plea of self-defence?

Answers to tasks and self-test questions are on my website at www.drsr.org/publications/tasks. For some interactive exercises, click on 'Free Exercises'.

Chapter 18 Duress and duress of circumstances

"Necessity would open a door which no man could shut" – Lord Denning

By the end of this Chapter you should be able to:

- **Distinguish between these defences, whilst noting the overlap between them**
- **Explain how the law applies in practice by reference to cases**
- **Identify possible criticisms**

With duress, D is arguing that there was no alternative to committing the crime. It was necessary due to a threat, or to the circumstances.

Example

Don tells Dave that if he does not rob a bank he will kill his family. Dave can use duress as a defence to a burglary charge.

Dave is attacked by a violent gang whilst waiting at the traffic lights. He jumps the red light to get away. Dave can use duress of circumstances to the driving offence.

In **Shayler 2001,** the CA suggested that duress and necessity were the same. Both were available to a charge under the **Official Secrets Act 1989**, but not unless there was a threat of harm, there had to be an 'imminent threat to life or limb'. The dividing line between duress of circumstances and necessity, if any, is very faint and the terms have been used interchangeably by the courts. In fact in **Quayle 2005**, discussed below, a new term, 'necessity by circumstances' was used. For application purposes it is enough that you understand the defences of duress and duress of circumstances, but I have added a little on necessity as it relates to the development of the law, as well as suggesting a lack of clarity, so can be used for evaluation purposes.

Duress of threats is where there is a specific threat of harm to D if a particular crime is not committed. **Duress of circumstances** is where there is also a threat of harm. However, here the threat comes, not from another person, but from the surrounding circumstances. Necessity is similar to the latter. We will look briefly at necessity and then look at duress and duress of circumstances in more detail.

Necessity

Necessity is rarely a defence in itself. Stealing because you are starving is still theft, though your sentence may be reduced because you had some justification. In **Southwark London Borough v Williams 1971**, homelessness was not accepted as a reason for squatting. Lord Denning said that if it was, "no-one's house could be safe", and continued with the opening quote. He also said that if hunger could be used as a defence to theft, it would open another door through which "all kinds of lawlessness and disorder would pass".

In **Dudley and Stephens 1884**, the Ds had been shipwrecked and after several days in a lifeboat with no food they believed they would die. They killed and ate the cabin boy in order to save their own lives. The defence of necessity was rejected. It has since been confirmed that it cannot be used as a defence to a murder charge.

One of the very few cases where necessity was successfully raised is **Re A 2000.** A hospital sought a declaration that it would be lawful to operate on Siamese twins in the knowledge that one twin would die. The operation was the only way to save the life of the other twin. Although they may not have been prosecuted, they *could* have been charged with murder. They operated in the knowledge that one twin would die and so intended that consequence, even though they didn't desire it. The CA granted the declaration and confirmed they would have a defence of necessity. They made a distinction between cases of duress by threats or circumstances, and cases of real choice. In the latter, the question is one of justifying a choice between two evils. This is the defence of necessity. It would only succeed where the act *was necessary to avoid an inevitable evil, and the evil inflicted was not disproportionate* to the evil avoided.

It was confirmed in **Quayle 2005** that 'necessity' and 'necessity by circumstances' should be decided on a case-by-case basis. There are, however, certain requirements which will apply generally. We will look at duress first, as this is where the rules were established. Then we can look at some cases to illustrate duress of circumstances. There is an overlap between the two. Where the rules have developed, or reconfirmed, the law on duress generally I have included them in the discussion of duress. You should note in particular that the HL reconsidered the whole issue of duress in **Hasan 2005** (duress of threats), and this was applied by the CA in **Quayle** (duress of circumstances) with approval.

It is for D to provide evidence of duress, but then the burden of proof is on the prosecution to disprove it. If the defence succeeds then D will be acquitted.

Duress

The test for establishing the defence of duress was laid down in **Graham 1982**.

Key case

In **Graham**, D was a homosexual who lived with his wife and another man. He was charged with the murder of his wife. He alleged that the other man had threatened and intimidated him, and argued duress as a defence. The HL upheld his conviction and established a two-part test for duress. The jury must answer two questions:

Was the defendant impelled to act as he did because he believed that he had good cause to fear that if he did not so act he would be killed or caused serious injury? If so have the prosecution made the jury sure that a sober person of reasonable firmness, sharing the characteristics of the defendant, would not have responded that way?

Put more simply:

- Did D believe that there was good cause to fear death or serious injury if the crime was not committed?
- Would a sober person of reasonable firmness sharing the same characteristics have responded that way?

The test is therefore in part subjective and in part objective. However, the first part is not fully subjective because D must have 'good cause to fear'. Unlike self-defence and mistake, where as long as a belief is genuinely held it need not be reasonable, for duress it must be a reasonable belief.

The threat

The threat has to be a serious one. Firstly, it must be a threat of *harm*. In **Valderrama-Vega 1985**, it was said that financial pressure and a threat of disclosing that D was a homosexual was not enough. In **Shayler 2001**, the CA said that duress was only available where the threat was to 'life or serious injury'. In **Wadsworth 2009**, a woman pleaded duress to a charge of theft. She had stolen from the bank where she worked over a period of time, due to demands made by her boyfriend. She argued that she was in fear of violence and believed he would kill her or her family if she did not bring him the money. She had good cause to fear serious violence and the defence succeeded. However, in **Van Dao 2012**, the defence failed in a case where D had cultivated cannabis under threat of being held prisoner, as this was not sufficiently serious.

Secondly, the threat must be *imminent*. The rule was that if D could seek police protection or take evasive action then the defence was unavailable. Thus in **Gill 1963**, the defence failed because although there was a threat of harm if D did not steal a lorry, he had time to escape and seek help. This rule was relaxed in **Hudson and Taylor 1971**. Two young girls had lied in court because they were told they would be harmed if they testified against the accused. They successfully appealed against their conviction for perjury. The CA rejected the prosecution's argument that the threat wasn't imminent. They said that it was irrelevant that it could not be carried out immediately; it could be carried out on the streets late that night. The CA clearly recognised that the girls may not have received effective police protection from the threats. In **Abdul-Hussain 1999**, the Ds successfully appealed against a hi-jacking conviction. They believed they would be executed if returned to their own country, which they thought was imminent, and hi-jacked a plane to escape. The CA accepted duress of circumstances did not need an *immediate* threat, as long as it was *influencing* D at the time the crime was committed.

However, in **Hasan 2005**, Lord Bingham referred to both these cases and disapproved them on this point. He thought the limitation that D must have no chance of evasive action had been "unduly weakened". This HL case reaffirms that the threat must be immediate, or at least there should be no possibility of taking evasive action.

Key case

In **Hasan 2005**, D had fallen in with a drug dealer who was known to be violent. He told the dealer about a house where there was a lot of money kept in a safe. The dealer then told him that if he didn't burgle the house his family would be harmed. When charged with burglary he argued duress. Lord Bingham said that the defence was excluded where, due to a 'voluntary association' with criminals *"he foresaw, or ought reasonably to have foreseen, the risk of being subjected to any compulsion by threats of violence"*. He also said that if the harm threatened was not *"such as he reasonably expects to follow immediately or almost immediately"*, then there was little doubt that D should take evasive action *"whether by going to the police, or in some other way, to avoid committing the crime"*.

In **Hasan**, Lord Bingham restated the essential requirements for duress. These are:

- The threat relied on must be to cause death or serious injury
- The criminal conduct which it is sought to excuse has been directly caused by the threats
- The threat must be directed to D or a member of D's family, or to "a person for whose safety the defendant would reasonably regard himself as responsible"
- D may rely on duress only if there was no evasive action that could reasonably have been taken (such as going to the police, disapproving Hudson & Taylor)
- The questions for the jury were both objective (did D 'reasonably believe' there was a threat, approving Graham)
- The defence is not available where, as a result of a voluntary association with criminals, D "ought reasonably to have foreseen" the risk of violence

Examination pointer

Look for any evidence of a threat in the given scenario. If there is a threat from a person then duress will be appropriate. You will need to apply each of the rules from **Hassan** to decide whether you think the defence will succeed.

Sober person of reasonable firmness

In **Graham 1982**, D had been drunk as well as threatened but the court said that voluntary intoxication could not be taken into account. The test refers to a *'sober person'*. *'Of reasonable firmness'*, means factors such as timidity and susceptibility to threats will not be taken into account. In **Bowen 1996**, D had been charged with obtaining services by deception. He said he only did it after he and his family were threatened. The court refused to take his low IQ into account. However, as well as age and sex the CA did say that pregnancy, a recognised mental illness or serious physical disability could be relevant characteristics because these could affect D's ability to resist.

Self-induced duress

In **Sharp 1987**, D had been involved in a plan with a gang to commit a robbery, he then tried to withdraw but was threatened. Someone was killed during the robbery and his conviction for manslaughter was upheld. The CA made clear that the defence would fail where D knew that the gang he had joined might put pressure on him to commit an offence. This is self-induced duress as D had a choice in the first place. The key issue is what is known about the gang. In **Shepherd 1987**, the defence succeeded as there was no evidence of any violence prior to the threats. It is now clear that this is an objective test. Even if D didn't know of any violent tendencies, the defence will fail if these would have been obvious to anyone else. This was made clear in **Hasan**, which is an example of self-induced duress. The question is whether D *should* have known, rather than whether D *did* know, that there was a risk of being threatened. The words "or ought reasonably to have foreseen" in **Graham** had indicated this.

In **Ali 2008**, D had been charged with robbery. He did not deny the robbery but said that another man had forced him into it. His parents had warned him the man was a criminal and to stay away from him. He pleaded the defence of duress. The CA held the defence was not available where, because of a voluntary association with others engaged in criminal activity, D foresaw, or 'ought to have foreseen', the risk of being subjected to any compulsion by threats of violence to commit criminal acts. If so, the duress will be deemed voluntary and the defence will fail. The main question was whether he had voluntarily put himself in a position where such a risk was reasonably foreseeable, and it was made clear that this was an objective test.

Duress of circumstances

Duress of circumstances arose during the 80's in driving offence cases. Recognising that necessity was rarely allowed as a defence, lawyers had started to argue that duress could extend beyond the traditional 'threat by a person' to situations where D has no alternative but to commit a crime. In **Conway 1988**, D was in his car when he was approached by two men. He believed they were going to attack him and he drove recklessly to escape from the perceived threat. The CA accepted the defence and said it was 'convenient' to refer to such a defence as 'duress of circumstances'. In **Martin 1988**, D had driven his son to work whilst disqualified. He argued that his son might lose his job if he was late and his wife had threatened to commit suicide if he did not take him. The judge said that English law recognised a 'defence of necessity' in extreme circumstances. In such cases, where the threat came from dangers other than a threat from another person, *"it is conveniently called duress of circumstances"*. In the early days, it was most commonly used for driving offences. In **DPP v Bell 1992**, D drove whilst drunk, again to escape from a threatening gang. The defence succeeded because as soon as he was out of danger he stopped in a lay-by. In **Mulally 2006**, a woman drove whilst drunk but was not in danger at the time, so the defence of duress was rejected.

This shows that as with duress, the threat must be effective at the time of the crime or the defence will fail.

The defence is not confined to driving offences. In **Pommell 1995**, D was charged with possession of a firearm and successfully argued duress. He said that he had taken the gun from someone who was threatening to use it in a revenge attack. As this was in the early hours of the morning, he kept it overnight, intending to take it to the police in the morning. The police had, he said, arrived before he could do so.

Although coming from circumstances rather than a person, in all these cases there was a threat of physical harm, either to D or to another.

Examination pointer

If there is no evidence in the given scenario of a threat from a person, look for any circumstances that may be threatening, and consider duress of circumstances. Apply the rules from **Hassan**, but note in particular that there needs to be a threat of physical harm, whichever defence is used. If there is any evidence that D belongs to a gang, look at how **Hasan 2005** confirmed the rules on self-induced duress seen in **Sharp** and **Shepherd**.

Task 45

Look at the following situations and decide if I can successfully use a defence of duress, using a case in support:

- I am threatened with being exposed as a cheat and a drunk if I do not steal a packet of smoked salmon from the supermarket. I do so and am charged with theft.
- I am chased by a man who is threatening to hit me. I steal a car to escape. I drive to a nearby house where I have friends. I am charged with theft.
- I am at a party and a bit drunk. As I live 50 miles away, I intend to stay overnight. An old enemy turns up and threatens to beat me up. I run outside and see my car in the drive. I get in and drive all the way home. I am charged with driving with excess alcohol.

Duress and mistake

Conway 1988 shows that D can use the defence even if there is no actual threat. It turned out that the people D thought were going to attack him were plain-clothes policemen. However, he was able to rely on duress even though he was mistaken as to the threat. He was judged on the facts as he honestly, and reasonably, believed them to be.

In **Safi 2003**, the judge had suggested there had to *be* a threat but the CA said that this was wrong. They confirmed that the **Graham** test was still the law. Thus both types of duress could (as with self-defence) be used with mistake. However, there is a difference. With duress the mistake must be reasonable. This was implied by the test in **Graham** (did D have *'good cause to fear'*?) and has now been confirmed by the HL in **Hasan**. Lord Bingham said *"there is no warrant for relaxing the requirement that the belief must be reasonable as well as genuine"*.

The overlap

Duress of circumstances has mostly replaced necessity, but both terms may be seen in judgments. In **Quayle 2005**, D had argued necessity in defence to a charge of growing cannabis. He argued that it was necessary for medical reasons. He was in pain and it was the only drug that allowed him to sleep without knocking him out. He did not want to take anything that knocked him out as he had children to look after. The CA rejected his appeal. They referred to the "defence of necessity where the force or compulsion is exerted not by human threats but by extraneous circumstances". They relied on **Rodger and Rose 1998,** where the Ds had been suicidal because they were in prison and when caught escaping had argued duress of circumstances. The defence had failed and the earlier cases were distinguished on the basis that the threat was not from an extraneous source, it was the suicidal tendencies of the Ds themselves. The CA in **Quayle** confirmed that the threat could come from circumstances rather than a person but restated that it must come from an external source.

The CA in **Quayle** recognised the overlap between the defences and said that both "duress of threats and necessity by circumstances" should be confined to cases of threats of physical injury. They did point out, however, that there was no 'over-arching principle' which applied to all cases. They referred to the comments of the CA in **Abdul-Hussain,** that in the absence of parliamentary intervention, the law should develop on a case-by-case basis.

Evaluation pointer

Developing the law on a case-by-case basis may be achieving justice but is it at the expense of consistency? The courts have clearly stated that Parliament should address the issue. In **Safi 2003** (another hi-jacking case), the CA noted that the courts had 'repeatedly' emphasised the urgent need for legislation on duress. It appears from the detailed discussion in **Hasan 2005** that the HL has decided to try to clarify the law itself.

Limits to the availability of the defence of duress

We have seen some of the limitations in the cases discussed. They were restated by the HL in **Hasan 2000**:

- Duress does not apply to murder – Howe 1987
- Nor attempted murder – Gotts 1992
- D may not rely on duress as a result of a voluntary association with others engaged in criminal activity where there was a foreseeable risk of being subjected to threats of violence – Sharp 1987/Hasan 2005

In **Wilson 2007**, a teenager was accused along with his father, of murdering his mother. He argued that he only helped in the murder because he was scared of his father. The CA confirmed that however much duress a person was under the defence was not available for murder.

In its **2006 Report (No. 304)** the Law Commission proposed that legislation should provide that the defence should apply to all offences including murder and attempted murder but these proposals have not been implemented.

Criticisms and reform

The defence has not been without its critics and in its **1978 Report** the Law Commission acknowledged several criticisms of the defence of duress. These included:

- It should not be justifiable to do wrong or cause harm
- The defence could be used as an excuse to commit a crime
- It should not fall upon an individual to balance wrongdoing against the avoidance of harm to themselves or to others
- It could encourages terrorists and kidnappers

There are some fair points here. However, the Commission proposed that legislation should provide a defence and recommended that:

- Duress should be a general defence applicable to all offences including murder and attempted murder
- Threats of harm to individuals should be allowed but not threats to property. Self-induced duress should not be allowed
- The burden of proof should be on the defendant to establish duress

Evaluation pointer

Many of the Commission's recommendations have been incorporated by case law. The proposal in regard to murder is one that hasn't. It is somewhat contentious. It is arguable that it is not up to D to decide whose life is worth more. In **Hasan 2005**, the HL noted the logic of the Commission's recommendation, but also noted that the recommendation had not been adopted *"no doubt because it is felt that in the case of the gravest crimes no threat to the defendant, however extreme, should excuse commission of the crime"*. One problem is that the defence results in an acquittal. It could be argued that allowing it to be used as a partial defence to murder, reducing murder to manslaughter, would be more satisfactory.

Essentially, the defence needs to be clarified by Parliament, as requested by the courts.

Summary

Defence	Requirements	Limits
Necessity	The evil avoided is greater than the evil done	Case by case basis. Could justify a killing (**Re A**)
Duress	Imminent threat of death or serious injury (from a person) D had 'good cause' to believe such a threat (**Graham/Hasan**) a reasonable person would have acted as D did	Not murder or attempted murder (**Howe/Gotts**) Not where D voluntarily associates with those foreseeably posing a risk of threats No evasive action possible (**Hasan**)
Duress of circumstances	Imminent threat of death or serious injury (from circumstances) D had 'good cause' to believe such a threat (**Graham/Hasan**) a reasonable person would have acted as D did	Not murder or attempted murder No evasive action possible (**Hasan**) The threat need not come from a person but must be external to D (**Quayle**)

Links to the non-substantive law

ELS: For links to the English legal system, look back at the diagram and examples in the introduction to Part 1. Again, the jury has an important role with this defence. The **Graham** test includes consideration of what a reasonable person would have done, always a matter for a jury to decide.

The nature of law: The role of law is to protect both the individual and society as a whole, so it is right that duress should not apply to murder. However, if D is forced to act because of a serious threat of harm there is a lower level of fault but this cannot be taken into account. The sentence for murder is mandatory so the judge cannot take into account any reduced level of fault. In cases other than murder and attempted murder, the defence achieves greater justice. The law balances the interest of the public in being protected against those of D, who has only committed the crime due to a threat of serious harm. In this case, unusually, the private interest prevails. A final point is that justice requires clarity, especially in the criminal law. It is arguably the case that the defence of duress does not meet these requirements, and, as the Law Commission suggests, should be clarified by Parliament.

Self-test questions

1. In which case was the test for duress established?
2. What did **Hasan** confirm in regard to the first part of this test?
3. Is the test for self-induced duress an objective or subjective one?
4. What point was confirmed in **Quayle** about the source of the threat?

For answers to the tasks and self-test questions, please go to my website at www.drsr.org and click the button 'Answers to tasks'. For a range of free interactive exercises, click on 'Free Exercises' to see what's available.

Summary and evaluation of the defences and their effect

An important thing to note is the *effect* of defences. This will help you decide which one is most appropriate.

Defence	Main points	Which crimes	Effect
Consent	May be express or implied e.g., in sports - A-G's Reference (No 6 of 1980) 1981	Makes a battery, and thus ABH, lawful so the *actus reus* is not complete	Acquittal
Insanity	Defect of reason caused by disease of the mind (internal factor) M'Nagten rules	All	Not guilty by reason of insanity
Automatism	Must be total loss of control (caused by an external factor) Broome v Perkins 1987	All	Acquittal
Intoxication—voluntary	Must remove *mens rea* Kingston 1994	All crimes requiring *mens rea*	Acquittal
Intoxication—involuntary	Majewski 1977	Specific intent crimes	Reduces to basic intent crime
		Basic intent crimes	Guilty
Self-defence	Force must be reasonable Martin 2001	All	Acquittal
Duress	Must be a threat of imminent harm Hasan 2005	Not murder or attempted murder	Acquittal

Task 46

Note the principle and brief facts of the cases:

- A.G.'s Reference (No 6 of 1980) 1981
- Sullivan 1984
- Broome v Perkins 1987
- Kingston 1994
- Majewski 1977

- Williams (Gladstone) 1987

Key criticisms

All these can be used in a discussion of whether justice is achieved. As with all defences the law is recognising a lower level of fault, so many also relate to fault.

- There is a problem with finding insanity in respect of people whose conditions are not normally associated with mental disorder
- The stigma of an insanity verdict may mean people who genuinely have a mental problem do not plead the defence
- The insanity defence originates from an 1843 case and should be updated because of medical advances
- Majewski 1977 seems to dispense with the requirement of *mens rea*. If D is drunk that shows recklessness, no other evidence is required
- The Majewski 'rules' are not fully clear as to which crimes are specific intent and which are basic intent
- Duress should not be available to justify wrongdoing, especially where harm is caused

Chapter 19: The A-level Examination (7162)

About the exams

This Chapter covers information for all three papers so you will have a complete idea of what is required. The guidance and actual paper are just for Paper 1.

The A-level is a two-year course with an external examination at the end of it (the first being in May/June 2019). There are three papers. Each is 2 hours long, worth 100 marks and is a third of the A-Level.

All papers are a mix of multiple-choice, short answer and extended writing questions. The nature of law and the English legal system come into all three (see table below for what goes where), the difference being the core substantive law.

Paper 1: The nature of law and the English legal system (25 marks) plus criminal law (75 marks)

Paper 2: The nature of law and the English legal system (25 marks) plus tort (75 marks)

Paper 3: The nature of law and the English legal system (25 marks) plus contract OR human rights (75 marks)

The assessment objectives (AOs)

These apply to all A-level courses and all examination boards. The examination will test you in the following ways.

AO1 tests your knowledge and understanding of the English legal system and legal rules and principles (13.33%)

AO2 tests your ability to apply legal rules and principles to given scenarios in order to present a legal argument using appropriate terminology (9%)

AO3 tests your ability to evaluate and analyse legal rules, principles, concepts and issues (11%)

Weighting is the same for all three papers and is given as a percentage (of 33.33% for each paper) in brackets. You should be aware of these weightings so that you plan your time accordingly. AO1 for the three papers together is 40%, AO2 is 27% and AO3 is 33%. This makes a total of 100% of the A-level.

For specimen papers and mark schemes visit the AQA site at www.aqa.org.uk.

For teachers: Please visit my website at www.drsr.org for a Guide for teachers including the changes to the specifications and examinations.

The English legal system and the nature/role of law: What goes where for A-level 7162?

Paper 1 Crime	Paper 2 Tort (including balancing competing interests)	Paper 3 Contract or Human rights (HR)
Statutory interpretation	Parliamentary law-making	The rule of law
Precedent	Law Reform	Delegated legislation
Criminal courts	Civil courts	The European Union
Lay people	Alternative dispute resolution	
Legal personnel	Judges and their role in civil courts	Judges and their role in civil (contract) or criminal courts (HR)
Judges and their role in criminal courts	Access to justice and funding in the civil system	Independence of the judiciary
Access to justice and funding in the criminal system	Law and society - fault	Access to justice and funding in the civil (contract) or criminal (HR) system
Law and society - fault	Law and morality	Law and society – balancing conflicting interests
Law and Justice		Law and Justice
		Law and morality

Note that where the English Legal System fits in has changed slightly from the AS papers.

Statutory interpretation was on Tort Paper 2 and is now on Crime Paper 1.

Law reform was on Crime Paper 1 and is now on Tort Paper 2.

Independence of the judiciary was on Crime Paper 1 and is now on Contract or Human Rights Paper 3.

The European Union was on Tort Paper 2 and is now on Contract or Human Rights Paper 3.

The rule of law was on Crime Paper 1 and is now on Contract or Human Rights Paper 3.

Delegated legislation was on Tort Paper 2 and is now on Contract or Human Rights Paper 3.

As for the nature of law, here is a quick summary

Law and society – fault: Papers 1 and 2

Law and society – balancing competing interests: Paper 3 (but note it is included in the substantive law for tort in relation to injunctions as a remedy)

Law and morality: Papers 2 and 3

Law and Justice: Papers 1 and 3

Although the non-substantive law is assigned to a particular paper, you are not limited to using only that area of law to illustrate the concept.

Types of question and apportionment of marks

For each paper there are 5 multiple-choice questions on the substantive law and the English legal system (total 5 marks). There are 2 short answer questions at 5 marks each one on the substantive law and one on the English legal system (total 10 marks). There is one 10-mark question on the substantive law (total 10 marks). There is one 15-mark extended writing question on BOTH substantive and non-substantive law (ELS or nature / role of law) total 15 marks. Finally, there are two extended writing questions at 30 marks each (total 60 marks). One of these is only substantive law, the other mixes substantive and non-substantive law (ELS or nature / role of law).

It looks like this:

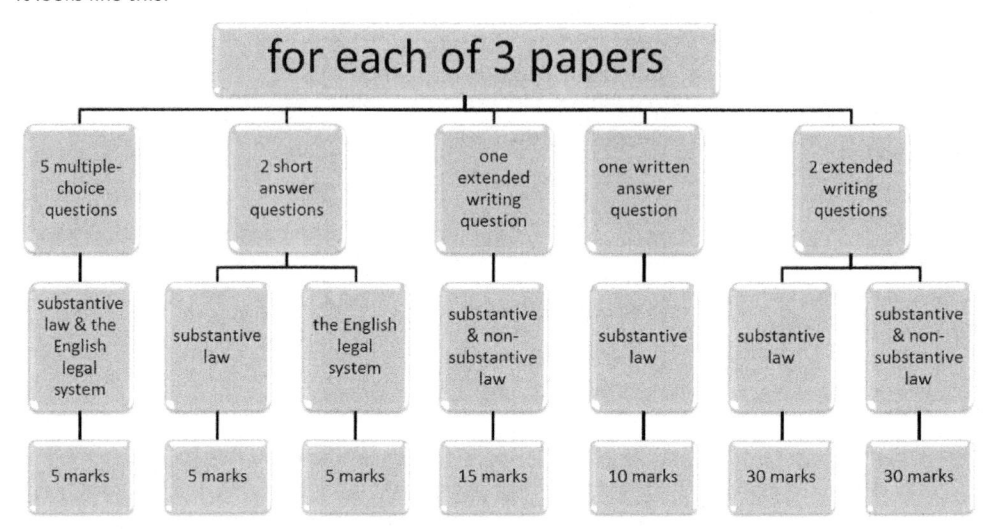

for each of 3 papers

- 5 multiple-choice questions
  - substantive law & the English legal system — 5 marks
- 2 short answer questions
  - substantive law — 5 marks
  - the English legal system — 5 marks
- one extended writing question
  - substantive & non-substantive law — 15 marks
- one written answer question
  - substantive law — 10 marks
- 2 extended writing questions
  - substantive law — 30 marks
  - substantive & non-substantive law — 30 marks

Note that where for AS there were two extended writing questions, there are three for A-level. In each of the papers, you have to answer **all** questions. Two questions are a mix of criminal law and either the English legal system or the nature of law. One of these is not scenario based but requires analysis of the concept or legal system to evaluate the substantive law topic. Look back at the introduction diagram and the links at the end of each chapter for guidance on these.

In each of the papers, you have to answer **all** questions.

Examination guidance

As you see there is a mix of questions and sometimes a question will include both application and evaluation of the law. What you need for application and essay questions cannot be divided completely but there is a difference. For both, it is important to know and understand cases and principles well. This is because the examination is not merely a test of knowledge, it is also testing your ability to *use* that knowledge, whether in applying what you know to a set of facts, or in evaluating what you know and connecting it to other areas of law.

In either case, you should structure your answer. As this is a test of **law** you need to state the legal principles involved and apply them to the particular question. A solid start is worth a lot and gets the examiner on your side.

Don't be tempted to write all you know about the area. Being selective is a skill in itself and an examiner won't be able to give you marks for stuff that isn't relevant, even if it is correct. If you ask a solicitor for advice, they won't tell you everything they know, they will pick out the law that suits your case. You have to do the same in answering an examination question.

In precedent, you learnt that the important part of a case is the *ratio decidendi*, the reasoning behind the judge's decision. As you revise a case, think about this and look for the legal principle.

It is important to:

Explain a case briefly but show that you understand the principle

Show that you understand the relevant law well enough to be selective

Before going on to look at an examination paper here is some general guidance for the two types of extended writing questions. See also the AS examination guidance for the two summaries for application and evaluation in the mixed questions. Note that for the A-level there are still two mixed questions on each paper. However, this time one is based on a scenario and one is not.

Application advice

For application of the law to scenarios (problem questions) you need the same logical approach as for AS. Read the scenarios carefully to make sure you understand the question. Sometimes you will be directed to a specific offence and sometimes not. It may be necessary to discuss more than one offence as there is often an overlap, however, if you are told to discuss a particular offence you cannot get marks for discussing any other offence(s). An example is the overlap between **s 18** and attempted murder where it is only a matter of chance that V did not die, as in **R v Z 2017**. Always read the questions carefully to see if you are being directed to a particular offence, if not discuss both possibilities.

Try to summarise the facts in a few words. It is valuable when time is short. The principle forming the *ratio decidendi* is the important part, although you may need to discuss the facts briefly to show why you have chosen that particular case.

Example

In **Roberts 1971 and Pagett 1983**, the principle was that a foreseeable act will not break the chain of causation. If the scenario involves someone being injured when running away from the threat of an attack, **Roberts** is the most appropriate case. You don't need all the facts but should refer to the fact that she tried to escape an attack, and this was foreseeable. The principle of the case was based on this, i.e., a foreseeable act does not break the chain of causation. This case therefore supports a conclusion that the chain wasn't broken so D is guilty for the injury caused.

If you can't remember the name of a case that is relevant don't leave it out but refer to it in a general way, e.g., 'in one decided case....' or 'in a similar case....'

Read the scenarios carefully to make sure you understand the questions (I say this often as it is really important). Make a few brief notes; these can be a useful checklist later when you are tired and possibly short of time.

You need to use the current legal tests, which come from statutes or cases. Some crimes (including murder) are common law offences so *all* the law comes from cases, and even if the law comes from a statute, that statute has to be interpreted by judges. **Key cases** highlight those which are particularly important. Use these to apply only the law that is both *current* and *relevant* to the given facts. Use the ***examination pointers***, plus the ***diagrams*** or ***summaries*** at the end of each Chapter as a guide for problem questions. An answer to a problem scenario should be rounded off with a conclusion as to liability. If it is not clear cut do the best you can; the main thing is to use the law and apply it sensibly. If you do that, your conclusion is likely to be sustainable. This means you should never start an answer with "D will be guilty of ...." What you need to do is to:

Identify the appropriate area of law – this will tell the examiner you have understood the focus of the scenario and will shape your answer. Sometimes you are directed to a specific offence in which case deal only with that.

Apply the relevant rules in a logical way to the facts– this will be the substance of your answer. Define the offence(s) then take each part of the *actus reus* and *mens rea* in turn. Do this for each offence if there is more than one, and for any possible defence. If you do this logically you won't leave anything out. If the area is covered by a statute quote the law from that statute accurately and with section numbers if possible. Then consider if a defence is possible and define and apply the law on this.

Add a little more detail if there is a particular issue shown by the facts – there will often be something particular to focus on so look for clues in the given facts to see if you need more on anything e.g., causation.

Support your application with relevant cases – only use cases which are relevant to the particular scenario, and only state those facts that are essential to show why that case is relevant.

Conclude in a way that is sustainable and supported by what you have said and the cases you used – it is useful to look back at the question at this point. If it says "Advise Mary ...", then make sure your answer does so. In your conclusion you should pull together the different strands of your answer and then say that based on that application you would 'advise Mary that ….'.

It is good policy to refer to the facts of a scenario as often as you can when applying the law as this indicates that you are answering the specific question and have a sound enough knowledge of law and legal principles to know which cases are relevant to the particular facts.

Application practice Task 47

In **Freaney 2011**, a woman was charged with the murder of her severely autistic 11-year-old son, Glen. Mrs Freaney denied murder but admitted manslaughter on the grounds of diminished responsibility. Her son needed 24-hour care and help with dressing, washing, brushing his teeth and eating. He was not toilet trained and still wore nappies. She killed her son using her coat belt and when she was sure he was dead she lay down on the bed beside him and tried to commit suicide. She was suffering extreme mental stress at the time she strangled her son.

Apply the law to this case to decide whether she will succeed with the defence of diminished responsibility.

Evaluation advice

Essays require more discussion and evaluation of the law or legal issues. The **key criticisms** in the summaries are designed to help with this, along with the **evaluation pointers**. The **'links to non-substantive law'** should help you see how a particular area of law connects to the English legal system and the various concepts of law. The law is not cut up into sections that can be dealt with in isolation, the topics you cover in your course are interwoven and you will need to show you understand the link between various areas of the substantive and non-substantive law.

In an essay question, you may need to form an opinion or weigh up arguments about a particular area of law, or a certain principle or issue. Here a broader range of knowledge is needed, showing you understand any problems with the law and are able to assess these and discuss possible reforms. You should always round off your answer with a short concluding paragraph, preferably referring back to the question. This shows the examiner you are addressing the given question and not one you would have preferred to have been asked! Planning an answer on an area of law is fine, as long as you are prepared to adapt it to the specific question. Not doing so is a common failing which examiners' reports frequently comment on.

Example

If the examination question asks you to discuss both criticisms and reforms, make sure both these words are included in your concluding paragraph. An example for a question on the non-fatal offences would be to discuss the problems and proposals for reform and conclude something like this: *"As can be seen from the above there have been many criticisms of the law in this area over a long period of time. Despite the calls for reform, especially those of the Law Commission, very little has been done. These offences remain unnecessarily complex and case decisions are unpredictable. If the law is not clear and accessible it cannot achieve justice. "*

Examination practice Task 48

Look back at some of the evaluation pointers and links to the non-substantive law. Make a few notes on the problems with the law and the difficulty these pose in relation to achieving justice, e.g., because the law is not sufficiently clear or there are conflicting cases. Keep these for revision and for using when answering the mixed question on the criminal law and the concepts of justice or fault.

As with application of the law, you should try to take a logical approach. The beginning, should introduce the subject matter, the central part should explain/analyse/criticise it as appropriate, and the conclusion should bring the various strands of argument together with reference to the question set. Where possible, try to consider alternative arguments. A well-rounded essay will bring in other views even if you disagree with them. Here is an idea of how you might structure an essay. This is only a rough guide; in the central part you will of course need to cover any specific issues raised by the question e.g., a discussion of reforms, or of the development of an area of law, or of whether the particular law achieves justice.

State the issue – quote from the question

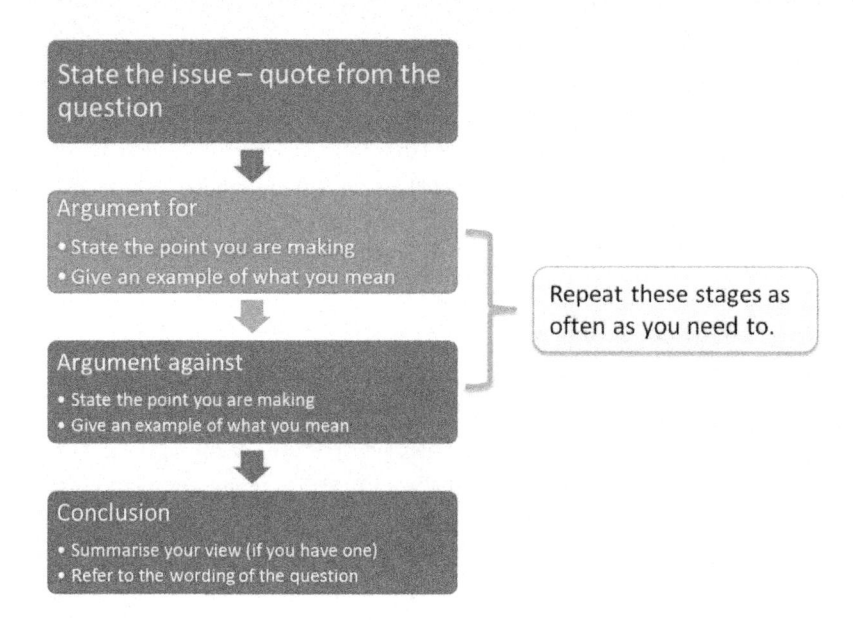

Argument for
- State the point you are making
- Give an example of what you mean

Argument against
- State the point you are making
- Give an example of what you mean

Repeat these stages as often as you need to.

Conclusion
- Summarise your view (if you have one)
- Refer to the wording of the question

Finally, if you are confused by a case, or you see cases which conflict, don't despair. Just think 'I can use this to illustrate an argument that the law has not achieved justice'. If there is confusion or uncertainty then there will be a valid case for arguing that the law is not fully satisfactory so does not achieve justice.

Examination practice Task 49

Look back at any of the tasks that you had trouble with. Do these again and then check your answers before attempting the examination paper.

Examination paper Task 50

For each of the three papers that make up the A-level examination there are 100 marks in total and a time of 2 hours. Each paper is worth 33% of the full A-level.

What's assessed in Paper 1?

The nature of law and the English legal system (25 marks out of 100)

Criminal law (75 marks out of 100)

It is unlikely an examination paper will cover everything but I have included a wide range here so that you get practice on as many topics as possible.

Note that because of this I have used a scenario in Question 9. In the actual paper this question is not based on a scenario.

A-Level law Paper 1

Answer all questions

Tick the correct answer for multiple-choice questions

[1] Which **one** of the following statements best describes **absolute** liability? **1 mark**

A Liability without *actus reus*

B Liability without *mens rea*

C Liability without motive

D Liability without *actus reus* or *mens rea*

[2] Which **one** of the following statements is **false**? **1 mark**

A Automatism is caused by an external factor

B Automatism is caused by an internal factor

C Insanity is caused by an internal factor

D Insanity can be caused by a physical disease

[3] Which **one** of the following statements about the *ratio decidendi* of a case is **most accurate**? **1 mark**

A The *ratio decidendi* of a case is a persuasive precedent

B The *ratio decidendi* of a case is a clear statement of the facts

C The *ratio decidendi* of a case is a binding precedent

D There can only be one *ratio decidendi* in a case

[4] Which **one** of the following statements best describes a persuasive precedent? **1 mark**

A A precedent which must be followed

B A precedent which may be followed

C A precedent which will not be followed

D A precedent set in a higher court

[5] Select the most **junior** judges in the list. **1 mark**

A Circuit judges

B High Court judges

C Recorders

D Appeal Court judges

[6] Damon is charged with ABH. Briefly explain the plea before venue and mode of trial hearing to him and tell him what the terms burden of proof and standard of proof mean. **5 marks**

[7] Brad approaches an off licence carrying a fake gun, intending to rob it. As he approaches the door he sees a police officer coming towards him, so walks away. The police officer saw the gun and arrests him on a charge of attempted robbery.

Explain why, in law, the charge is likely to fail. **5 marks**

[8]

Dave throws a brick at Tommy as he passes nearby. Tommy falls awkwardly and suffers a sprained wrist. Later Tommy is still in pain so goes to the hospital. The doctor puts his wrist in a splint incorrectly and he suffers a permanent injury.

Advise Dave as to his liability under **s 20** of the **Offences against the Person Act 1861. 10 marks**

In question 9 you are required to provide an extended answer which shows a clear, logical and sustained line of reasoning leading to a valid conclusion.

[9]

Luke and Jill were teenagers and were bored. They went into a derelict building and started a fire by setting light to an old duvet. The fire spread and Billy, a homeless man, who, unknown to them, was squatting there was killed by the fumes.

Examine the rules on constructive manslaughter as they apply to Luke and Jill. Discuss the importance of fault in the criminal law and the extent to which the rules on constructive manslaughter meet the usual requirement of fault (*mens rea*) and whether liability should always depend on fault. **15 marks**

In question 10 you are required to provide an extended answer which shows a clear, logical and sustained line of reasoning leading to a valid conclusion.

[10]

Olga called in at the supermarket on the way back from the pub where she had drunk several glasses of wine. She put a few items in her shopping basket, then picked up a packet of coffee and while no-one was looking put it in her pocket. When she got to the check-out queue she got scared and put the coffee in her shopping basket. She paid for it and the other items with a £10-note but was given change from £20. She saw she had been given too much change and rushed to leave before it was noticed. In her haste, she pushed another shopper out of the way.

Consider Olga's liability in respect of the coffee and the excess change under the **Theft Act 1968** and also consider what effect it will have if she says she would not have taken the coffee had she been sober. **30 marks**

In question 11 you are required to provide an extended answer which shows a clear, logical and sustained line of reasoning leading to a valid conclusion.

[11]

Darpak killed a man after returning home to find his wife asleep on the sofa with him. The marriage was volatile and Darpak had left the house in a temper after a row, and his wife did not expect him back. She had invited a male friend for a drink and they fell asleep after consuming a lot of vodka. Darpak hit the man with his fists and then threw the bottle of vodka at him. The man picked up the bottle by the neck and swung it at Darpak. Darpak got a knife from the kitchen and the next time the man came at him with the bottle he lashed out and the knife caught the man in the neck. The man died and Darpak was charged with murder. Darpak said he didn't intend to cause serious harm and anyway was acting in self-defence.

In **Clinton 2012**, the CA used a purposive approach when interpreting **s 54** and **s 55** of the **Coroners and Justice Act 2009** on the rules relating to sexual infidelity.

Consider Darpak's liability for the man's death and whether he might have a defence to the charge of murder. Assess the effect of the principle of law which resulted from **Clinton** in a case like

Darpak's. Also assess the purposive approach to statutory interpretation and how judges can find out what Parliament's purpose was when passing an Act. **30 marks**

END OF QUESTIONS

Appendix: Abbreviations and acknowledgements

Acknowledgements

With thanks to the AQA Portfolio Curriculum Team for their help and support in interpretation of the 2017 specifications and to my husband Dave for the diagrams and proof-reading.

The following abbreviations are commonly used. In an examination you should write them in full the first time, e.g., write 'actual bodily harm (ABH)' and then after that you can just write 'ABH'.

General

Draft Code – A Criminal Code for England and Wales (Law Commission No. 177), 1989

CCRC Criminal Cases Review Commission

ABH actual bodily harm

GBH grievous bodily harm

D defendant

C claimant

V Victim

QBD Queen's Bench Division (of the High Court)

CA Court of Appeal

HL House of Lords

SC Supreme Court

Acts

S – section (thus **s 1** Theft Act 1968 refers to section 1 of that Act)

s 1(2) means section 1 subsection 2 of an Act.

OAPA – Offences against the Person Act 1861

In cases – these don't need to be written in full

CC (at beginning) chief constable

CC (at end) county council

BC borough council

DC district council

LBC London borough council

AHA Area Health Authority

J Justice

LJ Lord Justice

LCJ Lord Chief Justice

LC Lord Chancellor

AG Attorney General

CPS Crown Prosecution Service

DPP Director of Public Prosecutions

Index of cases

Abdul-Hussain 1999	184
Adebolajo 2014	84
Adomako 1994	113, 118, 130
AG's Reference (No 1 of 1992) 1993	154
AG's Reference (No 6 of 1980) 1981	44
A-G's Reference (No2 of 1992) 1994	166
AG's Reference No 1 of 1983	139
AGs Reference (No 3 of 1994) 1997	84
Airedale NHS Trust v Bland 1993	18, 19, 83, 84
Ali 2008	185
Allen 1988	170
Alphacell v Woodward 1972	36
Anderton v Ryan 1985	154
Asmelash 2013	98
Attorney-General for Northern Ireland v Gallagher 1963	172
Attorney-General's Reference (No 3 of 1994) 1997	87
Bailey 1983	167, 173
Bailey 2002	103, 109, 129
Baillie 1995	95
Bamford 2016	95
Barnes 2004	45
Beard 1920	169
Belfon 1976	56
Bilton 2005 (unreported)	162
Blake 1997	18, 37
Blaue 1975	24, 80, 85
Bollom 2004	55, 58
Bowen 1996	185
Bratty v Attorney General for Northern Ireland 1963	161, 163, 165
Briggs 2004	136
Bristow 2013	120
Broome v Perkins 1987	166
Brown 1994	14, 53, 77, 79, 80
Burgess 1991	162, 163
Burns 2010	177
Burrell and Harmer 1967	45
Burstow 1996	55
Byrne 1960	104, 107
C v Eisenhower 1983	54, 56, 80
Cahill 1993	144
Caldwell 1982	31
Campbell 1987	107
Campbell 1991	153
Carey and Others 2006	122
Cato 1976	122
Chan-Fook 1994	49
Chua 2015	22, 86
Church 1967	119, 124
CICA v FTT 2014	84
Clarence 1888	54
Clarke 1972	161
Clinton 2012	95, 99, 100, 200
Clouden 1987	149
Cocker 1989	93, 129
Codere 1916	163
Coley 2013	165, 166
Collins v Wilcock 1984	44
Constanza 1997	42
Conway 1988	185, 186
Corbett 1996	23
Corcoran v Anderton 1980	149
Courtie 1984	48
Cunningham 1957	31, 56, 87
Dalby 1982	122
Daley 2016	108, 180
Dantes 2015	108, 164
Davidge and Burnett 1984	139
Dawes 2013	96, 178
Dawson 1985	120
Dawson and James 1978	149
Dias 2002	122
Dica 2004	54
Dietschmann 2003	105
Doughty 1986	94
Dowds 2012	98, 106, 107, 171, 172
DPP v A 2000	56
DPP v Bell 1992	185
DPP v K 1990	45
DPP v Ross Smith 2006	50
DPP v Smith 1960	27, 86
Dudley and Stephens 1884	182
Dytham 1979	19
Elliott 1983	31
Elmi 2016	164
Evans 2009	115
Evans 2012	95
Fagan v Metropolitan Police Commissioner 1969	17, 20, 32, 45
Fairweather 2016	107
Faulkner and Talbot 1981	44
Fenton 1975	105
Freaney 2011	104, 105, 112, 196
G 2008	36
Galasso 1993	136
Gammon (Hong Kong) Ltd v AG of HK 1985	36
Geddes 1996	154
Gemmell and Richards 2003	31, 33, 80

Ghosh 1982	141
Gibbon 2015	105
Gilderdale 2010	88, 90, 111
Gittens 1984	105
Gnango 2011	85
Golding 2014	54
Gomez 1993	135, 140, 150
Gotts 1992	187
Graham 1982	183, 185
Gullefer 1987	153
Hale 1979	149
Hancock and Shankland 1986	28, 119
Hardie 1985	167, 169, 173
Hargreaves 2010	58, 180
Harrow LBC v Shah 1999	35
Hasan 2005	183, 184, 186, 187, 188
Hatton 2005	180
Haystead 2000	45
Heard 2007	170
Heath 2015	86
Hennessey 1989	162
Hibbert & McKiernan 1948	138
Hill v Baxter 1958	166
Hinks 1998	136
Hitchins 2011	176
Holley 2005	95
Howe 1987	187
Hudson and Taylor 1971	184
Ibrams and Gregory 1981	94
Inglis 2010	88, 105, 112
Ireland & Burstow 1997	41, 54, 55
Ireland 1996	41, 43, 50
Ivey v Genting Casinos 2017	142
Jackson 2006	37
JF 2015	119, 121, 123
Johnson 2007	164
Jones 1988	45
Jones 2007	154
Jones v First-Tier Tribunal 2011	56
Jones v FTT 2013	56
Jordan 1956	21
K 2001	35
Kelly 1998	137
Kemp 1957	161
Kennedy 1999	122
Kennedy 2007	122
Khan and Khan 1998	114, 115, 119
King 2016	108
Kingston 1994	170
Lamb 1967	119
Larsonneur 1933	19, 20, 34, 79
Lavender 1994	144
Lawrence 1971	135
Leicester v Pearson 1952	17, 20, 34
Lidar 2000	114
Lipman 1970	165, 170, 171, 172, 173
Lloyd 1967	107
Lloyd 1985	144
Lockley 1995	149
Luc Thiet Thuan 1996	97
M'Naghten's case 1843	160
Madeley 1990	26
Madely 1990	140
Mair 2016	57
Majewski 1977	170, 171, 191
Malnik v DPP 1989	177
Mann 2015	108
Marshall 1998	137, 144
Martin 1988	185
Martin 2001	104, 178, 179
Matthews and Alleyne 2003	29, 86
Mazo 1996	136
McInnes 1971	177
Meade and Belt 1823	42
Meah v Roberts 1977	35
Mellor 1996	22
Millard & Vernon 1987	155
Miller 1954	49
Miller 1983	19
Miller v Jackson	76
Misra 2004	114, 116, 118, 130
Mitchell 2016	106
Mohammed 2005	97
Mohan 1975	27, 155
Moloney 1985	27
Morhall 1995	97
Morris 1984	135
Morrison 1989	57
Mowatt 1968	56, 73, 80
Mulally 2006	185
Nedrick 1986	28, 86, 119, 123
Newell 1980	92, 97
O'Grady 1987	172, 175, 180
Oxford v Moss 1978	137
Oye 2013	178
Pace and Rogers 2014	155, 159
Pagett 1983	22, 66, 87, 119, 195
Palmer 1971	177
Parker 2012	94
Pittwood 1902	18, 79, 115
Pommell 1995	186
Press & another 2013	57, 171, 178

Prince 1875	36
Quayle 2005	182, 183, 186
Quick 1973	161, 166, 167
R v DPP; B v DPP 2007	150
R v R 1991	49, 78
R v Z 2017	65, 155, 195
Raphael and another 2008	143, 148, 149
Re A 2000	182
Redfern 2014	108
Rickets 2010	138
Roberts 1971	22, 43, 50, 66, 80, 123, 195
Robinson 1977	148, 151
Rodger and Rose 1998	186
Safi 2003	186
Saunders 1985	55, 86
Savage & Parmenter 1992	43, 50, 55, 56, 72
Savage 1991	58, 80
Savage1991	43, 48
Seymour 1983	113
Sharp 1987	185, 187
Shayler 2001	182, 183
Shepherd 1987	185
Shivpuri 1987	154
Sian 2016	94
Sindall 2014	86
Small 1987	140, 144
Smedley's v Breed 1974	35
Smith (Mark) 2012	161, 163
Smith 1961	55
Smith 2000	97
Smith v Chief Superintendent of Woking Police Station 1983	42
Smith1959	21
Southwark London Borough v Williams 1971	182
Stephen-Port 2016	120
Stone and Dobinson 1977	19, 79, 83, 115
Stringer 2008	29, 87
Sullivan 1984	162
Sutcliffe 1981	109
Sweet v Parsley 1970	35
Tandy 1989	105
Taylor 2016	36
Thabo Meli 1954	32, 124
Thomas 1985	41, 44
Thomas 2008	162
Thornton 1992	93
Toothill 1998	154
Topp 2011	58
Tosti 1997	154
Turbeville v Savage 1669	42
Turner 1971	139
Valderrama-Vega 1985	183
Velumyl 1989	144
Venna 1976	46
Wacker 2003	115
Walker and Hayles 1990	28
Warner 2014	116
Watson 1989	120
West 1999	149
White 1910	20, 82, 153
Whybrow 1951	155
Wilcocks 2016	109, 112
Williams & Davis 1992	23
Williams (Gladstone) 1987	177, 179
Willoughby 2004	117, 131
Wilson 1955	42
Wilson 1984	54
Wilson 1996	49
Wilson 2007	187
Windle 1952	164
Winzar v Chief Constable of Kent 1983	19, 20, 34, 79
Wood 2008	106
Woodman 1974	138
Woollin 1998	28, 86, 89
Zebedee 2011	103

Printed in Great Britain
by Amazon